The Exile S Daughter A Biography Of Pearl S. Buck

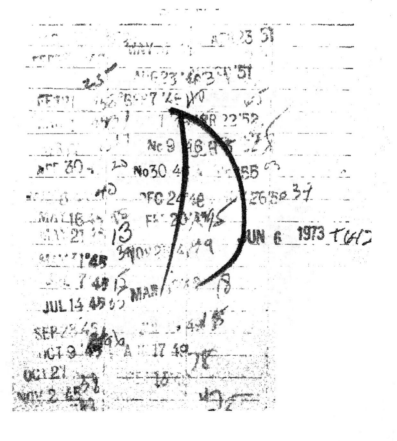

THE EXILE'S DAUGHTER

At home in her own country "the exile's daughter" with one of her own daughters (*Photo by Perles*)

THE
EXILE'S
DAUGHTER

A BIOGRAPHY OF

PEARL S. BUCK

BY

CORNELIA
SPENCER

ILLUSTRATED

NEW YORK   COWARD-McCANN, INC.   PUBLISHERS

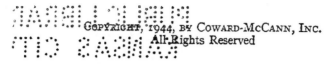

To My Sister

NOTE

The author wishes to acknowledge the copious use of the writings of Pearl S. Buck, as well as to express appreciation for permission to quote from personal letters, and to thank those who have kindly contributed through correspondence or interviews.

For the sake of clarity it has seemed wise to retain the family names used by Pearl Buck in the biographies of her parents All other names are authentic.

The quotation on page 227, from "America, The Beautiful," by Katherine Lee Bates is used by permission of E P. Dutton & Co.

LIST OF ILLUSTRATIONS

"I want to be the best wife in the world, the best mother I want to make a lot of lovely things in stone and bronze, perpetual things I want to see the world and people .. There isn't anything I don't want to do."

This Proud Heart
—Pearl S. Buck

THE EXILE'S DAUGHTER

PART ONE

I   Pearl sydenstricker was born in the little town of Hillsboro, West Virginia, early on the morning of the twenty-sixth of June, 1892 Aunt Anna bathed the baby and wrapped her snugly in her blankets and laid her beside Carie, the mother. Then she went quietly out closing the door behind her. Mother and child were alone.

Carie gazed intently at her baby. She saw she was pretty—prettier than any of the other babies had been. Even in its deep sleep, the tiny face gave an impression of definite personality. Carie was satisfied.

She lifted her eyes and looked with infinite happiness at the view to which the window near her gave. She had loved that view as far back as she could remember. For she was lying in her own canopied bed and this was her room in her own old home in America, and the view was her own view. Now because she was a little weak and weary, the passionate affection for it all made her eyes grow for an instant wet. As quickly she was smiling. The waving branch of the sugar maple tree, the tips of the apple trees in the orchard, the sweep of the meadow ending, it seemed, in the distant soft hills, all belonged as they were. The fragrance of the flowers in the little garden next to the house on the side where she lay came distinctly in at the open window and she breathed it in remembering the times in China when she had hungered for this very thing. Today all that was her home seemed more than ever hers because it was hers and the child's.

Swiftly, in this first moment of pause since the birth, she determined that all that had been hers in the background of her life, was to be this child's. Of goods there was nothing except the beautiful old house, built after the remembered pattern of the old home of her grandparents in Utrecht, Holland. Of the inheritance of the heart, there was much. There was the staunch Holland Dutch blood of her grandfather, Mynheer Cornelius Stulting, who had led three hundred souls to the raw Virginia woodlands for the freedom of their worship There was the keen sense of beauty and fastidiousness of her own father, Hermanus, who through all the years of struggle had never faltered in his meticulous personal habits nor in his determination that his children should be bred to love of the beautiful. There were the liveliness and courage of her French Huguenot mother that had put the sparkle in her own brown eyes and given her an unending sense of the comical. There were all these—courage and daring and humor, yes, and talent, for all of her brothers and sisters had an ear for music, clever hands at painting, down-to-earth appreciation of hard work and the fruit of their own efforts.

But there was more than this in the child's inheritance from the Stultings. There was love for America. How well she knew that! It was not the flag-waving kind of patriotism but love for their free land, so strong and deep-rooted that every year of the ten that she had spent an exile in the land of China to which she had gone as a bride, and where now lay buried three of her children (two within the last year before they left for furlough), only made America richer and dearer until it seemed sometimes that she could scarcely endure it. This love of country would be the baby's. She would build it into her, for this was her home.

There was the inheritance of Andrew, the baby's father. It was a good inheritance. She thought back to that family of German giants as she had first known them. Seven sons and two daughters, there were, all people of strong will, single purpose, clear minds. The family had come to America before the Revolution in which some of them had fought. With Andrew six were preachers, and one was an elder in the church and throughout Virginia and West Virginia the Sydenstricker family was known for its towering men who loved books, and was honored for the lives that they led.

Andrew had hovered at the door all night. She remembered this

4

and a sudden warmth, near pathos, swept her He was a man, all student, whose heart longed to meet the needs of life even when that longing was covered and made useless by incurable shyness and uncertainty as to what to do. She smiled now remembering how his long fingers clasped and unclasped each other as he had stood waiting, and how again and again he had asked Anna and Doctor Wallace, who had come from the village, whether or not all went well She heard again his light, cautious step as it passed up and down the hall, it must have been all night. From Andrew there would come a good mind and unmovable determination.

Thinking of Andrew made her think of their son Edwin, for Edwin was in many ways like his father—how much like her, she could not tell. Edwin had come to the door once in the night, too, she remembered, and had been sent quickly back to bed Edwin was eleven. He had been waiting for the coming of the baby with passionate excitement which he had carefully tried to hide. Dear Edwin! For an instant she longed to have him here, to hold him close. But he would have hated that, for he was tall for his age and reserved except in sudden gusts which made her wonder—was he like her after all? Now she smiled to herself. After his loneliness, this little sister would make him gay. They would all be gay now, for there would be a baby in the house again—a pretty, healthy baby, born in her own old home.

She sank into half-sleep. The journey home to America from China by Europe came to her again in flashes. They had come the long way around to avoid the sea as much as possible because she was always so ill on the water. Remembrance of beauty in things seen came back to her like bright gleams of color. Conversations with all sorts of people, for she must ever talk with everyone, were suddenly clear in their every word. Little incidents made her smile again. But over all and through all like a melody singing its way through accompanying harmony there had been the one predominant thought that she was coming home.

She re-lived that moment when her elder brother Cornelius had met them. Nothing changed him or could ever change him. He was the rock on which her life had been built as a girl. She felt again the unbearable delight of the instant when the house had come into view as the surrey in which they rode, rounded the bend. It was a beautiful house, more beautiful even than she had remembered it. The columns running to the roof in front, the broad steps leading to the porch, struck her with their simple dignity. But then there had been time for no more than that instant appreciation, for already she had seen her father coming down the walk to meet them As though she had not been away she saw him—white shirt, snowy hair and beard, short quick steps. His words were as clipped as ever as he said simply, "Carie, you're back!"

Then Cornelius had stepped ahead and stood waiting at the open door which led into the broad hall, as if to welcome her. He had not said anything, seeming to know it was a moment not to be spoiled with words. She was at home and he knew how her heart had ached for this moment.

The people in that house were the dearest in all the world to her. Here were her father, her brother, his wife, their daughters and their son. Here as in the days when she was a girl, there were music and painting and good reading and excellent cooking. There were all the familiar rooms—but all this the baby would be too small to see this time. They would wait until she came again. This time when she saw everything Carie had thought not only for herself but for Edwin and the one she carried.

When winter came they went to search for a school where Edwin could be sent when he was too old to be taught at home as there was no American school for him to attend in China. They went to live in the village near the preparatory school, Hampden-Sidney. It had been a happy winter with Edwin in school and America all around them. Carie hungered to satiate herself with American beauty. She took some painting lessons from a friend and feeling the thrill of a brush in her hand tried to record some of the things she saw—one day a little farmhouse snug in a valley beneath a blanket of clean snow. She sang as she used to sing as a girl and her voice had a fullness and abandon it could never have in China Yes, she could push away all that had been, for she was waiting for birth. . . . Now the moment had come. The baby was here. No sadness was to shadow this one. No alienness was to bar her from the birthright of America even though she might have to be a child in China—there was Andrew with his passion for preaching to the Chinese—because she, Carie, determined it. . . . She fell at last into deep, soft slumber.

It must have been mid-afternoon when she awoke. The maple was in shadow, and there was the odor of supper being cooked in the basement kitchen and the soft clatter of dishes in the dining room.

6

Someone was at the door watching for her to wake. All of them seemed to be waiting there! Anna came in smiling. She lifted the baby and held her for the others to see. They gathered around exclaiming. Edwin slipped in shyly and stood looking not at the baby but at her. He came to her when she held out her hand He blurted, "Mother, I'm awfully glad you've done it all so well." He stopped, turned hastily and then stared at the baby. "She's just like a doll," he burst out, forgetting himself. "I didn't think she could be *that* small!" Everyone laughed. Then he laughed, too, and thought of a letter he could write to his cousins in Virginia. Suddenly he wanted to laugh and laugh. Of course he wouldn't. Instead he ran out, and clattered down the stairs and into the orchard where he strode about kicking the fallen summer apples and swallowing the shouts that seemed to want to come.

Anna would let no one touch the baby She changed her and laid her carefully in the cradle which stood ready near the bed. "You must have something to eat," she said to Carie. "I thought you would never wake. But sleep's the best thing. Andrew, you come with me and fetch the tray. It will be ready in a minute." She went swiftly and the baby's father glanced hastily at Carie, his clear blue eyes showing nothing but simple pleasure and anxiety to please.

Cornelius came to the bed. "I'm glad it's done," he said simply. "You look fine and rested." In the moment he stood there looking down at his favorite sister, the past swept over him. From the time when he was a boy in his 'teens he had watched over this sister especially. Life had always been serious for him He was the only child of all of Hermanus' children born in the Old Country and on him had fallen early responsibilities which Hermanus for his very fastidiousness and love of fine things and for his trade, which was that of jeweler, was not fitted to handle. Seeing how poor the schooling the village offered, Cornelius had determined that Carie should go away to school In those days it had been like reaching for Heaven. He had saved and saved from his tiny teacher's salary and she had gone. That journey to Bellewood Seminary in Kentucky came back. They had had to go by surrey, then by boat and train. He had planned carefully about money. Yet when he came to leave her, so far from home it seemed, in panic lest she run short, he had emptied his pockets of their change. Anyway, he would not need extra money to get home. The horse and surrey waited at the house of the preacher, Andrew's brother John. There would be a meal waiting the

7

next day when he was sure to come there. But when at last he reached the preacher's he was a little late for dinner and they had already eaten. He remembered now how his stomach had growled and protested and how he refused to speak of it. Instead he had said he would walk a little in the orchard and there found a few apples to make shift until the next mealtime came along. . . . He smiled suddenly, looking down. What a strange thing to remember now! If only he could have had more to give her But he said nothing of his memories. Words had never been many between the two. Now as life passed and grew richer with suffering and joy, they were needed even less.

Hermanus, Carie's father, came no further than the door It seemed to him indelicate to stride into the room where she lay abed. Instead he paused a moment stiffly, bowed his head a little, smiled, raised his hand in friendly signal and then went briskly down the hall and stairs and into his room from which Carie seemed to hear even at this distance the ticking of the innumerable clocks and watches which he was either mending for the villagers or which he simply tinkered with because it was his habit. Her father was growing old. An instant sadness swept her.

So the first day passed into evening and in the evening, as dusk fell over the meadows and hills, there was music from below. Carie, lying in the dimness of her room, heard above this the light breathing of the baby and reached out her hand and touched the warm bundle in the crib. The years in China seemed hidden as by a curtain that is drawn. It was here in this house and here in this country that the new life must be rooted. In that security Carie lay, her heart planning, her voice eager to join the singing from the music room downstairs.

II   "HER NAME is to be Pearl Comfort," Carie said. In later years Carie came rather to regret the name "Pearl" and said that she wished she had named her child "Jean" And sometimes after that she called her Jean, and that is the name used intimately in her family today.

"Carie," Pearl's mother, as a child

The mill where the grain was ground

The house in which she was born, at Hillsboro, West Virginia

This picture of Pearl at the age of five months was taken in San Francisco, just before her parents sailed with her for China

Edwin wrote to his cousins:

"Last night I heard a noise in Mother's room. It sounded like cats fighting on the roof. I went to see what it was but Father sent me back to bed. This morning I learned that I had a nice little baby sister."

He told them what the baby's name was to be. He wasn't sure of the "Pearl," but "Comfort" was all right, surely. He sealed the letter and stamped it carefully looking hard at the stamp. It was not the old dragon stamp he had used in China but a good one of George Washington. Today he couldn't settle down to any of the things he usually loved to do, like making little sketches with a sharp pencil, or carving a knot of white pine, or sitting curled up with a book in one of the deep chairs. He looked oftener at the portrait of his great-grandfather, Mynheer Cornelius Stulting, where it hung above the carved and fluted mantel in the parlor, because it seemed important to think that there was another in his family. He wanted to rush up and stare at the baby and see whether she looked like the portrait. But he would not do that. Anyway, as he remembered, she was not like anyone but herself.

It would be nicer when his mother was up again, of course He missed her even among the relatives. He always missed her when she was not right there. It was as though something had been taken from the air, for he did not breathe with the same fullness; and as though a dankness and chill had crept into the house; and as though a quality of lightness had left the room, or half-heard music had been stilled. He could not think what it was that changed everything when Mother was not up and around, running quickly in and out, talking merrily, singing snatches of things, making little jokes at which he laughed even when they made him embarrassed, mimicking funny people until his raw ha-ha suddenly rasped out in spite of himself. No one was like her, he decided. My, but he would be glad when she came downstairs again!

It was not long, for in the brisk sunny air with fresh milk and the good food Anna cooked and plenty of rest, Carie was soon strong and once strong nothing could keep her in bed.

She went one day to the village and bought a length of eiderdown cloth to make Pearl a cape and hood. She would take it with her when they went to see her sisters in Virginia. Nettie was clever with her needle and they would sew it together. She chose a shade of delicate blue, blue with a touch of turquoise in it. It would suit the baby's eyes.

9

She studied the baby's eyes while she nursed. They were clearer than any baby eyes she had seen, and blue—not like Andrew's which were forget-me-not, and not like Edwin's which were like Andrew's and not like any blue eyes she had seen. They changed, sometimes a little gray, sometimes a little green, but always clear.

As weeks passed she saw Pearl grow prettier, and more determined. When she began to hold her head up Carie laughed to see how demanding she could be. But she was good except sometimes in the evening when she cried and Andrew walked the floor with her, holding her like a basket of eggs which he feared to drop, quite unsuccessful in quieting her, and yet painfully anxious to succeed. Carie, watching him play with Cornelius' youngest daughter, Grace, a child of three, knew as she had not fully known that his inarticulate heart had missed the dead babies, too. He could never play freely with children They knew instinctively that one word from him, one outstretched hand, one smile, one half-playful pinch signified as much as an hour of tumbling over someone else. So Andrew tried to quiet Pearl, striding up and down the room with his step which was less set to the lulling of a baby, than to covering miles of country road on his way to a preaching place among the Chinese valleys.

Carie knew his heart but at last took Pearl from him and in a little while had her quiet and tucked safely in her crib. She knew Andrew's heart in more than this, for already she saw that he had been too long away from China. Already his heart was turned there and he was counting the months until they should set out again for the land where his work lay.

She would not think of it except to make the most of every moment of the summer. She took part in all the cooking and the canning She put on a sunbonnet and picked berries, eating as she picked, the sunwarm fruit. She sat with Anna's daughters in the shade of the porch and sewed on tiny dresses while they sewed their ruffles. She listened to Cornelius as he told of the people of the village, and was part of it again. She went to church with Andrew and again her voice rang out in the old hymns she loved—hymns she sometimes could not sing in China when her throat was tight with homesickness. She did everything as she had done it before.

At last, as it seemed to Edwin, they set out for Highland County in Virginia where three of his aunts, Carie's sisters, lived and where there were his cousins. Here, even more, it was country. There were miles of fields and meadows, glorious mountains, mists, brilliant sunsets and air so keen and bracing that all of them were filled with vigor.

Here, with Nettie, Carie cut a cape and hood, cut them cleverly so that only a few scraps were left These were gathered carefully by Nettie's small daughter, Eugenia, to make a jacket for a doll. But the jacket was never made, Eugenia deciding instead to keep the soft and beautiful pieces to be fondled years later as bits of memory Here Carie laughed with Nettie and Kate and her younger sister Gradda, remembering things that had happened years before and rarely telling of the ten years she had been away. Of those ten years it was hard to tell, for it was a life too remote from all they knew and a life she would as soon not think of now. Everyone praised the baby and said how pretty she was and Carie held her upright, brushing up the fair hair which now covered her head and cooing at her and making her coo and smile. "Each baby is the best," she said.

It was a happy summer for Carie not only because of Pearl and her own delight in the things of home, but because of Edwin who ran barefoot over the meadows to rush in and eat enormously and to talk more freely than ever he had talked in all his life. In China— no, she would not think of China. There was this day and she must live it to the full.

Because Carie had been ill when they left China, she and Andrew were granted extra time for furlough. So it was not until autumn came again and touched the woods and turned them into the glorious colors Carie loved, that they began to think of returning. Even yet Carie thought more of America. She walked in the woods and came back laden with bright boughs and red berries, gathered nuts, helped with the smoking of good hams and bacon. All the goodness of America seemed heaped around her and she lived it all, for she had to store in herself not only enough for now but for the years ahead. She gathered in the beauty. It would be not only for her but for the children. She would bring it all back to Edwin in the days to come. She would tell Pearl of it and make it part of her life. She would remember it again and again and refresh herself with it, for nothing could take from the storehouse of her mind.

But at last the time came. When Pearl was five months old they left the house in Hillsboro and set out for the west coast. Of all of them only Andrew was eager. The extra months had been almost too much for his patience. Carie saw his eagerness in the new timbre in his voice, in the shine in his eyes, the tremble of his hands as he tried awkwardly to help in packing. All that he did now was for the last time before he set out for the work that he had chosen and which was his life.

Andrew's last sermon in the village church was one of hope and victory. The Word of God could save and every day on which he did not proclaim it was to him a day of momentous loss.

Carie sang less clearly that morning but only Cornelius heard the difference. He looked down and saw the sudden, shamed tears she dashed away His hand holding the hymn book with her moved to touch hers and with instant control she glanced up at him and smiled.

In San Francisco Carie had a picture taken. It was the last chance to have one made in America. Pearl sat, tiny and straight upon a small table. Beside her stood Edwin, tall and proud Pearl wore her cape and hood, her eyes looking straight ahead, a little surprised, but not at all dismayed by the experience. Years later Carie was to look at the picture and laugh at the baby who sat there like a queen.

And now Carie set herself for the return to China which must be by the sea that treated her cruelly. And yet sick as she was when once they were on the sea she had to laugh to see the baby who refused the bottle on which she must now be fed. Andrew held her awkwardly and tried to feed her with a cup and spoon. It was too much for him and at last Pearl was fed across the Pacific by the combined efforts of Andrew and the stewardess. Carie smiled to see a mite so obstinate, small in body but mighty in will.

They came to Shanghai, Pearl having traveled ten thousand miles before she was six months old and thriving on it. During the weeks on the sea she had become more plump and humorous, more merry and demanding.

There was only one face Carie longed to see now and that was the face of the Chinese nurse, Wang Amah. Yet, longing to see it she must push back the memory of those others the Chinese arms had cradled. And she did this resolutely while she scanned the crowd which waited for the ship. It was possible that Wang Amah might have come to the coast to meet them even though it was a long trip by slow Chinese houseboat.

"Mother! Wang Amah's there!" Edwin shouted suddenly. To see her was to feel a quick belonging to what had been alien.

Once the gangplank was down they pushed their way ashore. Wang

Amah rushed to Edwin and held him against her blue cotton jacket. He drew away disgusted even though so short a while ago he had shouted out his pleasure.

She reached out for Pearl. It did not matter that the new one was a girl. She clutched the baby laughing and weeping. Carie stood back an instant, knowing that there must be time for this and feeling her own eyes stinging. When she wanted to take Pearl with her in her ricksha to the hotel, Wang Amah held tightly to the baby and said, "Mistress, it is so long. Let me take her with me," and fell to fondling her tiny hands and saying *"Gou-guo*—precious" in the way she had with all the babies. Carie saw that Pearl was all the babies back again for Wang Amah. The last glimpse she had as the rickshas started off on the smooth Shanghai streets was of the small face smiling up at Wang Amah, accepting her.

III   THEY STAYED only one day in Shanghai. Then they started to their old place where Andrew's work lay, going first by steamer up the Yangtze River, and later by Chinese junk up the Grand Canal to the city which was Tsingkiang-pu. Carie had now her two children and she set herself to make her home for them, bringing to it fresh memories of her own home.

Pearl's first memory is connected with this house in Tsing-kiang-pu, or more especially its garden The garden was a court, walled about as are all Chinese city gardens. But Carie had made this unlikely spot beautiful, and this beauty formed the background of the first picture Pearl remembers. She writes of it in this way:

"I remember one early spring morning in the court, where roses bloomed everywhere, festooned against the gray brick wall, glowing along the edge of a small green. I am clinging to Edwin's hand, staggering over the old flagged pathway. Ahead of us looms the big gate, always closed against the passing world outside. The gate is raised from the ground some six inches and underneath it marches an unceasing procession of feet—bare feet, straw-sandaled feet, velvet-shod feet. These are for me the outer and unknown world. I stop, and very carefully, for I am somewhat obese, I lower myself to the ground and peer under the gate. But all my peering brings me no higher vision than flowing robes knee high or to the feet, or bare brown legs on which the muscles stand out like ropes. I can make nothing of it and rise again, dusting myself.

"Just then she comes out, the person around whom our own inner world revolves. She is dressed in a ruffly white dress that sweeps the grass as she walks and she has a big, old straw hat with a red ribbon tied around it on her curly brown hair. She has a pair of garden shears and she goes snipping the roses, wet with dew as they are, until she has a great armful.

"One perfect white rose, as large, it seemed to me, as a plate, she holds at arm's length, gazing at it. It is covered with shining drops of water. At last she puts it to her nostrils delicately, and seeing the look of ecstasy on her face, I clamor also for this privilege. Whereupon she extends the rose to me and recklessly I bury my face in it. It is larger and wetter than I had thought, and I emerge from it, sneezing and gasping and drenched, with all the sensations of having been suddenly submerged in a cool pool."

Soon after this Pearl remembers that her mother was scarcely to be seen. The garden was empty. The house seemed empty, too, for all its life was concentrated in Carie's room. Carie lay desperately ill with one of the summer diseases. It is Wang Amah who watches over Edwin and over her. Twice every day she is washed and dressed, her hair newly brushed and curled before she is taken in to see her mother. She is too small to see more than that Carie lies there.

It was that summer which made Wang Amah one of the two figures most important in her life and for a time it seemed that Wang Amah was the more important of the two. Pearl writes of this memory:

"She was, even at this earliest memory of her, already old. . . . True, doubtless she would rather have had me a boy. But even a girl was better than none. Doubtless, also, she would have preferred a child who had my mother's dark eyes instead of my blue ones, and my mother's dark hair, instead of pale yellow floss . . .

"But I seem to remember a time when all my world circled about that small, blue-garbed figure. Then did I see no face but her brown wrinkled face bending over me, and I seem to remember a fairly constant attachment to her hard brown hand, its forefinger very rough with needle pricks. At night when it was suddenly too dark to breathe I remember being lifted out of my bed and cuddling down

14

with the greatest relief and comfort into a warm bosom."

When at last cool autumn winds swept away the summer heat they seemed to bring, too, a fat little blue-eyed, black-haired brother whom Carie named Clyde The change from heat to coolness brought health as well and soon Carie took her place beside Wang Amah in the memories again.

All of Pearl's world was in those days within the courts of the Chinese house in Tsingkiang-pu except for stories Carie told her already—stories of a place called Home where apples lay on clean grass under the trees, and berries grew on bushes ready to eat, and yards were un-walled and water clean enough to drink without boiling and filtering. Already the small girl had a picture in her mind. There was a house, large and beautiful, set on a green lawn There was a wide stair going to bedrooms upstairs, one of them Mother's. There were pretty ruffled curtains and pictured paper on the walls. There were closets with sweet-smelling linens. Down in the basement there was a big kitchen where someone called Aunt Anna made good things to eat, such good things as apple pies and cookies with a certain kind of sugar called maple sugar on them There were cheeses, and hams and a thousand more things she could not remember all at once. There was an old little man in the house and he was Grandfather. He loved watches and he had millions of them. He liked to wear white shirts—shirts as white as his hair. He walked very fast. There was another man called Uncle 'Nelus. He was taller and he worked in the garden and taught school and liked to take a child on his knee to tell a story. Oh, wouldn't she like to see Uncle 'Nelus!

So from the little house deep in the interior of China, Carie reached out and touched America and drew it to her children.

Wang Amah told stories, too. " 'And what stories can I tell, who am only an ignorant old thing and never learned the name of a letter in my life?' the old nurse would exclaim, squinting at the toe of the perpetual stocking she held over her hand to darn.

"The remark," Pearl says, "we both knew was merely polite, and I answered in like terms:

" 'You know more stories than any woman in the world!'

"It was true she had a hoard chiefly from Buddhist and Taoist priests. The Buddhist stories were about wonderful daggers that a man could make small enough to hide in his ear or in the corner of his eye, but which when he fetched out again, were long and keen and swift to kill. Or they were tales of this god and that and what they did to men. . . .

"But I liked the Taoist tales better, really. They were tales of devils and fairies, and of all the spirits that live in tree and stone and cloud, and of the dragons that were in the sea, and the dragons in the storm and wind. There was a pagoda toward the east and I knew there was a dragon head pinned under there. If ever he managed to wriggle loose the river would flood and swell until we were all drowned. But there was no danger for it was a great, strong, beautiful pagoda, and there the dragon was, imprisoned and helpless.

"Many and many a time when I was surfeited with magic I used to beg my old nurse:

" 'Now tell me about when you were a little girl!'

"Bit by bit she told me the story of her life. On rainy afternoons when we sat in the nursery, or on sunny afternoons when she sat in the servants' court, sewing, I put my bamboo stool beside her and leaned an elbow on her blue-trousered leg and listened by the hour.

. . ." 'You must know, child, that I had when I was fifteen a very pale smooth skin, and my hair was very straight and very black and my braid swung to my knees, and in front I cut it to a long fringe over my eyes like a veil. My mouth was so red I needed not to paint it. My only fault was that my eyebrows were not even, and I had to brush them black with my brother's ink and writing brush. But my teeth were white and as even as the grains in a pomegranate.'

"I was too polite to express distrust of this, for my old nurse would not tolerate rudeness in us, and I merely stared very hard into that brown and wrinkled face. She had not more than six teeth all told, at this time, and the mouth she had said had been so rosy was sunken now into her toothless jaws, and the lower lip protruded. Her greatest comfort was that two of her teeth were opposite three others and so were still of use to her. One of the accidents she had that grieved her greatly was when she later fell down the cellar steps and knocked out two of these serviceable teeth. We children laughed and she showed us one of her rare flashes of anger and called out a good hard name at us. But immediately she regretted it and fumbled in her deep bosom and produced a handful of watermelon seeds, warm from her body, for us to crack. This was by way of apology, and we apologized, too, and all was well again.

"As for her eyebrows, I could see they were too scattered. Her hair, as I sat staring at her, was still black, but very scanty, and the

16

patches of her bald head would have shone through except that on such places she had painted her scalp black. I knew this and took great interest in it. She used our black shoe polish and, after applying it, would ask us if any skin showed through now, and we advised on further touches. At a little distance it was a very passable deceit."

They were to be more isolated yet, for Andrew felt a need to preach in another town, more barren, less beautiful. The only house which could be rented was a small, earthen one. Here in the winter after they moved, Clyde came near to dying of pneumonia. This loss so barely escaped made Carie see that even though she would be willing to follow Andrew to the ends of the earth for herself, for her children she would go less far.

In the white hot temper which was hers when she was provoked too much, she said in a dreadful still voice, "You can preach from Peking to Canton, you can go from the North Pole to the South, but I and these little children will never go with you again. I shall take them to Chinkiang to that bungalow on the hill, and while it is empty we shall stay there where there is peace and where there are hills and fresh air.... I have no more to give away to God now."

Instantly she set forth with the children and Wang Amah and came to Chinkiang, a larger city and river port to the south, and settled in an empty mission bungalow. The house was to be theirs only a few short months before the family assigned to it returned but with those few months there is connected another memory.

There is a narrow front yard enclosed with tiny box trees and bordered with beds of violets. Pearl is clinging to Edwin's thin forefinger. He is fifteen and soon he is going away to school in America. She is four now. She does not know anything of the many letters that have crossed the Pacific planning for Edwin's return. She cannot know anything of the anxiety in Carie's heart, for Carie sings through the great square cool rooms and strolls through the garden; Clyde tumbles in the grass and even Wang Amah sits down in its coolness with her feet straight before her, her face serene or scolding when the little boy, toddling now and clambering, tries to perch himself on her shoulder.

"Cly, lo, lo!" she says, her lower lip protruding, unable forever to make the sound of *n*. But Clyde creeps to her through the grass and, smiling his sweetest at her, turns her anger into a vapor quickly melted away.

It is this summer that Pearl undertakes Clyde. After Edgar leaves suddenly she is the elder Carie watches and smiles half-sadly to see the little girl leading him gravely round the yard, showing him his picture books and pretending to read him a story from them. She listens.

"There is a great big house with a great big yard. There are apples and grapes and berries and cows and horses and bees. Grandfather takes care of the bees and they never sting him."

"Why?" Clyde puts in, his chubby face full of wonder, his eyes round, his lips apart.

"Because he never hurts them and they know he never will. That's what Mother says.... So they make honey in little boxes and it's very sweet, very, very sweet.... And there is a big tree near the house and there are flowers, more than here, and, and ..."

A faraway look comes into Carie's face. It delights her always to see the two together. Pearl is the little mother often intent as now on Clyde. Her hair curls around her face and the ends have been carefully turned around Wang Amah's finger with a damp comb. Sometimes in shadow it takes on a bronze darkness which changes it altogether. Her face is serious, absorbed in what she is saying to Clyde. She is still pretty with her baby prettiness which was always distinct rather than round and soft as with other babies. The nose is more slender, lips full but expressive. Her eyes as she looks suddenly up at Carie, feeling her there, are brilliant with interest. "That's the way, isn't it, Mother?" she asks. Carie nods and smiles and a twinkle comes into Pearl's eyes. In a sudden burst of feeling she throws her arms around chubby Clyde who responds with two very wet kisses. His eyes are violet, his lips deep red, his hair the rich chestnut of Carie's.

IV   BUT WITH AUTUMN the bungalow on the hill had to be given up. Andrew searched for another home and found at last a small three-roomed place above a Chinese compradore shop on the Bund, a street which ran along the shore of the Yangtze River where the city lay. It was near enough the hills for the children to be taken there every day for their airing.

In this house on the Bund, Pearl's continuous memories begin. There was the room which was the dining room and parlor combined. It was not large In the center stood a round dining table and when the chairs were pushed into place there was not more than enough room to pass around it. In one corner there was a fine Mason and Hamlin organ which Pearl knows Uncle 'Nelus sent. Mother often plays at it and sings, her voice carrying through the open window so that sometimes a farmer or a Chinese gentleman passing in the street below pauses and looks up. There was a little barrel stove for warmth. There were two or three wicker chairs, and a low-hung wooden rocker worn of paint. There were a few pictures—a framed magazine cover showing a shepherd leading his sheep home from pasture in the dusk; a garden bright with flowers; Jesus with the children around him. At the windows were ruffled white curtains.

There were two bedrooms, one for Mother and Father, one for Pearl and Clyde. There was a back porch not good for much but a passageway, for one end was enclosed for the bathroom which was a cubbyhole with a tin tub and enameled basins set on wooden stands, and Chinese wooden toilets. And the other end was the kitchen. Between these two was a trap door opening down to an alley. At night Wang Amah spread her bed on this closed door. Anyone going or coming after the family had gone to rest had to brave her, for she had to rise and roll her bedding before the trap could be opened.

But Pearl's world is no longer the house. Nor is it a garden. It is made up of the whole world of people she watches from the windows on the street. She cannot quite see in all directions because to the left a warehouse called a godown shuts off that part of the street. In front of her, this spring, a window box of brilliant geraniums hides the sight of a disfigured beggar crouching just beside the compradore's. But she can see clearly the crowds of people moving up and down the street and these hold the gaze of her gray-blue eyes. There is a farmer with his baskets of cabbages still dewy-wet from the sprinkling of river water; a candy man shaping monkeys and birds from the taffy which he twists with slender dirty fingers, while he inflates them through a reed buried in the lump of taffy itself. There is a sewing woman who sits in a doorway patching a man's blue trousers, and running her needle from time to time through her sleekly oiled hair to ease its way through the heavy cotton material

19

for a few stitches. An old gentleman is starting for the hills outside the town, his thrush cage in his hand, his eyes very peaceful because of the thought of waving green grass and trees on the grave mounds. There is the call of a vendor of dumplings—she would like to taste one although Mother will never allow it saying, "They are very dirty. Look at the cloth that covers them!"

If she looks straight ahead above the street she can see the Yangtze River. It is very broad, so broad that the distant edge of the opposite shore is only a dim, misty line, broken here and there by uneven hills.

On calm days the near shore is cluttered with boats. There are flat cargo boats, steam launches belching heavy coal smoke and chugging like a man hiccoughing. There are sampans to transport passengers. There are houseboats in which whole families live from one year's end to another. On stormy days there are not so many boats, for some go to wait in snug coves until the storm is past, Mother says. And sometimes when a great wind arises, Mother draws the curtain and says cheerily,

"Come, I'll read you a story. You choose the one that you like."

It was a pretty river when the sun was bright. Far to the right lay Silver Island with another smaller hilltop emerging beside it. Silver Island had lots of trees and up one side went a stone-paved path leading to a temple which showed brick-red among the green. Sometimes in the early morning, mists hung over it breaking into shreds and gradually melting away to leave behind them streaming brightness which tipped the waves with gold. Broad noonday sun was beautiful because its light made the sails of the junks seem whiter and the boatmen's jackets more blue.

Sometimes at sunset time Mother stood beside her to look out. Now the water was no longer brown and muddy. It had turned to gold and crimson, mirroring the sunset light and making long reflections of boats and people which rippled to the near shore in wavering lines of color. After a while the color faded away and instead there were soft grays and blues and the twinkling of tiny bean-oil lamps and the flickering of charcoal stoves being fanned beneath the rice pots for the evening meal Sometimes Pearl could hear the sleepy cry of a baby and the sing-song lullaby of a mother; sometimes a wailing which she did not know was the call of a woman for the flitting soul of a dying child. All the sounds wove themselves into the night and were lost at last in the deep hum of the city of Chinkiang.

20

There is another world she is beginning to discover. It is the world of books. As winter passes she learns to read well. She reads to Clyde, though not very fast, and Wang Amah sometimes watches and then goes off shaking her head and saying proudly, *"Nau-ching cheh mu ts'ing ts'u*—that clear a head!" Faster reading comes when she curls up on her bed with a book. There are scarcely any books but she reads anything because suddenly it brings her new people, new places.

That winter in the house on the Bund, Father and Mother talk often of the summers. Always Mother worries about the summer for that is the time of tropical diseases. Now Father says that some lovely high mountains have been found. Mother tells the children of them:

"An Englishman was hunting in some mountains in the province of Kiangsi, and he found a high valley with a fine stream running through it It was such a good place that he took a lease on it. That means that he can use it and build on it. Now some other people are building small cottages there where they can go and keep well in the hot weather."

"And are we going there, too?" Pearl interrupts. How fine it must be up there!

"Father is going to see the place and then we will decide," Mother says.

When Father comes back they can't wait to hear what he will say. Even Clyde is marching around the room like a soldier shouting in rhythm, "Going to the mountain! Going to the mountain!"

Then they are all still, waiting.

"It is more like home than any place I have seen elsewhere in the world," Father says.

That is enough.

"We will find a way to go and we will build a little house, perhaps no more than two rooms," Mother says and smiles at all of them.

That winter Father goes back and forth several times and each time he comes back there is something to tell. First there is a small lot on the mountainside above the stream; then coolies at work quarrying; then a tiny house almost done. Father says in his spare, shy way when Carie presses him for details,

"Carie, I saw wild grapevines full of fruit, just like I used to eat

21

on the farm at home. There is a fine spring at the bottom of our lot. I drank a cup or two and it was icy cold. There are clean pebbles and white sand."

That is all he says but instantly all of them see exactly how it must be.

There is a world she rarely sees but sometimes hears. This is the world centering for her in the compradore's shop downstairs. The Chinese compradore sets out very prominently his little stock of imported goods, such things as Allen and Hanbury biscuits in tin cans, Crosse and Blackwell jams, Golden Churn butter and Borden's condensed milk. But he is Chinese still and often there is the sound of loud Chinese talking and argument, the smell of Chinese food, and sometimes a curious sickening sweet odor which creeps through the floor even though Carie sees to it that the cracks are freshly puttied and the matting carefully laid. This world Mother never tells her about and when they pass the entrance to the store Pearl and Clyde look enviously but silently at the cans of biscuits which have come from far away and which they know they would be allowed to eat because they are quite clean. They pass the store only when they go and come from their afternoon walks.

Every day after their rests Wang Amah helps them get ready to go. Pearl feels fresh and merry and eager to run on the hills. When Wang Amah tries to comb her hair she darts from beneath her hand so that Wang Amah cries in mock anger, pretending to glare, "Per-r-r-h, laughty girrh!"

At last they are ready. Mother has on her hat. Clyde wears a fresh little blue sailor suit. Pearl is wishing she did not have to wear her big coolie hat of Chinese straw braid because it is forever slipping back, the elastic cutting her neck and the rough edges tangling her hair. Yet she likes the strip of ribbon around it and the two tiny bunches of forget-me-nots. But Mother insists that she wear the hat to protect her from the wicked Chinese sun which once made Father desperately ill and left him stiff in his arms even yet.

They go down the narrow stairs and into the side street called Horse Street. Horses rarely pass there for there are no carriages in Chinkiang, but next to the Bund it is the broadest street in the city and to Pearl it seems immense and almost unending.

Once the children are out they would like to rush around seeing

22

The Sydenstricker family in Shanghai in 1894, the parents, Edwin
Pearl and baby Clyde

Wang Amah Pearl's well-loved Chinese nurse

Golden Island, with its pagoda, was near her childhood home in
Chinkiang *(Photo: Methodist Prints)*

everything, but Mother holds Pearl's hand and Wang Amah Clyde's. Wang Amah is very stiff and proper now in a freshly starched blue jacket and trousers. She nods in recognition of a shopkeeper or two but says no word to anyone. The people who seemed so small seen from the windows, now seem to tower above Pearl. She wishes she could have a piece of that malt candy over there with the little seeds on it. But there is no use in asking Mother. She has asked millions of times and always Mother says, "No, dear, the flies sit on it."

But there is the peanut stand at the corner where the road forks, one branch leading downward to Golden Island, and the other up the hill to the fort. "But Golden Island is only a hill," Pearl says when Mother tells her its name.

"It used to be an island years ago before the river left it," Mother says. "One time a famous man came all the way from Genoa and went there. His name was Marco Polo."

Pearl has no idea where Genoa is but it must be very far away indeed. She looks at the mountain again. It is only a small mountain, nothing like the one where Father is building their cottage.

The peanuts smell delicious as they come near. They are piping hot and browned just enough. Mother buys two three-cornered packages wrapped in coarse straw paper. She gives one to Pearl and carefully shells a few nuts from the other for Clyde, saying,

"Chew them very, very well, Clyde." He looks up at her with solemn eyes as she pops one into his mouth. Wang Amah watches over him, her trousers crackling at every step.

Now their road leads between two lines of great trees. To the left stands the old Fort, enclosed by a thick mud rampart through which a few antiquated cannon thrust their blunt noses. To the right is a temple.

Soon they are climbing the hill up which the road leads and all the houses are left behind. At this instant the children are free. They drop the hands which hold theirs and dash ahead. Pearl spies a yellow flower and climbs the bank to pull it and gazes deep into its heart. Yellow is a lovely color—like sunshine, or like butter, or like Mother's ring—what is yellow like? She takes it to Wang Amah and says, "It's for your hair." The old woman stoops patiently while Pearl thrusts it in next her knot and says in Chinese, delighted, "It's pretty, very pretty, Wang Amah."

At the top of the first rise a wooden seat is set between two half-dead trees, very old trees, they must be. Pearl dashes to it, her hat

23

slipping back on her shoulders, Clyde puffing after her in his fatness. She has reached the seat and found it empty. The instant Clyde arrives she lifts him up and flings herself down beside him, her arm about him. Then she looks away. There before her is Golden Island with its delicate pagoda and curved temple roofs and the winding steps leading up. Below it lie green fields of rice and a length of street which dwindles away into a country road. She can see far now and everything looks large and wide and open. She draws a deep breath. It will be like this, only better, this summer in the mountains.

Mother and Wang Amah have caught up to them now and Mother sits down beside them while Wang Amah sits on a stone. No one says anything. Everyone is breathless and it is nice just to look.

Soon they are ready to go on. From here the road runs down a gentle hill, just steep enough to race down without tumbling. The road leads to Victoria Park, a spot which the British port people have tried to make look English. Here they play tennis and croquet and gather one day a year to celebrate the Queen's birthday.

Pearl likes the park. There are narrow pebbled paths which wind in and out, shrubbed corners where seats are set, flower beds and a few choice pheasants. The golden one is gorgeous when he opens his tail and the silver one is sleek and cool, making her think of icicles.

They cannot go as far as the park every day. Today they stop on a slope and let themselves drop on the soft grass of a Chinese grave mound.

Clyde flings himself down and then rolls over and over and shouts, "Sister, see me!" His eyes are shining and his brown curls are tumbled and his hat lies in Wang Amah's lap. Pearl stands a moment looking at him and then says to Carie, "Isn't he *darling*, Mother!" Carie smiles. Wang Amah is smiling, too. In a moment Clyde crawls to her and rolls into her lap.

Pearl watches some men on the other side of the road. They are digging herbs. Their baskets are full of small twisted roots. They look up at her and begin to ask questions which she answers gravely for she speaks as much Chinese as English.

"You are American, aren't you?"

"Yes, American," she says shyly.

"America is a good country," the men say agreeing among each other with a look.

"A very good country," Pearl says.

24

"You must be eight," another man comments.

"I'll soon be five," Pearl answers

"So big and only five! But then you drink the milk of cows and eat much meat."

"But I like Chinese food," Pearl says quickly. "It is better than ours, I think." They laugh, embarrassed.

The children do not want to start back when it is time. They are never ready to go home When they reach the street it seems to enclose them. Today a deep whistle from a foreign ship tears the air as they walk along.

When they come to the compradore's he is in a genial mood smiling at them and trying to engage them in talk. As they pass into the alley he goes into the store and brings out a small can of imported biscuits. The children thank him and race clattering up the stairs.

"Open it quickly, Mother," Pearl begs. Yes, they are the very plain ones she likes with tiny letters printed on them. There is A and there B and there C. She makes her name in cookies. She rather hates to spoil it by eating them. Perhaps if she eats enough she will have what Wang Amah is always talking about—"A stomach full of learning."

That night there is a great noise downstairs Wang Amah pulls her pigskin trunk so that it rests on the end of the trap door. Carie gets up a half dozen times and wanders in to make sure the children are all right A strong smell of whiskey creeps up, and there are shouts of drunken men and foreign oaths. There is the high laughter of young Chinese girls, an extra loud curse, a cry, and the crash of broken dishes. Carie knows a foreign gunboat is in port and the sailors have come ashore. "Good it always happens in the night," she says. "As for the broken dishes, I have told the compradore a dozen times it is justice for the serving of drinks." But in the dead of night her heart goes out to the American boys below and she plans to try to find a way to give them instead of this, a taste of home.

The noise makes Pearl restless in her sleep. She tosses about and flings one arm over the edge of the bed. She has a dream. That dream is to this day clear. Someone seems to have caught her loose-hanging wrist and is holding it tightly. Her terror is so great that she can scarcely breathe, much less call. She wants to pull her arm back but she does not dare. She lies perfectly still and suddenly her hand is released.

In the morning she tells Carie, "Last night someone caught my hand and held it very hard. I didn't like it It made me afraid."

"Just a dream, of course, darling. Perhaps you had too many cookies!" Carie laughs and hums a tune to cover her inward worry. That old rascal of a compradore with his peace offering!

Wang Amah's lip is out very far this morning. She grumbles over her work, dashing bucket after bucket of water down the stairs and scrubbing them thoroughly with a short-handled broom There is a strong smell of carbolic acid when at last they are dry again.

V   WHEN THE heat fills the valleys and mist rises like steam from the ponds and hangs over the river, and the Chinese babies are naked in the street, and coolies go bare-waisted, Carie begins to pack for the journey to the cottage in the mountains. She is gay and the two children sit together on the edge of the bed watching her. This is not like other goings-away. This is like going somewhere just for fun.

"We are going to have a great, big picnic," Carie says. "The house is tiny, only big enough to sleep in and for days when it rains. We will just live outdoors." Little chills of delight run up and down the children's spines.

They go first by river steamer, moving slowly up the Yangtze. In some places the river is so broad that the far shore can scarcely be seen. In others they pass through channels where rocky cliffs rise up seeming to impede their way. There are swirling whirlpools and currents which seem great enough to twist the boat about. Instead, it moves steadily through them.

There are fishing boats and houseboats and strange old steamers, sidewheelers and rusty sea-going vessels, freighters which can go all the way to Hankow. There are gunboats, low and gray against the yellow water, their officers very stiff and white on the bridge.

At the ports where they stop along the way, there are old hulks rocking and swaying beneath their loads of scrambling people.

Breathtaking the moment when the coolies, clinging by one hand to the rail, let go and leap for the deck of the ship. Pearl watches, but sometimes whirls swiftly around so that she cannot see. What if one misses? The narrow strip of water seething between the hulk and the ship seems like certain death. Yet no one misses. With a whoop and a shout each is across, falling on the ship's deck and then jumping up and brushing off his clothes and laughing.

There are dozens of coolies leaping across the water before the steamer can come alongside and then there seem to be hundreds of people coming aboard, passengers with their bundles of bedding and their baskets of food, vendors with their goods in boxes, on trays, in buckets, all shouting and scrambling and trying to make the most of the time before the steamer will blow the blasts which mean that she is about to start again. Pearl stands awe-stricken at the hubbub, yet fascinated.

Now the ship is ready to leave. The whistle blows and Clyde presses his plump hands over his ears, his big eyes suddenly turned on Wang Amah, who stands with him, to be reassured.

"*Pu yao-chin,*—it doesn't matter," she says and puts her arm around him. Pearl stands very still but for an instant she can scarcely keep from running inside the saloon. She does not like such a great noise. Then, all at once it is over and there is only the sound of many voices shouting and quarreling and laughing and all the vendors and coolies and visitors get off.

In the morning an English officer from the captain's deck comes quickly down the companionway. He smiles warmly at the two white children.

"I say," he says in his clipped British way, "now would your mother let you have some sweets? I've a bottle of them here." He takes a small square bottle of fruit candy drops from the pocket of his jacket. Pearl sees at once that they are like the ones in the compradore shop.

"Oh, thank you," she says quickly. "I'll run and ask my mother."

In an instant she is back, her eyes shining. The officer screws the lid off and each of them has one, Wang Amah and the officer, too.

The man wants to talk. He has watched them from upstairs

"I've a little boy in England," he says. "Would you like to see his picture?"

"Yes, very much," Pearl says. She is surprised at what is happening.

She looks carefully at the picture of a small boy in a sailor suit.

"Wouldn't you rather have him here on the ship with you?" she asks shyly. "England's very far away, I think."

"His mother is with him. I was afraid he might not stay well where it gets so hot."

"But we're going to where it's cool," Pearl begins eagerly. "My father's built us a little house in the mountains. The place is going to be called Kuling. I asked Mother whether that was because it made people cool, but she said it wasn't but from the name of a temple there. My brother and I are going to have a splendid time My mother says it is going to be one great big picnic." Suddenly she is overcome at having said so much, for usually she fears strange people. She drops her head so that her long hair falls forward and she has to sweep it back over her shoulders when she looks up again.

"I shall go up there one time when I am in Kiukiang where you leave the ship," the man says.

"Then you must come to see us," Pearl answers with a touch of grown-up courtesy in her voice. "We would be glad to see you. Mother always likes to have people come and see her." Her breath comes quickly because all this is exciting.

"How old is your brother and what is his name?" the officer asks, turning to Clyde.

"He's nearly three and his name is Clyde." Clyde is clinging to Wang Amah's hand. Now she stoops and whispers, "Clyde, speak to the man." He drops his eyes and says so softly that one can scarcely hear, "How do you do, sir." The children are less shy with Chinese than with white people.

The officer smiles and represses a desire to draw the chubby boy to him. "You're a wee gentleman, aren't you?" he says. "But I must go. They will be wondering where I've got to. The sweets are yours but mind you don't eat too many at once or your mother will be blaming me for it!" With a quick turn on his heel he is gone, running lightly up the stairs.

The second morning when they come out to the cool deck, Carie points quickly to something far away. "Look! There are the mountains!" she says.

There they are, seeming hopelessly far off, very blue and tremendously high because they rise from low plains.

Two nights and a day on the steamer and they are in Kiukiang where the officer said they would leave the ship It is very hot but they go to a friend's house and there it is pleasant. Clyde is entranced with the great punka or fan which swings over the dining room table, fanning them all as they eat that evening. It is the first he has seen

28

"A boy sits in the hall and pulls the rope that makes it go," Pearl whispers, seeing that Clyde cannot finish his supper until the question is answered.

Pearl watches the Chinese boy who sits in the shadow of the hall. Sometimes his white teeth glint when he smiles at her, but his pull is even and the breeze delightful.

"Oh! It's nice, isn't it, Sister?"

In the dusk they all go for a walk along the Bund. There are palm trees and hibiscus. Everything is different from Chinkiang. The clothes the people wear have different knotted buttons, and different decorations. The women's hair is twisted high on their heads so that it sticks out like a teapot handle; Pearl suddenly laughs to herself thinking how funny Wang Amah would look with her hair combed like that. The talking of the people in the street is different, too. It has a high singing quality ending sometimes with a long-drawn note which is comical to one not used to it.

The city lies in a lowland and that night not a wisp of breeze stirs the air. The mosquito nets seem to shut them in even more than at home because it is so close. But Pearl tries to sleep because early in the morning they are to start the long ride across the plain to the foot of the mountains, by sedan chair. The time will go faster, too, if she sleeps.

The next morning she will never forget. The sky is still red, streaking the river which lies near as they get into bamboo chairs slung between two poles. There is loud talking, and a fist fight or two among the chair coolies. They all want to carry Pearl because she is light and will sit in a chair by herself. Wang Amah has Clyde with her. The coolies demand that Mother ride alone because she is heavier than Wang Amah. There is a great deal of discussion about Father because he is so tall, but as one coolie says in the Chinese way, "He has no meat."

At last they start. The mountains cannot be seen at all now, hidden as they are by the city and all that intervenes. Now they are passing through narrow city streets. Soon they are outside the city and there is the country with its farmhouses and villages. Very far off they can see the mountains. It looks now as though it will take days to reach them.

While they cross the plain they stop several times so that the men can have a drink of tea. Children crowd around to gaze and old women ask Pearl how old she is and how old Clyde is and why their skin is so white, whether it is because they were bathed too often too young, and what makes Clyde's hair all curls, and what they eat, and why he is so fat

At last they leave the crowd and go on. Soon they will reach the station in the foothills where they change coolies for the climb. Already they are going up slowly There are small pine trees and new kinds of flowering bushes Mother calls once,

"Pearl, do you see the wild roses? They are just like the ones at Home."

There is the sound of a stream and the water runs over rounded stones. clear water over white stones. It is not like streams Pearl has seen before.

Now they are getting into other chairs and having fresh coolies at a stopping p'ace, Lien Hwa Tung. The trip is too long not to change them especially since the hard climb comes at the end. People from the mountain valleys gather to stare. They talk among themselves. They feel of Pearl's dress. "*Yang pu*—foreign cloth," they say. They touch the ends of her hair. "Fine," they say, "but a strange color." She does not mind their touching her, but it makes her uncomfortable to hear what they say.

They are ready to go but still they do not start. The coolies are arguing over price. Father is unwilling to promise more wine money. He sits, his face unchanging. The cicadas sing in the trees and the mountains loom against the sky. Many years later, Pearl writes from her home in the Pennsylvania country, "The cicadas are singing away just like Lien Hwa Tung, this morning. Do you remember how they used to sing there? It is associated in my mind with the hustle for chairs, and finally being swung up and starting on that lovely mountain ride."

At last they start, the chair-bearers half running along the rock-laid path of the foothills. There are feathery bamboos and pine trees and wild day lilies and many flowers. Pearl glances back at Carie. She is sitting upright in her chair, a hand on each arm, her eyes shining and straining to see every detail that they pass.

Now the coolies are going smoothly along a slow ascent and now they are running up two dozen steps shouting in unison and laughing when they have reached the top. Suddenly the foothills are falling away. The mountains grow bare. Great rocks tower above the path,

30

Pearl when she first returned to America at the age of nine

Those terrifying steps up to the summer place at Kuling

gray with lichen, beautiful, imperious. From a high point they look back and there, minute, in the distance, are a village and a slender pagoda. How far they have come already! Yet the mountains still tower above them.

Oh, but the air is cool now! There is a breeze and high above them the clouds shape themselves out of the upper valleys now hiding and now revealing the black crags.

They come to a resting place, a tiny mountain house clinging to a precipitous slope. The chairs are set down with a clattering of poles. An old woman comes to pour tea for the men and they wipe their sweating bodies and go to stand in a gurgling stream. When the cold wind comes racing down the ravine they beat themselves upon their backs and chests and whoop out into the nothingness and wait for the echo. Pearl has not seen Chinese men like this. They seem free, part of the mountains and streams and wind.

Now they are off again! The men joke heartily among themselves, take a steep path as though it were a game, half-teasingly let the chair get out of rhythm with their step so that she is thrown a half foot into the air. Everyone is having fun out of this climbing to the mountain valley.

But suddenly the laughing and teasing have stopped. Ahead is a very long flight of steps shaped irregularly of stones. On one side is a sheer wall of mountain. On the other is a straight fall to the valley through which like a silver thread flows a stream. The men pant, their breath coming hard through dry lips. Mother has two extra men at the back of her chair to help push upwards. There is no sound but the panting and shuffling of straw sandals on the dusty stones, and far away, high above, the song of the birds—mountain thrushes. Pearl glimpses Wang Amah as the road curves on itself. She sits tight-lipped, gray with pallor, clasping Clyde with one arm and clinging to the chair arm with the other.

The men's steps go faster and faster. Now they are on the mountaintop going along a level stretch. In front of them lies a narrow street with Chinese shops and a cluster of Chinese houses. They do not stop here but go on swiftly into the bowl-shaped valley to which this is the entrance. Suddenly, on the opposite slope, Pearl makes out a few tiny stone cottages. Father is pointing one out to Mother. Pearl looks with all her might, her heart pounding.

That first summer in Kuling was Pearl's happiest childhood summer. There was to be one more with Clyde, and many others, but this was the best.

The house was so tiny that they could do no more than camp, but there was the outdoors. Everything was clean. Pearl could run barefoot with Clyde. She had never been allowed to go barefoot before and now she knew the experience of soft cool grass beneath her feet. She could wade and wade for hours holding Clyde's hand and guiding him over the stones. She could pick any flower she saw. She could watch storms come up over the mountain behind the house and dissolve in thundershowers in the valley. Mother said so often, "It's almost like the Highlands of Virginia! It's almost like Home!" Pearl's picture of Home was clearer than before.

Something made everything different that summer. She knew suddenly what it was. It was Mother. This Mother was so full of fun and life, whistling or singing, or on a sudden impulse saying, "We'll picnic on the big rock tonight and see the sunset," or "We'll take our supper to the stream."

Every night they crept into bed, tired, with the cool mountain air blowing in the window. It was like dropping into down, even though the mattresses were homemade and only ticks filled with sweet hay from their own lot.

Clyde's cheeks grew rosy. No one was ill all summer. But the summer had to end. They went down the mountain to Chinkiang again. But they did not go back to the little three-roomed home above the compradore's. By some magic they never went there again. When Father came to fetch them there was much talking in the night about an empty house in a compound on Horse Street.

This house in the compound on Horse Street is their home when autumn comes again. The compound is wonderful. There are three mission houses in a row, and a chapel. They have the second house. The Lawtons, another American family, have the third, and they have a baby girl.

Every morning as soon as breakfast is over and before lessons begin, Pearl runs next door to help Mrs. Lawton bathe Mary. It is something she has never done before because she was too young when Clyde was small. Now she can stand ready to hand Mrs. Lawton all the things she needs—soap, towels, diapers, pins, and the dress. She is completely absorbed in it. Sometimes she is allowed to rub the soft soapy cloth over the fat little legs. Sometimes she shakes

32

on the powder. When everything is done and the baby is warm and clean, Pearl is allowed to hold her in her arms while the mother mixes the bottle of milk.

"When I grow up," she says to Mary's mother, "I'm going to have millions of babies They are just going to fill the house—a big house—an enormous house!"

And Mary's mother smiles.

The second autumn in the house on Horse Road, a family comes to live in the first house in the compound. They are Scotch. Mrs. Walker loves to chat with Carie. Mr. Walker is quiet and has what Carie calls "green fingers." Before the cold weather comes he has transformed the garden near the house into neat flower beds planted ready with hardy plants for spring. He has flower pots already growing well to take indoors for the winter. He builds a small barn and buys a cow for milk. There is Nessa, a little younger than Pearl, with soft brown eyes, and a quiet way like her father, and there is Willie, a small boy vivacious like his mother.

One delightful thing about the Walkers is their afternoon teas. Every afternoon they have tea, whether there are guests or not, and Pearl sees with astonishment the assortment of small cakes and biscuits and sometimes even minute meat pies. "The British always have afternoon tea," Carie says, "but don't spoil your supper." It is hard, for Mrs. Walker presses food upon everyone and Pearl can scarcely stay away, not so much because of the tea as because of Mrs. Walker's lively, continuous conversation. And her Scotch brogue is entrancing.

Often Pearl wishes Nessa did not wear glasses. Her eyes seen through the lenses are beautiful and soft. One day she finds her in her bedroom with the glasses lying on the dresser. Then she sees that the beautiful eyes are crossed.

Nessa wears a ring. It is a plain gold one set with a garnet. Pearl has never had any but a small Chinese silver one with no stone at all. The more she sees Nessa's the more fascinated she becomes. If only she had a ring with a stone! A red stone.

One day she goes in search of Nessa. She passes through her bedroom and there lying on the pincushion is the ring. Without thought she takes it and drops it into her pinafore pocket, and runs home.

33

She slips it on her finger and turns it slowly. It fits perfectly. She is not thinking of anything but that the ring is on her finger.

Carie comes into the room and sees the ring on her finger. "Why, Pearl, where did you get the ring?" she asks instantly. She knows, of course, but her voice is not sharp.

"I found it in the Walker's barn," Pearl answers at once without hesitation. Why did she say that? The words just came.

"Let's go and talk to Mrs. Walker about it," Carie says and holds out her hand. They go together It is easy with Mother like this In a moment everything is explained and Nessa is smiling But to Pearl only one thing is vivid. She has had a red-stoned ring on her finger. It was for only a moment, yet it was there.

Pearl plays with Nessa often now when lessons are done. Every day she has arithmetic, spelling, geography, and stories of history. Then in the afternoon she is free. The Lawtons have gone. The parts of the day that are not filled Pearl fills for herself with reading. Often Nessa comes to find her and has hard work to bring her to playing. There is an inner content in Pearl which makes the Scotch girl wonder.

That winter of 1899 when Pearl was six and Clyde was four was broken suddenly by disaster. Both children were very ill. Somehow diphtheria was carried into the house and Clyde took it first. There were only two western trained doctors in the city, and one was always drunk. The other was a kindly half-breed from India, and when he examined Clyde he said the illness was only tonsilitis. It was Carie herself who recognized the dread diphtheria. It was Carie herself who hunted through the Bund for the drunken port doctor when the Indian said he knew nothing of the new anti-toxin. The port doctor was a good doctor when he was not drunk, and Carie made him sober for a little while. But though he saved Pearl he was too late for Clyde. Clyde died and Pearl was too ill to remember more of his going than a January afternoon when a sudden gusty winter storm lashed the trees and Carie stood by the window watching something which took place along the front walk, her face broken with weeping; and an evening when Wang Amah came in to care for her, freshly washed and combed, but with eyes red and swollen. That night Pearl seemed to hear a Chinese woman crying as Chinese women cry for their dead. Then suddenly the sound was

34

hushed and there was stillness. Pearl knew she was the only child in the house.

When she was well again, she was lonely indeed. Carie spent more time with her and rarely left the house. She helped her with her first printed writing, a letter to the *Christian Observer*. But only reading made Pearl less lonely. She read everything she could find. Soon she began to pray to God every day to send her a brother or sister or both. She still remembers and smiles at the memory of that small six-year-old girl that was she Every morning regularly she went to the bathroom where she could be sure of being alone, locked the door and knelt beside the small wooden commode.

"God, please, send us right away, a baby with blue eyes and brown hair, like Clyde."

Although it seemed long, she did not have to pray for many months. One evening that spring Nessa came running to say she was to spend the night at their house. The next morning Father came for her. "Come home quickly and see what is there," he said and Pearl thought he smiled oddly.

She reached home before Andrew. There beside Carie was a tiny bundled baby. It was a sister, Faith When she looked into the face of the blue-eyed, dark-haired baby, her prayers were answered.

VI   THE PART OF Pearl's childhood lived so near the Chinese street ended there. Carie resolved that she would no longer keep her children in this compound where even though the walls were high, evil sounds and odors penetrated There were the mission bungalows on the hill. After the summer in Kuling, Clyde gone, and Faith so tiny, she would ask to be allowed to use one of these.

That house on the hill outside of Chinkiang is clear, for it was Pearl's home all through her girlhood. It was a square bungalow set on a foundation high enough to allow for good walking space in its basements. There was a dark cellar where in winter coal was stored for the large base-burner and the fireplaces and the kitchen stove; and a dry dusty one enclosed only with trellis work under the side porch where the children could play when it rained. Carie had a tiny cookstove made of kerosene tins and clay and here Pearl cooked for her dolls when she liked. There was the broad hall from which all the rooms opened and where at one end stood the base-burner. That hall brings back a memory of evenings when Carie was busy taking accounts with the cook and Andrew at work in his study and she herself and small Faith danced the seemingly great length of the room, singing with complete freedom and improvising their steps with abandon.

From the front, broad wooden steps led to a high porch which ran around two sides of the house. At its north end the porch was sheltered by a clambering white rose, sweet with fragrance and nesting a dove who raised her brood there each year.

Of the rose Pearl wrote years after, remembering the picture of Carie in that bungalow garden: "At one end of the long veranda a white rose hangs heavy with bloom, and if you go near it, she will call you sharply away, for there is a turtle dove's nest there and she is guarding it as zealously as the mother bird guards it. Once I saw her angry—and she can be angry often—because the lounging gardener robbed the nest, and she poured on him a torrent of well-articulated Chinese, and he skulked astonished from her presence. Then in passionate pity she turned to the fluttering mother bird and her voice fell until one would not have said it was the same voice, and she coaxed the mother bird and twisted the rose branches this way and that and picked up the despoiled nest and put it tenderly back, and sorrowfully and angrily she gathered the broken eggshells together and buried them. And who more joyous than she when the mother bird laid four more small eggs in the replaced nest!

" 'Now that was good and brave of her!' the woman cried, her eyes flashing."

On the south end of the porch the sun shone warm in winter and that was Pearl's favorite spot for reading. She spent many hours there curled over a book, her pocket full of peanuts or roasted broad beans to eat while she read. This was the porch where sometimes Wang Amah brought a bowl of her specialty, piping hot rice with vegetables, grumbling that Pearl did not even stop in her reading but ate meditatively from the bowl with chopsticks, one eye on her book.

But the best room of the house was Carie's bedroom with its wooden bedstead, the old rocker, a wardrobe, a straight chair, a trunk, a fireplace, and her bureau with a sandalwood box full of

36

precious things—a silver leaf brooch, a tortoise-shell comb, some treasured baby curls tied carefully with narrow ribbon. The room was never quite neat, for it was too much lived in. A door opened from this room into the children's room next to it.

The best part of the children's room was the bay window with the seat beneath it. Plants in the window never did well, for the sun was not strong after it had crossed the porch But the seat was broad enough for Pearl to sit on, curling her legs beneath her. In bad weather, this was her place to read

Pearl writes of the bungalow on the hill,

"I remember that home as a place of delight to us all, for its simple order and cleanliness and its grace of flowers, and the sweet smell of the grass mats is in my nostrils yet. There I began to grow into womanhood, and there Faith began to walk and talk and grow into girlhood. From this house Andrew went forth refreshed and encouraged for his long tours of preaching and teaching From it, too, went out the refulgent outpouring of Carie's hospitality.

"It was about this time that Carie's mother heart took in one not her own. A Chinese woman whom she had helped died and left her her little ten-year-old girl, Precious Cloud. Precious Cloud became part of the household except that Carie sent her always to a Chinese mission school feeling that she must belong to her own race." ... It was of this girl grown to womanhood and married that Pearl a long time after was to write the merry children's story, *The Chinese Family Next Door.*

In the memories of this bungalow on the hill Wang Amah has large part, too. Years later Pearl wrote, "And what pleasure she gave us in the things she did for us! Chief of these was in the hatching of chicks to be our pets. Every spring this was an event, and as soon as the edge was off of the spring wind we went through the little farms in the valleys about us and with her we searched until we found a setting hen she liked. Then she bought here and there fresh eggs until we had twenty, and when we went home again she made a nest in an old box she kept from year to year for the purpose, and the nest was put into her own room where she could guard the whole process, and the hen established.

"We were never allowed during these three weeks to touch either hen or egg, for the old nurse assured us that Chinese hens would run right off the eggs and never come back if children with white skin and yellow hair showed themselves before her.

37

"In spite of everything, however, the hen would occasionally abandon the task, and then if she was too flighty to be coaxed back to it, the old nurse would dispose the eggs carefully about in her own capacious garments and hatch them with the warmth of her own body.

"At night she put the eggs under her quilt and slept half awake lest she lie on them. And what a moment it was when we caught the half-absorbed look on her face and saw her shrug herself gently and pull her hand up her wide sleeves and fumble in her depths elsewhere! She would whisper in a hushed voice,

" 'Wait—a chick !'

"We waited breathless until she reached her hand out carefully with the little damp, new fowl in it. How precious were such chicks and what tragedy if one died!"

The bungalow on the hill is connected with yet another memory. This has to do with the coming of the yearly order from Montgomery Ward. Pearl describes it:

"They were necessities, ordered months before, paid for and safely arrived. The children, (first Pearl and later Faith), anticipated for weeks the morning when Andrew, looking up from the letters before him on the breakfast table, would say solemnly, 'The boxes have come!' If he were not at home, they could scarcely bear it, for Carie would not open them until he came. But he was nearly always there in the early winter. There was a regular routine to be followed, always exciting. Andrew must go down to the Customs office on the Bund and present the bill of lading and get the boxes through the Customs. The children at home were waiting at the gate of the compound, if it were fair, climbing high so that they might catch the first glimpse of Andrew around the corner of the Buddhist temple in the valley. If it were raining, they waited at the front door, their noses pressed against the glass pane. Meanwhile Carie was preparing a place in the back hall for the boxes.

"There was no greater ecstasy than the moment when Andrew appeared from behind the temple, followed by four or five coolies with boxes slung on ropes upon their carrying poles. The sound of their rhythmic step-keeping call floated up the hill and came nearer and nearer—'Heigh-ho—heigh-ho—' Soon, soon the boxes would be dropped in the hall, and the men clamoring about them in the dear confusion of the hour. Andrew would be waging a war over the tips the coolies were shouting for, slapping their sweaty breasts, pointing to the welts upon their horny shoulders.

" 'These foreign boxes are full of lead!' they would shout. 'They are fit to kill us—and we came up the hill—and what is this mite upon my hand!' They would throw their coins down and spit upon them, and Carie would implore Andrew, 'Give them a little more, Andrew—just this once!' And then very unwillingly he would give them a little more, and they would subside into grins and go away. And there were the boxes!

"Some child always had the hammer and the big nail puller that Andrew had bought for such days, and breathlessly they would watch while the strong iron teeth sank into the wood as Andrew pounded and clutched the nail head and the nail came up screeching with reluctance.

"Every board was saved as it came off, because the boards were good American pine, dry as no wood in China was ever dry. All our bookcases and bureaus and the chests in the attic were made of the Montgomery Ward boxes. Under the lid was strong brown paper. Carie pulled it away, and there were the things from America! It was our most real, most tangible touch with our own country.

"Now, looking back, these things seem very simple, such things as the Americans order every day from their grocers and think nothing but necessities. But to us they were the dearest luxuries, things that could be bought nowhere around us, foods to be tasted and savored and enjoyed as precious, tools that seemed magic in complexity, garments made and ready to wear, marvels of fashion.

"But really there were tins of coffee and bags of sugar, cakes of yeast and soap, a round keg of molasses for Carie's famous gingerbreads, and spices which perhaps had grown in the Orient and now were back again ready to be used. There were needles and pins, hairpins and threads, all the small things not to be found in the Chinese stores—some ribbon in gay colors to be used to tie back little girls' curls on Sundays (dyed tape on other days) and there were other little luxuries. . . . At last there was always a little special thing that each child had chosen out of the fabulous catalogue. Oh, the lovely hours we all spent poring over the catalogue, searching for the one thing, costing no more than the dollar that we were allowed, the heart-burning decisions as to whether it were better to have several small things costing less or the one beloved costing a full dollar! And the agony when the one beloved cost a dollar and nineteen cents! There was no use in going to Andrew . . . but Carie could be persuaded. . . .

"Each child then had his little package, precious to receive, precious to unwrap and to look at and to fondle and play with and put under the pillow at night. Yet the catalogue was a book of heartburning, too. So many things cost much more than a dollar! There was one of Andrew's little girls [Pearl herself] who yearned deeply over years for a certain large doll. To this day she has not forgotten that doll The legend underneath read 'life-size.' That meant as big as a real baby. She remembers its round bisque face in a frilly lace bonnet, its chubby hands, its long dress and little knit jacket. But it cost three dollars and ninety-eight cents and was of course hopelessly out of possibility. She bought a little doll or two, but they were never the same. She prayed resolutely for years that some Christmas— but there never was such a Christmas. She had little cheap dolls, dressed exquisitely and completely by Carie's hands. But they were not life-size. . . . If Carie had realized, she would have somehow seen to it, by some prodigious slashing sacrifice, that that small heart had its desire. But she never knew, for the child never spoke, not dreaming that the fabulous sum was within her parents' possibility to give. . . . So the doll remained upon the pages of the catalogue to dream over and at last to relinquish, except to this day that child, now long grown, cannot pass the doll counter in a toy shop—cannot have her fill, for that matter, of real babies."

The arrival of the Montgomery Ward order was almost like a second Christmas, for "every year of her life she (Carie) made Christmas the happiest, merriest time for her children. The trimming of the house with holly (cut from the nearby hills) and greens, and the stirring of the plum pudding had always been rites in the family life. Here as elsewhere she had had to provide all, for there were no toy shops, no Christmas display to help her. But she could make Christmas a very orgy of gingerbread men and ladies and toys she manufactured, or things both useful and nonsensical, of stockings hung at the hearth on Christmas Eve, and on Christmas morning a tree trimmed with what she had made of bits of bright paper and ribbon she had saved through the year. It was one time in the year when she gave herself whole-heartedly to gayety, and nothing was allowed to spoil the pleasure of the season and to shatter the sweet mystery of Christmas Eve and the Manger Story told about an open fire and carols sung at the organ before bed time. In the morning

40

her brilliant voice rang through the house at dawn, 'Joy to the World, the Lord is Come!'

"So she created Christmas for her children. So she built into them the tradition and deep meaning of Christmas so that they never forgot it and to this day . . . Christmas stirs them with profoundest memories. Yet she took pains always to make them realize that it was a time of sharing and each child was taught to prepare gifts not only for parents and each other but for servants and little Chinese friends and any whom they knew to be in special need, also. Well she knew the pleasure of sharing and the good content that follows it."

Yet the bungalow on the hill, pleasant and comfortable as it was, could not hold Pearl now that she had escaped from the streets of the city where she had been forbidden to play. Beyond these garden walls the whole world seemed waiting to be explored.

There were purple-blue hills in the far distance, and soft splotches of green that were bamboo groves, and shining ponds in the valleys. Close beneath the hill where the house stood were thatched-roofed farm houses, each with its hard-beaten threshing floor. There was the Buddhist temple, too, against the far end of the hill. Its gong rang through the dusk, quivering and awesome, and faintly the chanting of priests rose sometimes in the lull of mid-afternoon.

Early in the spring in the valleys farmers beneath great straw or bamboo-braided hats were plowing for the planting of rice, the water buffaloes turning up the coils of rich black earth as they plodded slowly along. Sometimes there was a long, high call and the crack of a whip if one grew too lazy in working. After this plowing, the fields would be flooded, then harrowed before the planting began. All over central China the low fields and the terraced fields were being made ready for rice, which was the food of the people.

And the vegetable gardens were as pretty as flower beds, each neatly outlined with not a weed to be seen. Pearl watched the people at their gardening and saw the sowing and setting and weeding and harvesting. There were the baby cabbages, and there the next in size, and there the large ones almost ready to be cut for market, their stems glistening white, and their leaves shining and dark. The broad beans were beginning to blossom. Their flowers were like little lavender moths with spots of black on their wings. They were sweet

41

to smell when the sun shone hot upon them. Watching the life in those valleys Pearl began to learn the ways and the talk of the farmers and their families.

But in the rainy season of early summer she could not roam the hills and valleys. She had to stay in the house. She was just seven when, one day in her hunger for something to read, she discovered Charles Dickens.

High on a shelf stood a row of books all exactly alike, bound in dull blue cloth. Years later she looked back and thinking of that day wrote,

"I have long looked for an opportunity to pay a certain debt which I have owed.... Debts are usually burdens, but this is no ordinary debt, and it is no burden, except as the feeling of warm gratitude may ache in one until it is expressed. My debt is to an Englishman, who long ago in China rendered an inestimable service to a small American child. The child was myself and the Englishman was Charles Dickens. I know of no better way to meet my obligation than to write down what Charles Dickens did in China for an American child.

"First, you must picture to yourself that child, living quite solitary in a remote Chinese countryside, in a small mission bungalow perched upon a hill among the rice fields in the valleys below.... However kind the people about her might be, and they were much more often kind than not, she knew that she was foreign to them ... To this small isolated creature there came one day an extraordinary accident. She was an impossibly voracious reader. She would have liked to have had children's books, but there were none, and so she read everything—Plutarch's *Lives* and Fox's *Martyrs*, the Bible, church history, and the hot spots in Jonathan Edwards' sermons and conversations out of Shakespeare, and bits of Tennyson and Browning which she could not understand at all Then one day she looked doubtfully at a long row of somber blue books on a very high shelf. They were quite beyond her reach. Later she discovered it was because they were novels. But being desperate she put a three-cornered stool on top of a small table and climbed up and stared at the bindings and in faded black titles she read *Oliver Twist*, by Charles Dickens.... She took *Oliver Twist* out of his place—it was fat and thick for *Hard Times* was bound with it—and in great peril descended....

"How can I make you know what that discovery was to that small,

42

lonely child? ... I cannot tell you about those hours. I know I was roused at six o'clock by the call to my supper, and I looked about dazed. ... I remember twice I closed the book and burst into tears, unable to bear the tragedy of Oliver Twist, and then opened it quickly, burning to know more. ... I went to my supper in a dream, and read as late as I dared in my bed afterward, and slept with the book under my pillow, and woke again in the early morning. When *Oliver Twist* was finished and after it *Hard Times,* I was wretched with indecision. I felt I must read it all straight over again, and yet I was voracious for that long row of blue books. ...

"I resolved to read straight through the row and then begin at the beginning once more and read straight through again. This program I carried on consistently, over and over for about ten years, and after that I still kept a Dickens book on hand. ... Today I have for him a feeling I have for no other human soul. He opened my eyes to people, he taught me how to love all sorts of people, high and low, rich and poor, the old and little children. He taught me to hate hypocrisy and pious mouthing of unctuous words. He taught me that beneath gruffness there may be kindness, and that kindness is the sweetest thing in the world, and goodness is the best thing in the world. He taught me to despise money-grubbing. People today say he is obvious and sentimental and childish in his analysis of character and yet I have found people surprisingly like those he wrote about. ... He gave me that zest, that immense joy in life and in people, and in their variety. ...

"He made Christmas for me, a merry, roaring English Christmas, full of goodies and plum puddings and merriment and friendly cheer. I went to his parties over and over for I had no others. ...

"He made me love England. ... When I went there years later, London was my city and the countryside I knew. I was not strange. The people were my own people, too. England is the mother of a certain part of my spirit. ...

"This Charles Dickens did for me. His influence I cannot lose. He has made himself a part of me forever."

Pickwick Papers was one of Pearl's favorites in the long row of blue books for it made her laugh, and she loved to laugh. She laughed over the Wellers and the widow and Mr. Pickwick that first year in the bungalow. Dickens' people were a real part of her life, a normal, pleasant life, entirely her own.

The next winter Carie thought Pearl should learn to read Chinese.
An elderly tutor came three times a week to the house and spread on
the dining room table the few books which he wished to use. This
was the ordinary method of instruction in the Chinese language and
although Pearl spoke Chinese as readily as English, she had not yet
learned to read it.

It was this Chinese scholar who led Pearl to discover Abraham
Lincoln. Carie and Andrew had never made statements in recogni-
tion of Lincoln's greatness for they were uncertain in themselves,
Andrew saying always, "Lincoln was a very much over-rated man."
Many years later Pearl in a speech delivered in honor of Mary Mc-
Leod Bethune, said, "Certainly the Chinese among whom I lived
knew very little about America or the Civil War, and yet somehow
even to those remote regions there had come rumors of Abraham
Lincoln. I think the first time I heard one of these rumors was when
I was quite a young child, perhaps not more than nine or so, and I
heard it from an old Chinese gentleman who was my tutor in Chinese. I don't think he knew any more about America than that for I
never heard him make the slightest comment on anything else American. But one day when we were reading a little story about a runaway slave—he stopped and said suddenly, 'In your country the dark
people were slaves until A-ba-la-hen Lin Kung said, "There shall be
no more slaves now and henceforward forever in America." Now
do you understand the word slave?'

"I had later, a little book of easy Chinese prepared by some Chinese writer, in which were stories of the great men of all countries,
and Abraham Lincoln was the only American in that book. There
was a picture of him. I remember, a very badly printed blotchy picture of that tall, plain man, never handsome even at his best, except
in the beauty of his nobility."

Now there were American neighbors in the bungalow next door
There was the Bear family and James was near Pearl's age. He loved
reading, too, and often he and Pearl read together, sometimes books
from Mr. Bear's curious collection which was forbidden to them
But their real interest together lay in a museum which they hid in a
small tool house near the deep cold well. Here they collected strange
things from the hills. Writing years later, a story for children, Pearl
says, "There were old graves (on the hills) made long ago, and the

44

winds blew on them and the rains soaked them and sometimes the sides wore away, and I found old jars and bowls in them, that the long-ago people had put there as we put flowers now. These jars I dug out and washed and kept in what I called my museum."

But James was there in the next house only the one winter, and congenial as was that childhood friendship with the thoughtful, imaginative boy, it passed quickly and Pearl's life went on in her reading and in the events of the lives of the valley people.

VII   P EARL WAS to feel her foreignness during the summer of 1900. All over China new hostility was rising against white people. There were reasons for it. Pearl felt anxiety in the house as sometimes Carie packed a few suitcases or talked quietly with Andrew in the night. When Pearl asked about it Carie made it as clear as she could.

"The trouble began a long time ago, dear. Foreign traders drove their way into China with warships and guns. The Chinese do not like to fight and they had none of the things to make war with. They wanted to be let alone, too, for they were quite content as they were. But at first traders and then their governments fought wars against the Chinese to make them buy opium from India so that business could go on in a way that pleased them. The Chinese lost these wars and to settle up the matter had to let the foreigners have land to live on and had to pay large sums of money called indemnity to other governments. Of course it isn't strange that the Chinese really don't want the foreigners here."

"But what about the Boxers? You and Father are always talking about the Boxers," Pearl asked, puzzled. "Who are they?"

"They are a group of Chinese belonging to a secret club or brotherhood. They do peculiar gymnastics and call themselves the Righteous Harmony Fists. That is what the name comes from."

"And why are we afraid of them?"

"Because they have sworn that they would fight the foreigners and push them out of China. They weren't really dangerous until the Old Empress Dowager—."

"The one Father calls the 'old Buddha'?"

"Yes, that's right—until she gave them permission to go ahead and do what they liked. She wants China to be free of the foreigners, too, because she is afraid of modern things they are bringing in, things like railroads and machines and schools."

Pearl knew that the news grew worse. In bits it came to her that a group of American missionaries in the north had been killed. Their wives and little children had been killed, too. The killing spread and soon everywhere in China there was the dreadful word that the Empress Dowager had said that all foreigners were to be killed.

It was curious to look down into the valleys and watch the farmers peacefully at their work and think that if they wished they could steal up in the night and kill Mother and Father and little Faith and herself. But it was incredible. She was not afraid. These neighbors would never carry out such an order no matter who gave it. But suddenly she was more alien than ever before. Suddenly she was more than ever conscious of America and of being an American. It did not matter how good Father was or how he worked to help the Chinese, nor how Mother gave medicine to the sick women who came to her or helped care for their babies when they hadn't the proper food, or taught women to read, or had her meetings. They were still Americans away from their own country.

One day Father said suddenly at the table [Pearl writes],

" 'I've had to close up three more chapels this last month. The landlords would not let me keep them I can't find another place—no one will rent me a place to preach in now.... We're having meetings at the houses of the different church members. We have to have them as the Christians did of old—at midnight, secretly, as we are able.'

"Many and many a night the children woke to hear the clang of the compound gate and to see the flicker of Andrew's big old kerosene oil lantern which he carried at night and kept spotlessly clean himself ... When we saw the flicker upon the white-washed wall, we knew that it was Andrew coming home from a secret meeting of the Christians.

"The whole house came somehow to be filled not with fear but with a sort of solemn waiting. One by one the servants, on some pretext or another, left, until there were only the nurse (Wang Amah) and her son. And Andrew was at home more and more, his face daily growing more grim. He went several times to see the American

46

consul and came back to say to Carie, 'He can't do anything—they're all waiting.'

"And one night he never came home at all! It was nearly noon of the next day before he came in, and his wrists were bleeding where thongs had held him.

"When Carie, frantic with anxiety, cried out, he answered soberly, 'Be glad I am alive. I was at Lin Meng's administering communion to his old mother when soldiers came in. They took Lin Meng away and tortured him until he died. . . . I was left bound, and the old woman died as I stood there, bound to a post.'

"His face worked as he sat down and groaned."

It was a curious summer. Day after day no one except a few old, old Chinese friends and workers came to the house, and these came secretly. It seemed as though the hill where the bungalow stood was an island. Mother had time to play more than usual. They rarely left the house and no white people came. Pearl did not know until later, when they went to Shanghai themselves, that it was because all other foreigners had already gone. Because the viceroy or governor of their province was especially friendly to white people, they had felt it safe to stay on. But the American consul had said that if there were danger near, the flag at the consulate would go up and down three times. Then they must go at once to the river and catch the first steamer that they could.   •

One August afternoon it was very hot and Mother was saying, sighing a little, "If only we could be in Kuling! Our empty house stands waiting for us. But of course we would not dare go further inland, nor would we be allowed to do so," when the door opened and Father rushed in.

"The flag's gone down, Carie," he said "We must make haste to go to the river at once." They flew to the bags they had kept packed and stowed more canned milk and fresh bread in a basket. Wang Amah was spluttering and grumbling as she folded garments.

In ten minutes they were starting out the gate. They went, not by the big road, but by little paths, and keeping always to the narrow back streets, they reached the steamer, walked up the gangplank and were aboard. To Pearl it was a miracle. In an instant everything was changed and they were going to Shanghai.

Father did not go with them. He would not leave his work whatever the danger. They waved to him as the steamer pulled away,

47

until they could no longer see his tall figure in the white suit and sun helmet It was then that Pearl thought with sudden pride, "Father's not afraid of anything!"

"It is not possible to know fully what was in Andrew's mind when he went back, the solitary white man in that whole countryside," Pearl writes. "Never, then or after, did he leave his post when danger came. He went back quietly. On the way he was spat upon many times, and curses were shouted after him. But curses were common and he paid no heed to them. He entered the empty house, bathed and changed his clothing, and sat down to his supper. One young lad, (Wang Amah's son) remained to serve him.

"He stayed on stubbornly in the square mission house with the one Chinese lad all through the hot brilliant summer. The lad hanging about the streets at night, brought him rumors each day of new massacres of white people in other places. Andrew was the sole white man in the region He came and went quietly, preaching openly in the streets until the fury of the passersby and their shouts grew too threatening for him to be heard. Then with that high serene stubbornness of his, he handed out his tracts, saw them dropped or torn, and went away to try in another street His quietness, the extreme dignity of his tall figure, his lack of any fear seem to have preserved him I know that from Ma, the Christian, who stayed by him still. Once he said to me of Andrew, 'I thought many times he would be killed. . There were stones flung at him—once a stone cut him on the cheek, but he did not even put up his hand to wipe away the blood. He did not seem to feel it.'

" 'Were you afraid?' we asked Andrew when he was an old man, remembering.

"He considered. 'There have been times in my life when I have been afraid. But it was always over small matters. . . . I never was afraid when I was on God's business.' "

All through China the Rebellion was increasing in fury. The Empress Dowager had the young emperor put in jail because he wanted China to learn new ways. She had many of his friends killed. She thought that if only she could get rid of the greedy foreigners, China would have peace again. Yet she herself was not a true Chinese. She was a Manchu and long ago the Manchus had invaded China and now ruled it. Though the Empress Dowager had yellow skin, her

48

imperial dress was a long Manchu robe coming to the floor instead of the short jacket and skirt which the Chinese women wore.

In Shanghai Pearl knew that things were not getting better but worse. White people began to pour in by every steamer, by slow boats or by overland chairs. Some of them had been traveling for weeks.

"Everyone is coming here, Mother," Pearl said.

"The consuls have told the white people they had better come to the coast at once," Carie answered. She did not want to frighten the child and yet it was best to help her to understand. "You see the Empress Dowager has begun to urge not only the killing of foreigners but of the Christians who are their friends."

"Just like the man Father said they took," Pearl said.

Instantly she thought of the Chinese she had seen in the church in Chinkiang and of the men and women who came to the bungalow They were ordinary people just like the farmers and small tradesmen she saw every day. It was cruel that these had to suffer for the white men even though they meant well in their teaching

It grew so bad that foreign troops left Tientsin to go to Peking to protect the legations there. They could not reach there and had to turn around and come back. Within the next few days the papers said that Tientsin itself was in danger and the foreign troops had taken the Taku forts on the river leading to the sea The Taku forts were familiar even to Pearl, for often they were mentioned in conversations among the grown-ups. The Manchus said that the taking of the forts was an act of war and the legations were ordered out of Peking. The white people in Shanghai seemed to be clinging to the edge of China, waiting to be shoved off.

The Rebellion rushed along like a huge wave which grew higher and stronger as it came Word got out that the foreigners in Peking were beleaguered and no help could get to them. The German minister was killed. The old Dowager believed that her day had come at last and that she could rid China of this Western nonsense.

In Shanghai Pearl listened as fresh refugees came and told of their experiences. Every time a new group arrived there was rejoicing when friends met, and sadness over some lost, and a great new store of incidents to be told. There were stories of brave Chinese who had risked their own lives to save their Western friends; stories of escape, men let down over city walls in carrying baskets, or swimming canals in the dark of night, or lying in grain fields for days, or

49

hiding themselves in empty coffins. There were stories Carie tried not to have Pearl hear, stories of how whole foreign communities were killed, women and little children along with the men But Pearl could not be kept from hearing, for talk of the Boxer Rebellion was everywhere, and she absorbed it until it was part of her.

For the first time Pearl knew the feeling of being hunted because her skin was white. Mother had known it before, and Father, but not she. Although she knew that they were safe in Shanghai, the feeling was there, underneath. Through the years there has still come no answer to that problem which even as a child she saw The foreigners did not belong in China, even though most of them, like Father and Mother, were good, and there with the purpose of doing good. Years later writing of that time she said, "They had no right to be there. . . . They were innocent, for they believed that what they did was of God."

But there were experiences of other kinds, in those months in Shanghai. America was made more vivid and clear to Pearl. Carie and the children used often to go to the park beside the Whangpoo River where junks and sampans and launches and even great steamers passed. They watched with eager eyes when one of these ships from far across the ocean slid into its dock and Carie told how when it had changed its cargo it would set out again to go to America. This very ship would reach America! Carie's eyes were glowing.

"How soon will we be going?" Pearl asked one day.

"When Father feels the time has come when he can leave his work," Carie answered. There was then no regular time for furloughs among the mission workers.

Mother told them again of meadows and orchards and fields and cows and white houses and steepled churches and all of them seemed nearer because they were where one took ship for America.

There were experiences, too, of seeing people never seen before. Here were tall turbanned East Indian Sikhs standing guard before imposing entrances. Here Indian women swathed in yards of bright silks, carrying often their small soft-eyed babies whom Pearl longed to hold herself. Here were half-breeds who were called Eurasians, some more Chinese than white, some more white than Chinese, but all going about their business as though longing not to be seen, furtive and unhappy.

Even the Chinese were different from those of Chinkiang or the Kuling mountain, small and lithe and with a liquid dialect which she

50

could not understand at all. Wang Amah was often out of patience with them, arguing as to the meaning of what they said and grumbling, "Their food is not fit to eat, this food of Shanghai people!"

At last the foreign nations sent armies against the Empress Dowager and only then when the Empress was put to flight and Peking was taken was the Rebellion over.

But Andrew found the people still sullen They threatened him and set their dogs upon him and still refused to rent him places for preaching Twice chapels were burned.

"It occurred to him that it had been nine years since he had seen his country and that a furlough was due him. Carie, too, living in close rented rooms in Shanghai was ready for a change. . . . A year of furlough and then he would come back. . . . He shut up the square mission house and went to Shanghai. His children had almost forgotten him, although every night they had prayed, 'God, please keep our father from the Boxers.'

"He appeared taller than ever to them, thinner, and his eyes were more hoary blue in the burned red-brown face. And he was shy with them and did not know how to talk to them."

But with wonder and delight they thought, "Now *we* are going on one of the ships sailing to America!" To Pearl, now nine, it was a dream coming true. To little Faith it was a promise of things like red apples lying on clean green grass. To Wang Amah it was parting. To Carie it was the return of an exile.

PART TWO

VIII   Soon they were aboard ship.

The great funnels rose above them as they stood on the highest deck. Black smoke was pouring out as the engines were being fired for sailing. There was a blast from the small whistle alongside the funnel and the children shrieked and ran, more excited than frightened The ship began to move away from the dock. The cables were loosened. There was the grinding of wood against wood and the spinning of windlasses. They were turning and nosing out. They had started for America!

Now there was only sea and sea. It was beautiful, this water, yet Pearl feared it and was ever to fear it, feeling it too deep, too powerful and remindful of the strong currents of the Yangtze.

All day long she played with the other children on the ship. There were wonderful spaces for hide-and-seek. There were times when they could race down the decks, and times when the captain stopped to talk with them and tell them stories of typhoons and fogs and ships gone off their courses. He never told enough but no one dared ask for more. When he was done he simply strode away and left them aching with longing and lying in wait to see when he might linger with them again.

The ship did not stop at Honolulu and at last they knew one night that when the day came they would see land. When they looked out into the mists of early morning, the land was there. They had come through the Golden Gate in the darkness and now before them there lay bluffs and hills and the city of San Francisco. They were looking at America.

It was all wonderful and beautiful and clean and rich and un-believable—high buildings and elevators and running water and electric lights and people well-dressed, nobody seeming to be poor. But one thing was surprising to Pearl and this was the sight of white men handling trunks and white men doing errands in the hotels and white girls coming in to spread the beds. "Even the coolies and servants are white people," she said in a loud whisper to Carie as soon as they were alone.

"But we don't have coolies in America," Carie laughed. "Every-one works and no one is ashamed of it. It's the right way, of course."

The same day that they landed they took the train eastward across the continent The two children sat next to the windows and gazed transfixed at all they passed. They climbed mighty mountains and saw snow lying on the rocks; they dropped into valleys where streams rushed and gurgled and wild deer grazed; they passed lonely little towns on arid deserts—before they came after nearly a week to the country which Carie said with shining eyes was like her coun-try. Here were soft hills and cupped valleys and clustered trees and rich fertile fields, all beautiful beyond imagining. The houses snug and white and gabled, like pictures in the magazines! And the white fences and great barns! The people so clean and healthy and all speaking American! It was hard to get used to this.

Before they came to the white house which was Carie's home, there was Edwin He had finished college now and was ready for the university and they were planning to spend the most of this year in America in the college town where he was to be Yet it could not be that this tall man with curly dark hair and a pince-nez on his short-sighted eyes stooping to kiss Carie was Edwin. That morning when Pearl had held his thin boy's finger came back in a flash. He kissed her gravely now and as gravely her eyes clung to him. She did not know him for the years had changed him from boy to man.

Now Pearl saw the old home in America. She saw it with all that Carie had told her of it mingled in with her own impressions. There was the big white house with its columns running the full height embracing the porches, upstairs and down. There was the great yard fenced in with its white fence. There was the enormous sugar maple with the stile under it where Carie had told her she often as a girl had mounted and dismounted from her horse. There, again, was the fragrance of flowers from the garden at the side There was the Delaware grapevine, hanging full of fruit turning already to a soft pink and throwing a flickering shadow. There were the butterfly bushes flanking the lower porch. Far behind the house lay the orchard and the vegetable garden and the berry bushes. Everything was beautiful and free and open. . . . The big white door with its huge brass knocker and a fan-shaped window looked straight into a broad hall and opened at its other end into a back lawn with trees and phlox beds which intervened before the green mass of the orchard.

All this she saw in one vast, hungry, sweeping gaze. It was halted by two men who came towards them. With eyes no longer those of a baby she saw them. She says, "I remember. . . . my first glimpse of Cornelius, Carie's beloved brother, who had stood next to God all my life. He came out of the big white house in which I was born, his white hair glittering in the sun. He looked the oldest man in the world, and I thought he must be Hermanus and I cried out, 'Grandfather!' But Cornelius laughed and behind him I saw still another older, more silver-haired figure, and that was Hermanus."

Uncle 'Nelus led her through the downstairs rooms and she found them just as Carie had described them. On the left as they entered was the parlor, cool and dark and furnished with horsehair furniture —smooth and very slick and hard to sit upon because of its smoothness—and bookcases and a beautiful rosewood center table. There was a piano and on the piano lay violins and a flute. On the walls hung etchings and pen and ink drawings that Grandfather had made, and oils that his oldest granddaughters, the children of Cornelius, had painted. Over the mantel hung the portrait of Great-Grandfather Stulting. Pearl stood gravely studying it. He was the one who had led three hundred people here from Holland and he was the one who had started the building of this beautiful house. . . . A flowered carpet covered the floor under her feet. She loved the warm, rich colors feeling them luxurious after the plainness of Chinese mattings. Long French windows opened into the flower garden and she looked out with ecstacy. Cornelius felt the grasp of her hand tighten on his

54

and caught the shine in her eyes when she looked up at him and said carefully, "It is prettier even than I thought."

Opposite the parlor was Uncle 'Nelus's and Aunt Anna's room. Next to it was Grandfather's room Uncle 'Nelus opened the door and smiled to see the expression on Pearl's face when the sound of multitudinous watches and clocks rushed out with a steady whir.

At the far end of the hall was the dining room, moved up from the basement where it had been when Carie was last here, a cool simple room it was with only a few pieces of good furniture and an oval table which made her think at once of the table that they had in China. The windows of the dining room gave into the vegetable garden.

Carie called from the porch as they came back to the foot of the stairs. "Come, Pearl, I want to take you upstairs." Faith clung to the handrail of the dark walnut stairs and Carie and Pearl went lightly up. There were six bedrooms. Carie led the way to the front one on the left side of the house. She went at once to the windows which opened to the soft wooded greenness of the rolling meadows lying beyond the yard. There to the left was the sugar maple and below lay the flower garden. She stood a moment so, and then she turned swiftly and with a sweep of her hand pointed to what the room held.

"This is my room," she said, and her voice was warm with happiness. "Over there are the closets where I hung my hooped skirts. We needed deep closets for them. I told you, didn't I, how after the war we had to make everything ourselves, the flax we grew and wove into cloth and the wool of our sheep we carded and spun and used for winter clothes. ... We had to find our own hoops, too, and the best thing for them were the withes of greenbrier bushes. These did very well until they grew too dry and then sometimes they would snap. Did I ever tell you how once my hoop snapped?" Her eyes shone with merriment as she dropped into a low rocker and began to tell the story. " 'Well, one Sunday I went to church—of course we had to go every Sunday—but this Sunday there was a missionary speaking and the little church was very full and dear good Mrs. Dunlop, the minister's wife, sat next to me. She was a darling and I loved her, but she was very fat and she kept squeezing against me so that it seemed to me she just expanded more and more. It was a hot summer's day, too. Well, she kept expanding and she pushed against my hoop, and at last my hoop—it wasn't a big one, really, because my father wouldn't let us wear very big ones—but my hoop

55

just rose up in front of me and lifted my skirt shamefully high, and I tried to press it down and it wouldn't go down. Well, at last I grew desperate because a boy was sitting just behind and I could hear him snickering, so I gave a good hard push and there was a loud snap. My greenbrier hoop! My skirt went down all of a sudden then But you should have seen me when I stood up. My skirt hung about me and it was so long it trailed on the ground. Good Mrs. Dunlop stood in front of me and I walked out to the buggy behind her and climbed in right quick. Afterwards we laughed and laughed, but I was dreadfully ashamed that day, although I couldn't keep from laughing, too. I knew I looked funny. Father said it was judgment for my vanity. Maybe it was, but I always felt it was because the greenbrier was just too dry and couldn't stand the strain of Mrs. Dunlop's expansion!'"

Carie went quickly to lift the lid of the deep window seat. "This is where I kept my scoop bonnets," she said. "It still smells like it used to smell—like white pine and straw braid. . . . And the bed is the same one." She turned and stood now, her hands poised as though ready to touch something. "You were born here, Pearl," she said and her eyes grew soft with remembering.

It was such a pretty room. Pearl walked slowly around it examining the wallpaper with its tiny sprays of pink roses and pale green ferns, the pictures, three of them, a Madonna, a daguerreotype of Grandmother, and a print of a shepherd leading his sheep home in the evening. The floor was soft with its covering of matting overlaid with a rose-colored carpet. There were ruffled white curtains at the windows, held back by rose-colored loops. There were two chairs, the white rocker in which Carie had been sitting and a straight ladder-backed chair. There was a little rosewood dressing table and a bureau and above the dressing table a small oval mirror in a carved, pale gilt frame. Pearl caught a glimpse of herself in the mirror but her mind was too full of the room itself to see the intent face.

Someone called from downstairs. It was a girl's voice. At the foot of the stairs her cousins were waiting. There was Grace, three years older than herself, and Mamie in her late 'teens and Ena a grown young woman.

Cousin Grace's eyes were shining for she was impatient to begin playing. It was time to feed the chickens, and there were new kittens and there was Bundy, the old favorite doll, and Anna Zilla, the fine wax doll, and there was Grandfather's music box. And there was croquet set up in the back lawn. And old Shep, the dog, was barking with excitement.

They went quickly down and Grace appropriated Pearl and rushed outdoors with her. At first they scarcely spoke and then suddenly Grace burst out, "There's a robin's nest in the crab apple. Can you climb up to it? I've tried and I can't."

It was the beginning of their climbing trees. Pearl had climbed the trees of the bungalow yard and she climbed swiftly and well. But the robin had chosen a safe place At last Pearl was stopped. Grace watched progress from below and when she saw Pearl could go no further shouted up, "Shut your eyes and climb!"

They peeped into many nests that summer, never touching the eggs or the young. They dressed old Bundy and buried her, went through elaborate funeral services only to exhume her and repeat the ritual again. They fed the chickens until they clattered and crowed at the sight of the two girls. They picked sweet berries and summer apples, eating as they picked. They helped with the skimming of cream and the churning of butter and the making of cheese and watched the lump of salt-rising bread beneath Aunt Anna's strong hands.

When the sun was hot outside they came in to find Grandfather and begged him to wind up the old music box which he had brought from Holland. It gave out a soft tinkling music which Pearl loved. They watched Mamie paint china with delicate strokes before the cups and saucers and dishes and bowls were sent away to the kiln for the last baking. They gazed at a picture Grandfather had made in Holland. It was of an old lady who was supposed to have lived for forty years without food, yet she looked wonderfully well.

Pearl was always especially careful with Grandfather. The first morning he came to breakfast when they had already begun. He was eighty-seven but very straight and a little severe. His hair was pure white and brushed straight up from a forehead exactly like Carie's. He said "Good morning" to everyone at once and marched to his place. Later, he took Pearl to his room and told her about the watches and clocks, where they had come from and how old they were and to whom they belonged and what was the matter with them. Much of it had to do with the Old Country and all that he said was like a fairy tale.

But it was not through what he said that Pearl came to know Grandfather Stulting best. She saw him most clearly on the first

Sunday morning when they went to church. Sunday had always been different from every other day but here it was more different still. The whole house seemed set in a different key and everyone walked more softly and laughing was subdued and meals were prepared on Saturday as if the coming day were a holiday.

Promptly as the first bell rang in mellow tones over the village, they all set out for the small white church Grandfather walked in front and the others streamed behind him. Now she saw more clearly the line of his head and the shoulders drawn back to extreme erectness. Importance made the sound of his steps more rapid When at last they reached the church and filed in, Grandfather left them and went to the small choir loft and took out his tuning fork with elaborate efficiency. For years he had led the singing and even now his voice though weak was true.

Pearl herself felt a certain shyness of all the friendly eyes upon her. She wore a white dress and a leghorn hat which Carie had skilfully trimmed with a soft rich-colored scarf folded and knotted about its crown. Her hair, most often braided and fastened with bows behind her ears to be well out of the way on ordinary days, hung now in soft curls over her shoulders It was when the singing rose at the humming of Grandfather's fork, that suddenly she knew this for the singing that Carie had meant when she talked of singing in the church at home—so different from the half humorous, half pathetic singing of Chinese voices in the chapel in Chinkiang.

She learned to know Grandfather, too, through watching his small, dextrous hands working with the bees whose honey was his contribution to the table. He could handle them and move them from place to place and separate them when they swarmed, and never receive a sting. And while he did it the touch of a smile was always on his face.

She learned to know more about him and why always she feared him a little, because of Andrew. Andrew was away a large part of the time visiting his brothers and sisters and preaching at churches whenever he was invited. She writes of her memory: "I remember my anxiety when he was asked to preach in Carie's home church, that he would not be able to preach in English, and my amazement when he not only preached but preached very long indeed. He had, I felt, more than enough to say. . . . Andrew threw the family into consternation because he was so late in arriving the Saturday before the Sunday he was to preach. I felt quite miserable and somehow responsible for it. Hermanus kept watching and snorting about the delay and Carie kept apologizing, and I felt, since Andrew was my father, I ought to be able to do something about it. It was a hot August day and most of the afternoon I sat on the stile under the huge old maple, watching the dusty road. Around the supper table the aunts and uncles looked severely at Carie. 'Is he usually late like this?' they inquired of her.

" 'No—no, indeed,' she replied hastily. 'I can't think what's keeping him. He wrote me he was riding horseback from Lewisburg today over Droop Mountain.'

" 'He'll be worn out if he does get here now,' Hermanus said gloomily and added, 'He's not such a good preacher that he can get up and do us credit off-hand.'

"Carie did not answer, though I saw a kindling in her eye. I felt at once an odd aching—it was strange that she, my mother, should be scolded like a little girl, and I wanted to defend her.

"Then suddenly Andrew walked in, his suitcase in his hand, his shoes very dusty.

" 'Well, sir!' cried Hermanus.

" 'My horse went lame when she'd gone less than two miles,' said Andrew, 'so I walked.'

"They all stared at him.

" 'Walked!' cried Cornelius. 'Over Droop Mountain—and a bag!'

" 'There wasn't any other way to get here.' said Andrew 'I'll just go and wash myself ' He disappeared and I can still remember the clamoring and astonishment. He had walked fifteen miles over a great mountain, carrying his suitcase

"I was suddenly very proud of him and piped, 'There're always books in his suitcase, too!'

"But Hermanus said grimly, 'He'll be no good at all tomorrow,' and when Andrew came in presently, very washed and speckless, he shouted to my aunt. . . . 'Go and fetch some hot meat! The man's famished!' and sat there snorting a little from time to time while Andrew ate."

There were evenings when Uncle 'Nelus told stories out on the dusk of the porch. He liked to sit on the top step and run his hands through his bushy white hair so that it stood more than ever on end and tell things about the Civil War and about when Carie was little. Uncle 'Nelus had a way of telling something that was very funny without a change in his face, looking up when he had done

59

and then letting his eyes twinkle when they met the twinkle in other eyes Pearl loved Uncle 'Nelus

But Uncle 'Nelus did not tell of the hard years before the war when as the oldest in the family he did the work of a grown man, helping to finish this house begun by his grandfather, Mynheer Cornelius Stulting, and determining that those younger than he should have a better education, and planning to organize a village school and working on the farmlands and chopping wood and saving his father from hard work, since he was not bred to it, and caring for his little French mother who was delicate. He told them of the war which came when he was twenty. He was foreign-born and they could not conscript him. Nor could he volunteer for all these lives were mainly dependent on him Nor would he volunteer, for that matter. Hillsboro lay on the very border between North and South and many of the wealthier around them had slaves. But his father had taught him the hatred of slavery and would never own a man himself. It was clear and natural that all of Mynheer Cornelius Stulting's family should abhor all that was not freedom. Had they not come to this new, hard country for the sake of freedom?

No, they must be neutral, difficult as it would be. And Cornelius must do all that he could to take care of his little mother, she had a bad cough now, and his father who was dazed and depressed by the war and for all his sisters, Carie and the youngest scarcely more than babies, and his younger brother.

It was not easy to be neutral. There were taunts from other young men in the village. The armies of first one side and then another came and took all the food which the house held.

There was only one thing for Cornelius to do and this he did. He went by night to the mountains and stayed there day after day clearing a patch where the sun could shine warmly down on the rich woods soil. That lonely, secret life he painted for Pearl as she listened in the dusk of the porch and she writes of it, "The land he dug and planted with beans and corn and wheat, and when there were harvests he stole back by night to his home to take them food and to see his mother and to get what he needed for himself. When the Little Levels (that part of the foothills of the Blue Ridge Mountains where the house stood) were swept by the passing and repassing of the northern and southern armies, when fields were devastated and barns and stores robbed, these meagre harvests that Cornelius

60

brought were the mainstay of the family, and often all they had to depend upon for food."

There was another story Carie had told her of and now Uncle 'Nelus told it, too, his eyes catching the light in hers as she turned to him, and his voice taking on a touch of dry humor.

"Father had a big time with some watches during the war There wasn't much money around and people used other ways of barter. Watches or jewelry were good, for they could always be turned into money when the war was over. He made a point of getting hold of all the watches he could for of course they have always been especially interesting to him and he knew their value. One day he heard that the Yankees were coming. He was afraid he would be robbed of his store of watches. He put them in a small covered basket and carried them to the meadow beyond the garden thinking they would never be found hidden there beneath a little loose hay near a rock. In the afternoon when the Yankees came, to his horror they chose that very spot on the meadow for their camp. They sat on the stone near the basket or used it as a table. Father watched from his window in misery. He walked the floor all night and even slipped out a couple of times saying, if anyone questioned him, that he had come to see about a sick cow. Every time he passed the spot where the basket was he kicked a little more hay in that direction. At last dawn came and the soldiers packed up to move on. Father could scarcely let them get out of sight before he rushed to the meadow. But the watches were safe having been in the Yankee camp all night." Pearl could see Grandfather running back and forth with his quick step, hear him as he said each time he found them safe, "They are still there." She could see Uncle 'Nelus as a young man trudging over the mountains and bringing down bags of potatoes and baskets of corn and beans in the dark of night. But she must know more.

"And then what happened?" Her hand lay in Uncle 'Nelus', always a little hard from farm work even though for years now he had been a teacher.

"Well, there came the battle of Droop Mountain, over yonder." He pointed. "It was right up there that the little farm lay and the folks here worried about me while northerners and southerners fired back and forth at each other. I hid in a cave all day and after it grew dark I came down over a cliff and was pretty well scratched up when I reached home. But the field was ruined. We hadn't much for awhile after that. I remember a day when we had only some dried beans and Mother was going to cook them for us when a band of fugitive southern soldiers came by and she saw they were starving and her heart softened and she gave them each a bowl of bean soup instead. As I remember it she sent the children to look for dandelion greens for our supper that night." He ran his hand through his heavy hair, thinking.

"But if they couldn't take you for a soldier because you were born in Holland, then why did you have to hide?" Pearl wondered.

"They wouldn't believe me. As a matter of fact I was a little too young, too." Uncle 'Nelus went on, "but they tried several times to take me and twice took me as far as Lewisburg. It was only when it was proven there that they had no right to take me, that they let me go again. They were desperate for men, that was the truth of it. Mother always tried to tell them how it was and clung to me, but they never listened—only the last time when she convinced them. I'll never forget the look in her eyes and the way the man said at last, 'Ma'am, he's yours. Let him go, men' "

"And then soon the war was over," Pearl said.

"In four years the war was over. Your mother had taught herself to read just by pestering everyone she saw to tell her this word then that word. Her younger sister couldn't even read. . . . It was then I knew we would just have to have a really good school."

But he did not go on to tell how he organized the Academy, after which the town was named, and taught in it for years while at the same time he farmed for his parents.

They sat in silence in the dark that had crept over them. Carie was there in the shadow with Faith on her lap asleep. Edwin's long form was stretched beside her. Grandfather was there listening to the telling of the stories, too. Aunt Anna was still rattling dishes in the kitchen. There was soft music in the parlor. Father was away. A cricket chirruped suddenly in the long grass near by and there was the sound of something dropping, apples in the orchard, of course. The breeze stirred the cool fresh air and the sweet fragrance of ripening grapes came to Pearl where she sat.

62

IX   Pearl saw more American country and
      mountains and woodlands and streams
when Carie took the children to visit her sisters in Highland County.
This was the country which had made Carie say over and over how
much like America Kuling was. At night the air had a bite in it and
they slept beneath blankets. During the day the air was fresh and
cool. Here the only village which they saw lay nested in a cup-shaped
valley which they had reached by a long surrey ride from the railroad station. Cows roamed the meadows. There were horses lifting
their proud heads and tossing back their manes—horses ridden bare-
back by her older cousins. There were chickens and ducks and tur-
keys. There were haystacks smelling sweet when the sun warmed
them. There were berries and apples and sweet corn and melons. The
smokehouses hung full of hams and bacons and "sides" and sau-
sages. In no other place in the world could there be such plenty.

There was beauty. Mists clung to the mountain valley and were
dispelled only when the sun slowly melted them away. Sunsets were
vivid. Storms herded the cattle together beneath protecting trees and
sent people indoors to watch the crackling lightning. Trees silhou-
etted against the deep blue of the rarified sky were like pictures.

Carie helped first one sister then another with canning and washing and cooking and her voice was merry with talking and her eyes
clear and dark with pleasure.

Cousin Eugenia was Pearl's special playmate, leading her to the
best-loved spots, talking of China, asking her questions and trying
to reach out to that land which she knew only through the letters
from Carie passed always to everyone in the family, and through
letters from Pearl written rarely to the cousins known only by name
until now she saw them.

Those few weeks were for Pearl weeks of intense flavoring of
this beautiful country She grew more robust, more full of life and
vivacity, running and climbing and learning the ways of country
children.

But it was the beauty which stayed longest with her. She could
never forget that beauty of American country.

Autumn began to touch the high mountain air. Andrew wrote that
he would start to Lexington where Edwin was to enter the university, to search for a house where they might live that winter.

This rambling old house on the edge of the town famous from the days of the Civil War was Pearl's first home in America. It stood on a sloping lawn dotted with trees. The kitchen, after the fashion of the time, was removed from the house in what had been slave quarters so that Carie had to pass through a tangled garden as she went back and forth. But she did not mind the inconvenience, for as she walked she could look out over the hill to the woods beyond, could stop to study each bird and flower. The work seemed nothing because she had only her own and there was none of the burden of Chinese poverty and sickness and trouble upon her. Often her voice rang out in song as she worked and the children felt her mood and loved each day as it passed.

And now Pearl for the first time went to school. She entered the third grade. The grade school stood only about two blocks up the quiet street. Each morning Edwin went to his studies at the university and Pearl to her school nearer home. Faith romped on the lawn and followed after Carie.

In the school Pearl felt eyes staring strangely at her but she was used to curiosity. It was so much fun to have school properly and not in bits as always Carie, with her many interruptions, had had to teach her. Recess was pleasant with all the children in their pretty checkered and flowered dresses, with games to play and things to do. Lunch time was for talking and getting acquainted and finding sometimes that Louisa's great-grandfather had been wounded in the Battle of Lexington; or that Mary's mother had,—just think of it! —hidden runaway slaves during the Civil War although she was a southerner. The little old town was full of lore and scraps of it came out in the soft southern drawl of the girls, some prideful, some shamed.

It was here in Lexington that Pearl for the first time saw snow in America. And yet seeing it, she knew she had already seen it because of what Carie had told her years before in China.

"Snow!" she says, "how she made us see snow in America! Sometimes, once in a long time, we had a little drift of it in the southern Chinese city where we lived, sometimes on a damp, chilly, wintry day. We pressed our faces against the windowpane and watched it coming down, white against the gray sky, melting instantly as it touched the warmer black tiles of the roofs. Once I remember there was a corner in the courtyard where the wind had blown a tiny drift as faint as mist, but still made of snow. We went running out,

64

leaping and crying, 'Snow-snow!' One winter of unprecedented cold, real snow came down outside the city wall and there on the barren gravelands there was at least an inch of snow and if one did not look too closely at the stubble sticking through, the world looked white and clean. The bamboos were feathery dusty with snow and the small new wheat stood freshly green between white patches of graves. Carie nailed together some boards from a box that had held canned milk and tied a grass rope to it and we slid down steeply sloping Chinese graves on the contrivance and dreamed of tobogganing in America.

"Years later when I saw real snow in deep Virginia woods ... I knew that I had seen it all before. ... I saw meadows hidden, still and sleeping under it. I saw roofs under great blankets of it and windows peering out, cozy and merry, from beneath, and smoke curling against the still sky. It was all just as she had said. Before I had turned a corner of the road that led into the hills, my heart cried out that the shadows in the snow would be blue under the lee of the hills, and when I turned there blue shadows lay. She had shown them to me years before and ten thousand miles away, so I knew them."

The best of the year in Lexington came during those winter evenings. When Edwin came home at night, Andrew made a fire of wood and threw on great logs which lit the rambling room with blazes and Carie brought out ginger cookies and apples and cider and sometimes other college boys came in and there was talking and laughing and singing. Now Pearl grew acquainted with her brother, leaning against him in the firelight and listening to the endless talking. The talking of elders was always interesting to her and she had learned to listen to it long ago. Now she came to know stories of the War, of college, of aunts and uncles, of a thousand things only dim before.

Sometimes Edwin's hand, long and slender and delicate, so much like Carie's, so much like Andrew's, held hers. His voice was always quiet and he was never boisterous. But humor was often there in what he said and she came to wait for his soft, deep, hearty chuckle and loved him because he was exactly as he was.

Faith sat too in the firelight, most often on Carie's lap and begged to be allowed to stay up a little longer and frequently fell asleep there and was carried so to bed. But Carie knowing all this meant to Pearl let her sit and listen, sometimes putting in her bit of story of what that day in school had brought.

65

Sometimes when Faith had gone to bed Carie brought out her sewing and lighting a low light sat busy with her needle. She had seen that the girls' dresses made in China by a Chinese tailor, although copied faithfully from the pictures of some woman's magazine, were wrong when worn by the children. So she set herself to alter and replace, beginning with their very underclothes. She bought yards of muslin and lace and Hamburg embroidery and cut their drawers and petticoats and made them by lamplight in the evenings, looking up from time to time to laugh or join in the conversation. She bought gingham and flowered chambray and made them dresses which they wore proudly

Even Andrew mellowed in the warmth and comfort of the evenings in the old Lexington house, when he was not away preaching, and told bits from his experiences. When he talked with Edwin there was a touch of pride in his voice now for a quotation from the Latin or Greek authors, his beloved, found answer in the quiet repartee of this boy of his, grown now to a man and a student brilliant in his studies.

But it was one of Carie's new dresses for Pearl which brought a flash of Andrew's anger. Pearl says it is her only clear memory of her father in that house. "... We were all going somewhere to make a family call. I had, I remember, been dressed first, in a new frock of sprigged muslin. The skirt was smocked with blue silk upon a yoke, and the sleeves were short and puffed, and there was lace at the collarless neck. My long curls had been freshly spun about Carie's forefinger, and a blue bow sat on the top of my head, and I swung my big hat. Thus arrayed, and feeling perfectly satisfied with myself, I stood at the steps into the street, waiting and spotless, when two small boys paused to stare. I pretended to pay no heed to them, of course, although I was acutely conscious of them. Indeed, I was a little sore from a recent experience with a detestable boy, the dunce of my third grade class, who had chosen to subject me to his adoration in spite of my furious and loud protestations of my hatred.

"These two unknown and personable little boys, staring, were therefore in the nature of balm, although outwardly I appeared oblivious of them. At last one of them heaved a sigh and said to the other, 'Ain't she pretty?'

"But before I could answer I heard Andrew on the porch

66

" 'Oh, pshaw!' he exclaimed. He had come out ready to go, and caught the little boy's remark

" 'You go and find your mother!' he commanded me. And as I turned reluctantly, for I would not have dreamed of disobeying him, I saw the two little boys hastening up the street, pursued by his blue and baleful glare.

" 'Hm!' I heard him say loudly after them. And he stood there with a distasteful look upon his face, as though he had smelled sin afar off."

Spring had come again and soon after spring school was over, and to Carie's satisfaction, Pearl ranked highest in her grade for the last month's work There were the holidays and short visits to the beloved home in Hillsboro and to Highland County. There were good-byes—hard ones to Grandfather who was, they all guessed, though no one said it, not to be there when they came again—hard ones, too, to Uncle 'Nelus and to Edwin. The short year in America was done. Again before them lay the sea and the China shore—again the old square bungalow on the Chinese hill.

PART THREE

X   **Y**ET WHEN they came back to the bungalow on the hill, it was good to see the familiar garden, the great trees and the wall. The rooms seemed strange and bare and ugly. But old Wang Amah had been at the riverside waiting with the other servants and now she pottered about, smoothing the beds, fetching warm water and talking and wiping her eyes in a perfect dither of excitement. How old she seemed! Her bony shoulders were sharp under her thin, clean grass-cloth jacket and she had lost another tooth and lisped when she spoke. But it was comforting to have her about.

That night in bed there were the familiar yet half-forgotten sounds—the deep temple gong which seemed almost sinister after the church bells of America, the fierce barking of village dogs, wolf-like after the barking of the old shepherd dog in Hillsboro, the calling of a woman, half-frightened, half-angry. For a moment Pearl was lonely.

Yet when she awoke the next morning here was her bedroom with its bay window, her dresser, her wardrobe. For a moment they looked stark after the dainty prettiness of other rooms.... Then suddenly there was the sound of flails on the threshing floors in the valley, beating the repetition of a rhythm—three long beats and several short, grouped together, their number depending upon how

68

many were at work. She got quietly out of bed, dressed and went outside

The morning air was good to her and she ran swiftly over the hill A cicada from a grave tree wheezed out a wisp of song. The grass was long for the autumn cutting of fuel. It whipped her bare legs with dew-wet slashes as she ran Dampness rose like steam from the valley and dissolved in the sunshine striking now at the far side of the gardens.

There they were, threshing on the floor at the bottom of the hill! The men and women lifted their flails and let them fall. The pile of straw from yesterday's work was heaped to one side, the baskets for grain and the winnowing baskets stood ready. A man came along the path at the base of the hill and called his wares. He had fragrant melons, cold from lying in the stream all night and dew-covered now and ready for slicing. The threshing stopped and a thresher came forward, jingling the coppers in the pocket of his girdle. He selected three melons and had them peeled and sliced and carried them to the others. They sat, the women on the bank of the field, and the men on their haunches, and ate with relish, sucking the juice from the seeds There was laughing and talking. A woman came from the nearby house with a baby at her breast and stood and watched them. She swayed her body as she stood to keep the baby asleep.

The remembrance of the Rebellion came sweeping back, and still it was as though there had been no rebellion for the farmers were going about their work as they had always done. It seemed to make no difference to them that Peking had been stormed by foreign troops or that the Empress Dowager had had to flee. It seemed to make no difference that hundreds of white people and thousands of Chinese had been killed because of their connection with the outside world and an alien religion.

But in the days ahead Pearl found there was a difference. So thoroughly had the foreign troops shown their strength that from then on China was safe for the white man as it had never been before. To Pearl it was to mean, though she did not realize it until years later, that she could come and go among the hills and valleys in perfect freedom and safety The freedom was not to last forever. China did not forget her tragic defeat. But for those few years of her youth, this white child was free, and she made the most of it.

There was no end of the things for her to see.

Life was lived from its beginning to its end in the mud-walled, thatch-roofed houses down the hill from the bungalow. It began with the neighbor women running in and out of a doorway, a young husband coming in from a near field to see his first-born, and the shrill cry of a baby. The next day, or the next, Pearl would see the mother, a little white, a little weary as she walked, moving slowly about in the dim room. Then a few days later, the tiny bundled baby nursing at his mother's breast, his black head covered by his minute red satin cap, all the rest of him hidden by a padded quilt. Soon he would be a cunning thing trying to support himself on unstable legs, clutching at a cookie or a water chestnut peeled and slipped over a slit reed. Then he would be toddling and falling in the dust of the threshing floor, one of all the valley children.

Once, she knew that the daughter of a farm family was being wedded to a son in a house in the next valley. The red bride's chair came for the girl and she was carried out to it and put in protesting, and the chair curtain drawn so that none might see her face. Yet she must be glad to go to her husband's house, for now she would be a married woman and bear sons, and this was what every Chinese girl made herself ready for. The chair went swiftly, the bearers joking among themselves, a relative or two from another household going in front and behind with strings of firecrackers ready to be set off when they came near the bride's new home. When the chair was out of sight around the bend of the hill, Pearl heard the popping and smelled the gunpowder as it was carried faintly on the breeze.

Firecrackers were for the dead, too, she knew There was old Li who at last made use of the heavy fir-beam coffin which had stood in the main room of the house for years, a good fifteen, his daughter-in-law said. Last night the priests chanted and a soft-toned bell clanged and "fish-head" wooden drums throbbed under the beating of wooden mallets. Today the corpse was laid in its bed of lime, a corpse so dried and withered that it seemed a mummy, dressed incongruously as the custom is, in a red satin gown and velvet jacket and round skull cap. The coffin could not be moved in to the corpse, so the corpse was brought to it and streaming sunshine lit the scene for Pearl.

Pearl smelled the smell of hot sealing glue beneath the ponderous lid and heard the crying of mourners swathed in sackcloth and white unhemmed garments, from the threshing floor where they waited. She saw the emblems of mourning, reeds wrapped in fringed white paper stuck into the ground beside the doorway and laid ready to be carried to the place where the coffin would be set in the family bury-ing ground. There was good food cooking, she knew, for above every other odor there was now the odor of roasting pork, and baskets of rice stood ready and vegetables were being washed at the pond and fish scales lay in a shining heap in the ash pile which was for compost at the far side of the threshing floor.

The coolies gathered for the carrying of the coffin. They sat drinking tea and laughing. They were neighbor men who came to do their turn for the dead. Now they were tying strips of white cloth around their jackets for girdles in courteous sign of grief. There was a heaving and shouting when the poles were roped into place, a try or two before the enormous coffin could be lifted, a laugh when it tipped, and then slowly and carefully they brought it out through the door to the threshing floor, along the narrow path and painfully along the lower margin of the hill. They had to rest every twenty paces, so good a casket it was for the frail old man, but at last they set it beside another grave, a rounded mound on the bare hillside. That, then, was where it was to be placed. That was all they would do today. The coffin would stand so beneath the sky for many weeks, perhaps months, before it would be covered and its stone put properly in place, for the day must be propitious if the spirit was to rest.

But eager as Pearl was to watch any unusual event in the valleys below the house, the best days were those when there was no birth or wedding or funeral, but just what happened on an ordinary day. There was a family who lived in a cluster of houses on the far side of the hill. It was a big family with married sons and nephews, who were called sons, too, but in a different way, and an old grandfather and grandmother. Pearl went there often by the small back gate which opened from the kitchen yard. In the shade of the compound wall on this north side the tall grass and reeds grew rank, snake weed and pampas grass. But once out of the shadow there were the same tall waving fuel grass and wild raspberry vines of the whole hillside and the same narrow path leading to the valley below. She ran down it, the burnished grasshoppers making haste out of her way with a rasping and clattering.

Here at this clan farmhouse, on the threshing floor, or inside the courtyard enclosed by a low mud wall on the one side where the house did not bound it, there was always someone. The grandmother was there twirling her spindle to make the heavy cotton thread for

71

mending, or one of the daughters-in-law nursing her baby or sorting dried beans or cutting vegetables for salting, or an aunt, or an uncle, busy, or only sitting in the shade of a tree to smoke and to talk. Here everything was being done—grain threshed from its stalks, shed of its hulls by the buffalo walking his endless round, turning the great stone wheel in its groove to take the hulls from the rice, washed in the fine woven bamboo basket at the pond, cooked in the great thin iron cauldron so that the grains fell like snow when the wooden lid was lifted and all the bowls were filled at the table. Cabbages were grown from small round brown seed to tender young plants, then to thick-stemmed bunches, white and crisp and sweet when they had been tossed a few times in sizzling hot bean oil and brought to go with the rice.

The old grandmother made shoe-soles for the family, pasting layer after layer of cloth scraps on soft reed matting and letting them dry in the sun, then cutting and shaping the soles, sewed stitch on stitch with hemp cord The old woman pushed the needle in, twisting and pulling and saying always, "My eyes don't see to do other sewing." But when the soles were done they lay neatly bound in dark cloth and ready to be uppered to the blue or black tops which some other woman of the family had made. Then some day the shoe-soler would come, a cobbler with his traveling shop, and sitting on the edge of the court he would fit each top to its sole and sew it there strongly so that when he was done a whole row stood ready, made of scraps, paste, reeds, cord, and hard labor.

When Chinese New Year came, more than ever was happening in that household. For weeks things were slowly made ready for the great holiday. The best beans were dried and stored for making sweet bean paste, the best cuts of pork salted and smoked for the season, the best hens left to fatten. Sugar was brought from the city and hoarded, and rice flour carefully ground in the stone hand mill for the steamed rice cakes. Candied green gage and raisins, sesame seed and sunflower seed, gathered in summer, were looked over to make sure that the mold had not touched them, nor worms, now that they must be used soon for the "eight precious things rice" How good *that* was—glutinous rice steamed for hours with nuts and raisins and all the different fruits and seeds that could be crowded into it, and eaten piping hot with a china spoon! And everybody had something new to wear. The baby's shoes were cut out of brilliant red satin and his little new jacket was of peach pink and his new cap had an extra bangle of silver, and there was a paper and paste flower for the young mother's hair.

A few days before The Day the women made themselves ready, taking turns with each other. Pearl watched intently each step of the process. With a double-twisted string held stretched and then slackened and then stretched again, they plucked the hairs from the neat edge of the hair line, or from the forehead, or above the nose, or wherever an odd hair grew where it should not. "But doesn't it hurt?" Pearl asked, and the women laughed and made a joke of her question, not answering her. Then the long black twists of their hair were combed and oiled with fragrant oil and bound into place, and silver pins, betrothal pins, were pushed in and the earrings were hung in their places.

There were quarrels sometimes and anger when a strange man came and asked for money, for New Year's Eve was the day when debts were cleared and when tempers blew hot. But once the New Year was in no one could ask for a debt to be paid and there was much more laughing than anger. On New Year morning there was eating and leisure and more eating and soon, when the time had come, visitors and the drinking of New Year's tea, and when dusk came the drinking of wine with the evening meal.

But Pearl liked spring and summer and fall the best, for then the valleys were busiest. In spring there was the rice planting in flooded fields She watched always and once stood on the paddle pump with the others. In early summer the rice grew heavy and covered all the water, the ponds were padded with lilies, and rape and broad beans were full of blossom, and cucumbers and melons dropped their cones of petals to make their fruit. In autumn the air had a crispness and the sunshine a brilliance. Soon the winter wheat would pierce the rich black earth and winter cabbages would be cut for salting. *Han-ts' ai,* or salted cabbage, was good just as it came from the salting jar, and good, too, with rice gruel on a frosty morning.

This was the time of year to climb high in one of the trees with a book from the long row of dull blue ones and read and look and listen for the hot chestnut man who would soon be coming up the hill road. His piping whistle blew two notes and when Pearl heard him she always ran to buy a few coppers' worth to eat.

Here in the tree the whole world of hills and valleys was crystal clear. She could see in every direction and in every direction there were people living and working. Everywhere in China there were

73

people—too many, Carie said. But Pearl watched them and lived with them, for she knew what their lives were, and at home when it was cold or rainy she turned to her books and read of others far away in the America she knew now, or in the England Dickens had made real to her.

That first winter after the furlough in America Pearl began her first published writing. Carie had asked her often to write down bits of stories, tiny poems, incidents, and helped her with her ways of writing. These she sometimes kept for awhile and then threw away. But now Father began to take an English newspaper, published in Shanghai and called the *Shanghai Mercury*, and it had a children's page once a week. Pearl read this page from top to bottom. One day Carie said, "Pearl, why don't you write something for the *Mercury?*" A faint color crept upwards in Pearl's face. "I'm sure you could," Carie went on with energy, turning back to the plants she was setting in small pots for the winter windows. "You write whatever you would like to write about and I'll look it over to make sure there are no mistakes." She said no more, but when she went back to her work she tossed her head a little as she did when an idea took her.

A week later Pearl opened the paper carefully, scarcely daring to turn to the page where the children's writings were to be found. But there her story was, looking strangely dignified in the printer's type above the signature, "Novice." Carie had chosen the pen name for her and suddenly she liked it.

She wrote often in the winter about anything she wished, writing simply because she wanted to write and because it gave her pleasure to put into words many things she felt but had no reason to talk to anyone about. Carie always read what she wrote and made suggestions. Several times she won one of the week's prizes and received a letter from the editor. The check, small in reality, was much to her because she so rarely had money of her own and because she herself had earned it. It seemed that to be able to say what one wanted to say was a very important thing indeed.

XI   I T WAS SUMMER again With the first heat
       Carie packed the pigskin trunks for Ku-
ling and carefully put in the net-covered baskets the few choice pots
and pans and picnic plates and cups and saucers she had bought for
this.

Three summers they had not seen the cottage. One was that of the
Boxer Rebellion and two had been for the furlough. Now when suddenly the high mountain valley lay before them, it was changed. The
trees, before only bushes because every year before the lease of
the land they had been cut for fuel, had grown, softly half-hiding the
rocks And the cottages! They had sprung up like mushrooms. Where
before there had been a few dozen, now there was a village. Deep in
the valley near the stream stood a small stone church built of the
boulders and on the first Sunday its bell rang out making Carie feel
more than ever that Kuling was akin to America.

The terraces of the yard were half shaded. Behind the house had
sprung up a fern-like mimosa, pink with fringed bloom. Below the
porch blossomed Rose of Sharon and day lilies and trumpet lilies and
far beneath the ferns red spider lilies and Grass of Parnassus.

The roads leading to the church and the Chinese village lay spotted
with shadow and here and there wooden benches were set.

In the house next to Carie's lived old American friends known
since the days in Tsingkiang-pu, and now the friendship was warmed
and renewed. It was warmed for Pearl as well as for Carie for Fanny,
the elder daughter, was nearly her age and through the summer they
were always together.

The shade of the mimosa was a favorite spot for reading and
Fanny was as voracious a reader as Pearl. Through the long mornings they lay there on an old blanket, bolstered with cushions and read
and talked. Carie thought they read too much, and so did Fanny's
mother, but nothing could stop them. Books were read and exchanged
and argued and hated and loved. They tore characters apart and said
why they liked them or why they disliked them.

When it was rainy they sat on chairs on the narrow back porch
near the kitchen and went on with their talking. One day Fanny remembers, Pearl said, "If you could be anything you like when you
grow up, what would you choose to be?" Fanny answered instantly,
"An author."

But Pearl said, "I'd rather be a singer or violinist. I think a singer,

75

because a singer can put more of himself directly into his singing than a violinist through playing or an author through writing. An author can't *see* how what he writes affects people, but a singer can watch while he sings." Yes, she would rather be a singer.

Fanny looked thoughtfully at her. Perhaps Pearl was right, but still books were the best things in the world and there was nothing she would rather do than make them. She could not live without books even if sometimes she must hide beneath her bed to read when her mother grew impatient.

There were other girls that summer. There was Anna whom they called always by her Chinese name, Meifen She lived higher on the hill. She was tall and slim and fair with hair that fell in two long braids far below her waist. There was dark-eyed Lily, small and thoughtful. Sometimes the three of them made excursions down the stream together discovering quiet pools where they waded, small coves where ferns grew, falls which they could scarcely pass, or low cliffs of blue sandstone soft enough to carve and shape in tiny heart-shaped lockets to hang about their necks with ribbons.

There were races on the Fourth of July and the American children gathered and ran relay races and obstacle races and came in breathless for prizes and drinks of lemonade As nearly as it could be made so, Kuling was a bit of America and England set down in the Chinese hills. And yet Kuling was richly Chinese. The memories that come back are more of graceful temples tucked among the cliffs, than of foreign houses; more of pilgrim priests and straining coolies, than of European ladies sipping afternoon tea. Teas there came to be more and more as years passed, and whist parties, and glorified picnics. But the real Kuling was made up of the far cry of the men blasting the rocks from the mountain, the roar of explosion, the faint smell of gunpowder, then soon the sound of carrying, *"Wei-he-he-heh-heh-hei!"* It was made up of mountain people coming up through the valley on their way to a temple, bringing their small gifts of grain and of fruit and their sticks of sweet incense. Or an old hermit priest swathed in soft gray cotton, his face lined and lonely, his eyes dim with seeing only the mountains or the valleys far beneath. It was made up of simple excursions over the high open valleys to discover new lilies and rocks, and deep into threatening gorges—the Three Falls, White Dragon Falls, White Deer Grotto. Here were sudden coolness and deep blue-green water and the trickling of ice cold springs over banks of ferns and perilous cliffs. Picnics to these places,

76

after long hard walks in beating sun, clambering over risky rocks, plunges into breathtaking streams, were the real Kuling and it is these Pearl thinks of when she looks back Pearl says, "The thing I remember most about Kuling is the beauty of nature there—going out in the morning to pick ferns and flowers for Mother to decorate the house with."

Although Pearl was not conscious of it herself, she was entering adolescence Her reading had broadened and deepened her thinking. Her wandering through the valleys had explained simply much not known to other American children. But nothing could completely free her from the inward struggle which comes to everyone between childhood and maturity.

Carie watched that autumn as Pearl came running in from the valley below the bungalow. Why the child knew the names and ages, the worries and happiness of all these village people! That was her life A sudden anxiety swept her. "You're getting to be such a big girl, Pearl," she said, one day.

When autumn rains came Carie gave her longer lessons. But lessons could not hold her for she only studied harder and was finished with them as soon as before. She taught her to knit and sew and crochet and cook. She taught her how to make the yeast and set the bread and work it and let it rise and work it again and raise it for the second time before the baking. And Pearl learned what she was taught, but still there were the people of the valleys.

Then suddenly one day Carie said, "We are going to see Miss Robinson at the Methodist Girls' School, this morning." There was a firm little line near her lips. In the instant that she spoke, everything was changed.

Miss Robinson! She flashed before Pearl's eyes. She was the American principal of the mission school for Chinese girls. She had gray hair waving back from a center part, piercing eyes, a clear voice that was sometimes severe. She was very straight and walked erectly. The Chinese students were careful to be obedient to Miss Robinson. Something grew cold in Pearl when she thought of going to see this woman, even though she had been often to exercises at the school.

..."Then you think she could study right along with the other girls?" Carie said to Miss Robinson and listed some items on her fingers. "Chinese, arithmetic, religion, singing."

77

"And," Miss Robinson said, "I have a plan in my mind. Pearl could be a great help in our English conversation classes. She could teach the beginners and it would be splendid practice for her." She spoke definitely "as though it is all decided!" Pearl thought.

The door of Miss Robinson's study opened on the long hall. The school-rooms were very bare with their freshly mopped floors, blackboards, desks and potted plants. There was the sound of a piano being played methodically. Some voices were singing, English words pronounced as beginners in English pronounce them, troubled by the *l's* and *r's* and *n's.* The altos were confused. . . . How neat Miss Robinson was! There was not a crinkle in her lavender dress and the ruching of her collar was not even pressed down by her chin.

"It won't be hard to teach the girls English, Pearl," Carie said as they started home. "Just talk about any simple thing and be sure to pronounce distinctly."

But it seemed to Pearl at that moment that to talk would be the hardest thing in all the world. Always, even now, she was a little shy.

Yet in spite of herself she did feel grown up that Monday morning when she started for the school. She wore one of her American dresses and her hair was braided in two braids. She carried two pencils and a pad.

The road stretched along the ridge of the hill. In this direction the hill on which the bungalow stood did not fall away to the valley, but instead spread on upwards to the school and then to the old Fort which crowned its summit. The seat where Clyde and she had sat was beyond on the far side of the fort But here the ridge was narrow for a part of its distance and Pearl could see the valleys through spaces between the grave mounds.

There to the left was the beginning of the bamboo grove which surrounded the old Buddhist temple. And there to the right the farms which she knew so well The air was cold this morning. Smoke from the chimneys rose straight and was carried away by a breeze. The smell of burning hillside fuel was pleasant and clean. There was the shout of a farmer plowing his fields for winter wheat, and the far call of the harvest bird, "Kuh-ku! Kuh-ku!"

Now she has reached the gate of the school and the gateman smiles and bows and opens it for her. She is going toward the recitation hall along the damp walks and suddenly her knees are knocking together.

78

"Good morning!" someone says. It is Miss Robinson, smiling and taking her by the hand. How cold her hand is!

And then Pearl is sitting with the Chinese girls doing arithmetic. It is a little confusing to use the Chinese words for "multiply" and "divide," "subtract," and "add," but the figures are the ones she is used to One of the girls near her, a merry-faced girl, with twinkling black eyes and a deep dimple in one cheek, leans over a time or two to see how she is getting on. *"Pu ts'o, pu ts'o*—right, right!" she whispers.

It is more fun than she thought it might be, to work with the Chinese girls in school Already the rooms seem less bare. The girls look pretty this morning in their pink or blue or flowered jackets, with their hair all combed shining smooth It is warm and pleasant here with all of them. The sun streaming in the windows of flowers and the neat sums and writing on the backboard are all part of it.

When the bell rings for recess everyone runs out except one or two girls who still bend over their desks. The sun is bright on the playground and there are games. How merry everyone is! They are all running and laughing and doing everything with all their hearts. And now the bell is ringing again and they all come running into the hall. Some of the girls hang about her. One of them is smoothing the plaited yoke of her dress and pulling out the narrow lace edge. Another takes her hand gently and lays it on hers and feels of its suppleness and strokes it affectionately. But now everyone runs on to class, calling, "We'll see you before you go home! Wait for us to find you, Tseng-tzu." She is glad they are using her Chinese name. Her American one is especially hard for them to say.

Just before dinner comes the class in English conversation. There are eight girls in it, some of them older than she, and one a girl she played with on the playground a short while ago But how polite they are! All of them treat her exactly like a real teacher, looking down decorously at their books and waiting for her to speak. . . . It seems she will never speak again! Then suddenly she begins to talk easily, remembering not to speak too quickly, and the hour passes with no trouble at all.

When she goes out through the gate at noon and starts home she has the pleasant feeling of having tried hard to do her work well. When she reaches home Carie smiles at her and the rooms seem welcoming.

It was fun to go to the Chinese school every morning. Sometimes, quite often, she stayed for dinner, particularly if the girls had found out they were to have an especially good one. One of the girls was sure to come running to say that that day they were to have yellow fish since it was the season and they were so cheap and that she had asked Miss Robinson already. It was merry eating with the girls They talked so fast and ate so fast and there was such a clatter There were usually three "bowls" and a soup · That is, there were three meat or vegetable bowls in the center of the table for everyone to eat from, and then each one might fill her rice bowl as often as she wished. The rice stood in its wooden buckets on small side tables and one helped herself with the wooden ladle. Usually one "bowl" was mostly meat—pork balls or fish or shredded beef—and the other two were vegetables, perhaps with bean curd or perhaps with bits of meat for flavoring. Pearl's chopsticks flew as fast as anyone's and she could pick up a single grain of rice dropped on the smooth tabletop as easily as the other girls. She, too, had eaten with chopsticks, all her life, though Carie set her table in the American way.

But now that she went to the Chinese school each morning, the lessons which she did not have there had to be studied in the afternoon and sometimes heard at night She got them done, working by no set lesson but the amount she could do well in a day. And however late it was, and Carie would not let her be too late to bed, there was reading in bed.

The old volumes of Dickens were the ones to which she always came back. She tried Sir Walter Scott and finished what books of his were there. She still read some Tennyson and Browning, but best was Dickens. She went steadily on in the habit formed years before, the habit of reading through the long row, only to begin again.

When she was at home she was quieter than she used to be and Carie watched and tried to enrich and warm her life in every way she could. She taught her painting with a small easel and some tubes of paint bought at inconvenience in a small store in Shanghai. She taught her music, and somewhere bought a piano, paid for in part by exchange of some sort She required every week a composition, this in addition to whatever Pearl might choose to write for the Shanghai paper. She insisted upon calesthenics in bad weather when there could be no climbing of trees or running over the hills. These were done on the side porch, Carie leading the exercises and Pearl and small Faith following her, although they disliked it.

More often now Carie let her own sense of humor have flight.

These flights are still clear and Pearl writes, "Her humor was like a gay wind, beginning with a secret and keen sparkle of her golden brown eyes. A light seemed to radiate from her and then the children hung breathless on her words, for 'something funny' always followed that light, some absurd rhyme or quick twist of wit. She had a faculty for easy rhyming, and sometimes for sheer mischief would spin out one ridiculous verse after another from her head.

"This made the children shout with laughter, but such complete nonsense was always painful to Andrew. He would hold up his hand in protest, at first gentle, but finally fretful. 'Carie—Carie—please!' he would beseech her.

"But some imp of perverse enjoyment would seize her at his protest and she would rhyme more brilliantly than ever, her face alight, ending only, when she saw it really troubled him, with a fine flourish. Or perhaps she would come home from hearing some well-meaning but stupid person speak, and she would imitate the pompous intonations, much to Andrew's horror and the children's pleasure, for the children had her flashing humor and love of a joke. She was a born mimic and when she imitated someone, became in very truth that person, even almost in expressions."

And yet so often after she was merry she was sad, Pearl saw, as though after an escape into fun she came back to reality. And Andrew's protest at her humor only touched a deeper protest which Pearl, as she grew to adolescence, felt there between her parents. It was not something that could be helped for ever Carie spoke proudly of Andrew, his work and the man he was. And ever Andrew, although he never spoke, leaned heavily on Carie for all that home meant to him and all that her quick common sense and intuition saved him

There was Andrew's New Testament which stood a boulder between her parents. "Andrew had a keen and critical literary sense and he had for a long time been dissatisfied with the only translation which had been made of the Bible into Chinese. Gradually through the years there shaped in his mind the idea of making a translation at least of the New Testament and this directly from the Greek into Chinese. He was an excellent Greek scholar, and always in his own personal devotions read the Bible in the original Hebrew and Greek. I can remember the faded gilt edge of the small pocket edition of the Greek Testament he carried in the breast pocket of whatever suit he wore. When he died and we laid him to sleep for his eternity, we

81

knew he could not rest unless it were with him still, and we put it there forever.

"So he began to work on the translations in the evenings.... and as the years passed, the pile of manuscript, covered with the long lines of his somewhat angular Chinese writing grew higher upon the desk in his study.... But when the day came when the work was finished and must be published, there was no money.... except what we could spare from our already too meagre salary.... Carie looked at him and saw what it meant to him, and how it was his dream, and so at last she said, 'We will do it somehow'.... He was happy again, although thereafter the children came to think that Father's New Testament was sort of a well, down which were lost the toys they longed for, or a new dress a little girl hoped for, or the many books for which they hungered. They learned to ask wistfully, 'Mother, when Father has finished the New Testament, may we buy something we want?' They will never forget their mother's face when they asked this question. She looked angry but not at them, and she said very firmly, 'Yes! We will each one of us buy the thing we want most.' "

Pearl was old enough to see that between her parents lay an unlikeness too deep to meet in understanding, however it might be striven for, and this conflict coming sometimes, she could not but see, to the surface, cast a shadow.

In all the years of her life, and ever she loves life, those few years came nearest to being unhappy. She says in looking back to this time, "She (Pearl) was a tall girl now, a difficult child in many ways, passionate—if Carie had been able to see it, much like herself. But Carie could only see with a sort of fear and sorrow that this child of hers was so built that she must suffer in life as her mother had through too sensitive a nature and too much emotion, and Carie tried to teach her daughter self-control.... It was not always easy to make her (Pearl) submit to the daily routine. She could resist mightily and with gusto, and at last Carie saw that if she was to win it must be by approval and stimulation of ambition, for the girl would not be driven. Carie learned from that quick sympathy of hers to look at last into her own heart and see what would win the child's and thus the wayward adolescent period passed more easily for them both "

There was indeed much of Carie in Pearl and part of it was that directness with which Carie moved to sweep away any obstacle in

82

the flow of nature—things as they should be. It came perhaps from old Mynheer Cornelius Stulting who in his time had moved the obstacles to freedom of worship. It appeared in Cornelius who went his steady way through the War, who would not have ignorance and made a school himself.

Directness and determination and unconscious moving with the flow of basic rightness would increase, and as easily as she breathed Pearl was to take the course which would clear the channel of rocks and strengthen the flow of the stream.

And now she saw Carie, white-hot with anger, defying disease. It was the second autumn after their return from America. Every year after the summer a plague of cholera came and for weeks Carie lived in terror of it, watching with the utmost care all the cooking of food and boiling of water and washing of dishes. Cholera was in those days a swift disease which almost always brought death In the autumn of this year, Wang Amah took it suddenly one night and hating to call Carie said nothing. But the sound of Wang Amah's retching and groaning wakened Carie who ran barefoot to Wang Amah's room Already Wang Amah was fast sinking into unconsciousness. But she would not have Wang Amah die! Her valiant anger blazed and she set herself to save the Chinese woman.

The next morning Pearl woke to find the house strangely empty. She went to find someone. Andrew was standing beside the open door of the little tool house at the far side of the back garden and she heard Carie's voice speaking definitely and clearly. He came hurriedly toward the house, then, and said, "Pearl, you see to Faith. On no account are you to go near the back garden. Wang Amah's been taken seriously ill and your mother is caring for her."

It was not until that curious, lonely week was over, a week when they never saw Carie except at the far distance of the little tool house and then always flitting in and out and pouring and swishing and scouring until the aroma of strong disinfectant reached even the bungalow, that Pearl knew the full story. That night when Carie had found Wang Amah she sped to the kitchen and lit a roaring fire and heated an immense tub of water. Then she poured hot water and whiskey down Wang Amah's throat, chafed her hands and at last lifted Wang Amah into the hot water and immersed her up to her head. "It was terrific treatment," Carie said, "but I had heard the doctor say that the poison had to be purged out in every way, through the pores, from the stomach. . Well, I saw by dawn she would live, even though she was scarcely alive. . . . I guess it made me suddenly angry to see a wicked disease like that take Wang Amah. I just wasn't going to have it."

There it was. Carie "would not have it" if it was "not right." To Andrew those words meant right in the sight of his God. To Carie they meant right in the course of all life. Freedom was right, and beauty was right, and enough was right Unconsciously Pearl, too, began to determine the things that must be.

XII   A<small>ND</small> <small>NOW</small> there came a sweep of events.

The first was that the long-talked of building of the Shanghai-Nanking Railway pushed on and came to Chinkiang.

Shanghai was always for the foreigners of the interior parts of China a link with the outside world. It was the Mecca of imported goods and a haven in times of terror like the T'ai P'ing Rebellion and the last resort in serious illness. Shanghai had, besides the Chinese city, a foreign community of five thousand British and one thousand American residents along with hundreds of other foreigners. Beginning as a trading post hemmed in rigidly by the Chinese, it had changed into the greatest trading city of China, its business of export increased four hundred times in the span of half a century.

The railway was backed by British interests. It was a Chinese railway but it was also security for the British money invested in it.

Chinkiang was excited by the fact that the railroad carving its way between low hills, came at last to the one where the old Fort stood, and finding the hill too high for a cut, burrowed under it, making the first tunnel of China.

All possible workers were mustered and the poor, forever a weight upon charity, were set at work with hammers pounding the rocks for the road bed, and with shovels to scoop out the red clay of the hill. They came from the city and from all the country near by, refugees from famine areas, beggars, lost and lonely riff-raff, and set up their hovels along the side of the road. A small town seemed to have grown there through magic, and the magic was the eternal hunger of the poor.

As the hole grew larger and larger, merchants and gentlemen came out of the city and stood looking and talking together about the monstrosity of western civilization, which demanded entrance even to the stomach of the earth, comparing information on the speed of the "fire wagon," how many people it could haul, and what it might do to the wind and water of the city.

Gradually the workers disappeared into the depths of the earth, to come out white-faced and covered with moisture. Once there was a cave-in and panic stopped all work until it was clear that without work there was no food. Crowds watched more closely than ever, hungry for the excitement of further catastrophe. Guards fought off those who tried to go in saying with the stubbornness of the curious, "*K'an-k'an*—see!"

Soon the digging was going on at both ends and how the two ends should meet was a miracle possible only through what must be foreign magic. The people darkened the banks of the cuts where they entered the hill, standing for hours, watching and talking. The trains would go in there, it was said, and come out here. Unbelievable! But the white people thought with infinite satisfaction that now the trip to Shanghai would be only a few short hours, half a day, instead of a long journey by river steamer.

The opening day came. The first passenger train was to pass. On it would be distinguished guests who would stop to celebrate near Shanghai at a small place called Nanziang. The crowds gathered in Chinkiang, waiting for the train. The police fought off those who tried in every way they could to slip into the tunnel, climbing down over the stone-walled embankments, determined to see with the unreasoning curiosity of the ignorant. There were fights and accidents.

At last the train came, unexpectedly vomiting black smoke which suffocated those who insisted on standing perilously above the tunnel's mouth. One man was reported killed in the tunnel, though this was later denied.

On that day Carie and the girls sat on the old seat on the hill. They saw the train appear from the depths of the tunnel moving slowly with a certain majesty towards its red brick station.

Suddenly Pearl knew that the seat on Fort Hill would never be the same again. Now it no longer looked only on a Chinese street which dwindled into a country market place. It looked, too, upon a railroad which was to bring people from all the world into the old city. "What would Marco Polo think to see a train here?" she said, and her mind raced back through the ages.

With a certain sense of awe, a near regret, they went home that afternoon The West had pushed in. Like possessive arms of steel, the rails lay glistening in the sun.

The second event was the summer in Kuling when Pearl was fourteen. It was different from all the others. An Anglo-American school had been established and Carie feeling it might help Pearl, entered her there. There was study, that summer, but there were still hikes and picnics. The stream had been dammed to make a pool and here in what was called Duck Pond, Pearl learned to swim although she liked better to sit on the rocks. She was now as tall as Carie, and too thin for her height.

She had a group of friends that summer, some British, some American. Fanny was in America at school but there were still Nessa and Lily, and Meifen. And there were ruddy-haired Agnes and Isabel They roamed the hills together, read together, picnicked together.

When autumn came, Carie brought herself to decision. She would leave Pearl here in school. Autumn in the hills would be beautiful and bracing. There would be bonfires and nutting parties and snow and friends. And there would be school. With her heart at rest, Carie went back to Chinkiang with Faith.

Pearl roomed with Meifen and Isabel. She remembers how the three of them with what seemed adult abandon opened an account at the one foreign store, run by Mr. Duff, incurring a total debt of twelve dollars by Christmas time, for trifling items of candy, cakes, fruit, and soap. She remembers how Meifen scolded Isabel and her for their wastefulness since her own share was much less than a third of the total. But there were splendid hikes when they gathered chinquapins and ate the small sweet meats. There were the first frosts when fog froze on the branches and made the mountainside a fairy place of beauty. She remembers a Miss Hume who among all the teachers was the one she liked best. She remembers that this was the beginning of her period of poetry which she wrote in bits and sent to Carie. And Carie reading the adolescent rhymes, sent with a sober note from Pearl to the effect that this was to be her vocation, replied that two poems did not make a poet. It was the beginning of a feeling that Pearl came to have for a time, a feeling that Carie often "pricked her bubbles" and did not understand her. Strange contrasts there were in her these days. There was the dreamy poet and the practical joker. She writes, "I was at this age a dreadful practical joker and got into trouble for it more than once."

Her letters home were not happy and she seemed to have nothing to do. Carie saw that the work was too easy for her. Carie wrote in her diary, "The classes are not advanced enough. Pearl is losing time." When Pearl went home for the Christmas holidays, Carie thought it a waste to send her back to Kuling. She says, "Pearl did not stand it well and came home."

In Chinkiang on another hill there were the Longden girls. They lived near the road which went to Victoria Park. There were three girls. Mary was a year older than Pearl, Ruth a year younger, and Florence two years younger. Pearl and Mary became almost inseparable for the two years that Mary was there before she went to America to school. She was a sweet girl and Pearl went often to spend the night with her, and they slept in a broad bed together and talked into the small hours.

Pearl one day combed her hair in the round, forever-parting pompadour which was the style and one in which Mary combed her hair. Carie stared and said with a flash of sharpness,

"What on earth have you done to your hair!"

"All the girls do their hair this way, Mother," Pearl answered and sailed through the room. Nor did she comb her hair in any other way until the style had passed.

Carie saw that Pearl hungered for something pretty to wear. She sent to Shanghai for yards of good lace edging to be carefully whipped on. But Pearl with swift impatience sewed it on her petticoats with irregular running stitches to Carie's displeasure and her own complete satisfaction. The general effect was right.

It was the stage when Pearl felt it was ladylike to eat daintily and no urging of Carie could convince her that she needed more food. It was only when her own hunger led her to eat between meals that Carie decided the matter would settle itself.

All these small difficulties Pearl and Mary talked of and Mary's mother, gentle and gray-haired and restrained, overheard but said nothing.

Mary referred often to a certain other friend of hers, an Alcy Stuart who, it seemed to Pearl, must be the most fetching girl imaginable. Alcy was to come to visit Mary and Pearl half longed for and half dreaded her coming.

She came not once but many times and each time it was with a little rush and flutter of excitement. She *was* pretty, her nose straight and a trifle turned-up, fine freckles on her smooth white skin, and her hair a tumble of brown curls. But her clothes! Pearl locked with open envy at the modish things she brought. They were unlike anything a Chinese tailor could produce, however hard he tried, Pearl thought, and yet she learned a Chinese tailor had produced them, only a Shanghai tailor who it seemed sewed for wives of navy men and people of the consular services. And then, the girls soon saw that it was more than the clothes themselves. It was Alcy. She had a flair about her and it was their first experience of this sort. And she had friends among the boys! Mary and Alcy had long whispered conversations which at first included Pearl, but which later left her out, since suddenly she lost interest and reached for the nearest book.

It came to be that when Alcy Stuart visited Mary, Pearl automatically went to her old Chinese friends at the Methodist school. Mary went there, too, sometimes and often they went together so that the Chinese girls said they had a David and Johnathan friendship. But Dottie Wei and Su-i Wang were Pearl's closest friends and when Alcy came, she returned to them with complete satisfaction. Here she was not troubled by the style of her dress or talk of boys or conflicts of any kind Here was solid and exciting conversation of people and happenings and events in the lives of the Chinese.

And now as the summer came there was much fear of a bad season. Famines were common, for nearly every year there was a famine of some sort in some part of China. Either there was a drought; and irrigation, although perfect in many places, was not on large enough a scale to allow for it, or else the Yellow River, China's Sorrow, overflowed its banks and went wild, inundating all the surrounding country. But this time even the Yangtze Valley, China's surest farming area was threatened. The rains continued endlessly in the two neighboring provinces and in the province where Chinkiang was. *"Hwang nien"*—famine year—began already in the summer to have a worse meaning than in Pearl's memory, and the words were on everyone's lips.

When the first cold days of the autumn of 1907 came, the refugees began to stream southwards where there was still more food than in their own regions. They did not leave home until they had only so much as could be carried on their backs, and then they tied up their bundles of bedding and clothing and their little bags of grain and came as they could by wheelbarrow, slow boats, or on foot, making an endless stream as the small groups merged. The road was long and often the old ones and the children, already too worn and ill, dropped in ragged bundles of death along the way.

The refugees made it even harder for the southern cities Chinkiang had its own shortage and now it had as well thousands of extra mouths to feed. It had disease, too, and the panic of the starving.

The famine could not be kept from the bungalow, although Carie shielded it as best she could from the horror. There were no desserts that winter, and when Christmas came, they gave all that had before been spent on the simple celebration to the relief of the refugees. Andrew who was working on his translation of the New Testament and hoped soon to be ready for the printer, agreed that there could be no thought of printing until this was over. In spite of Carie's good cheer the girls came to know the truth of what lay beyond the compound walls.

Pearl could not go to the Methodist school that winter. It was not safe for her to go along the ridge of the hill alone because of the desperate people waiting sometimes outside the compound gate. There were her lessons and she worked swiftly at them Andrew heard her recitations in mathematics and Latin until he went north of the river to help with famine relief. Carie helped her as she could in the evenings. And there was reading. About this time Pearl bought with her own prize money a little set of books about modern writers. This she read and annotated copiously for she found she knew almost nothing about modern literature.

But that hard year was made much easier because now there were delightful guests in the home. Carie had for years boarded young missionaries for their first year in China while they grew used to the country and while Andrew helped with their study of the language. This year they had a young bride and groom from Texas, Mr. and Mrs. Hancock. Pearl watched them with keen interest. Mr. Hancock was lean and brown and full of the talk of the ranges and cattle and spoke with the twang of the West which Pearl had never heard before. He had humor, too, and laughed often with a caught-in sound of merriment, and tossed Faith high on his shoulder while she screamed with delight. Mrs. Hancock was slender and delicate and wore the most beautiful American dresses, too thin, Carie thought, for the Chinese dampness so that she shook the old base burner more often and had the coolie pour on extra coal.

Pearl saw that these two loved each other. It was what she thought of as a "love match" and the first she had seen She remembers an evening when Mr. Hancock went as usual to their room to review his Chinese after supper. Mrs. Hancock stayed a while with Carie and Pearl and then rose to join her husband.

"Why don't you stay here? Why do you have to go in there with him?" Pearl asked suddenly. And as suddenly and as simply Mrs. Hancock answered, "Because I love him."

Pearl came to know Mr. Hancock well for sometimes after Andrew went to help in relief he helped her with her Latin. Mr. Hancock was always interested in her Chinese way of thinking. One day while they were eating dinner a snake slipped in through the crack beneath the screen of the front door. He went after it with a cane. Pearl said quickly, "Don't kill it. You might hurt somebody's ancestors," and Mr. Hancock gave his short laugh.

He was studying hard to learn Chinese and Pearl watched him and listened but remarked seriously, "You'll never learn Chinese that way. You will just have to get out with the Chinese and talk it."

Sometimes Carie grew cross when fresh breads disappeared from the kitchen unaccountably. Once she spoke very strongly of it with old Wang Amah and the cook. Pearl stood up for them. "Oh, Mother," she said, "don't scold them. They were probably hungry and it is not stealing to eat when you are hungry."

Mr. Hancock laughed very hard one day when she stood watching him roll up his quilts and bedding for a trip to the country. "That's not the way," she said with finality when he was done With that she unrolled it and did it properly. She had seen it done too often not to know exactly how the edges should be turned in so that nothing could slip out

Her reading amazed the Hancocks, and the writing she was constantly doing. They remember one poem sent to the *Shanghai Mercury*, called, "The Chinese Wall Speaks." She was usually rather dignified by now but one day Mr. Hancock went out into the front

90

yard and she was sitting high in a tree. He called out, "What are you doing, Pearl?" And she said with a twinkle, "I'm cultivating the other side of my character."

One of the pleasantest experiences of that winter was to act as interpreter for the Hancocks. It came to be her regular work whenever a Chinese came to call or there was a tradesman there. It was nice to see the complete understanding on both sides, and it was easy to do.

In thinking back it seems that in those days Pearl spent only two or three hours at her schoolwork and for the rest she was free to read or do what she liked.

Determined to offset the sadness of that year, Carie planned a little series of musicales for the young people Pearl and Mary loved to sing duets together and that was their contribution. The smaller ones plodded catastrophically through "pieces" or recited poems, and while sometimes it was painful, still there was a cheerful gathering of white people, solid refreshments and practice in performance before an audience, which was far from waste.

But Carie's real life was for those months the desperate life she lived in the work of relief. A committee had been organized for this and Carie belonged to it. Every day she went out early and came back late, distributing food tickets by which the refugees could claim a bowl of thin rice gruel at the relief kitchen. She had to enter the mat-shed hovels and decide where the tickets were most needed. They all needed so much. Carie's lips were tight with pity, and her eyes were often wet. She came back home at night too weary to do more than bathe and try to swallow the food she knew she must have if she were to set out the next morning again although it seemed to choke her. And she was angry these days. Pearl first saw that anger, surprised.

When Carie spoke, Pearl knew why her eyes were flashing blackly, and her lips had that tightness. "It just doesn't have to be like this!" Carie burst out to the children. "There *is* rice in the country. They just can't get it where it is needed quickly enough, and then some rascals somewhere are hoarding it and trying to make money out of the suffering of the poor.... There is always *some way* if people will take it."

Suddenly Pearl shared Carie's anger. Mother was right. How large China was! Perhaps there wasn't enough rice but there were wheat and barley and *kao liang,* the Chinese grain of the north. This

91

suffering was stupidness or wrongness People shouldn't die for want of simple food.

After that moment her consciousness of the famine was mingled always with anger and the anger tempered the pain that everywhere people were dying.

Carie came to be known among the refugees because her warm heart gave them more than the food. With the little tickets she gave out, there always went a word of sympathy to a mother, a warm garment for a new-born baby, a tiny can of condensed milk to someone too weak for other food. Because they knew her they came to watch for her in the early morning and sometimes the voices of the people could be heard outside the compound gate and Carie when she went dared go only after she had called, "Wait a little now and give me room to pass I come to help in every way I can "

No, Carie could not keep the famine from the bungalow on the hill. There was the catch in her voice when she tried to force herself to sing, and the heartbreaking cheerfulness which the girls knew for what it was.

Yet there were touches of humor in that winter, too. As the year moved on and the famine grew no better, shiploads of relief gifts came from America and these brought laughter even though they were appreciated Americans sent clothes to be made over into garments useful to the Chinese. Unpacking the boxes and barrels, strange things were unearthed. High-heeled shoes—"every bit as bad as Chinese bound feet!" Carie said with a flash of disgust; low-cut evening dresses of sheer materials and corsets which could not possibly be used. But there were other garments of good warm cloth from which neat jackets and trousers were fashioned and distributed.

Strangest of all the strange goods which reached China for the relief of suffering was a shipload of damaged cheeses Cheese was the last thing the Chinese could eat, for it was made of what they called spoiled milk and thus was very vile.to them, and besides it was so strong a food that their systems, accustomed to simple rice and vegetables, even when not starving, could not tolerate it. But the cheeses were dumped off on a wharf and something had to be done with them. They were food and they had to be changed into something the Chinese could eat. They must be sold and the money used. All over that region scattered white people bought the cheeses, and as the list of foreign buyers grew, the cheeses were cut and found not spoiled at all but only ripened and hardened by sea water. Carie herself brought several and through this and her persuasion almost every foreign pantry in that part of China came to have its share while the rice and flour bought with the cheese money went to the famine huts.

At last, and Pearl could not think how, the winter passed and spring came. Slowly the skeletons who had survived gathered their ragged quilts and bundles of clothing and started again for their fields. The time for planting had come and if the next year was not to be worse than this, seed must now be laid in the ground. Seed, it was whispered, was being distributed, free. The streams of people formed and moved at snail's pace, northward, and peace came.

As soon as the seedling rice was planted in the paddy fields, Carie's thoughts flew to the mountains. Her old natural cheer came back, but her mirror reflected two distinct wings of white at her temples. Faith laughed aloud, for she loved laughing, and Pearl and the Longden girls spent long evenings on the porch. During those evenings before Carie set out up the river they sometimes sat and listened. Now there came the normal sounds of summer. There was the cheerful talking of the farmers, the call of evening vendors, the sleepy cooing of wild doves, the croaking of frogs now in their heaven with muddy water everywhere. The great famine was over.

XIII

THAT SUMMER Mary returned to America and in the autumn Pearl grew better acquainted with Mary's younger sisters. But her closest friends were still Dottie Wei and Su-i Wang. These girls were graduating from the Methodist school and already they were holding responsibilities in the school and talking quietly of the engagements which their parents had made for them years before in the old Chinese way, and of their determination to postpone marriage as long as possible.

"After all these years, after this opportunity, I am just ready for work!" Su-i said and her eyes flashed. "I will not marry now! I do not know the man. If Miss Robinson were still here I should not even be afraid of it." Miss Robinson had died that spring and the school missed her unwavering leadership

"But you won't change your mind?" Pearl asked anxiously. "Just because Miss Robinson is gone you are not going to change your whole life!" There was Carie's expression around her lips.

"Of course not! But it would be easier."

The three girls wandered off into the parlor and played the piano. Dottie hummed an English tune

"You *still* get your *th's* a little wrong," Pearl said and sighed "After all the years I've been teaching you English!" Her eyes lit with humor. Suddenly Dottie's arms went around her.

"Tseng-Tzu, you are not an American girl! You are Chinese!" she said.

Two other girls in the senior class were called home to be married Pearl saw Li-an the day she left. She was a beautiful pansy-faced girl. Her great eyes were swimming with tears. "I wanted to be a teacher," she said over and over. The other girls were silent with pity and with the inner heartaching fear that one day they, too, would have to obey the word of their parents.

When Li-an had gone, several of the girls gathered around Pearl and led her to a small music room near the parlor.

"Tell us how it is in your country," they pleaded. "Women there are not only for the bearing of children. It will not always be so here. But what ought *we* to do? You are one of us What would you do?"

Pearl looked around at them. What should she say? She thought of the Hancocks She thought of Carie. She thought of the farm families down in the valleys.

"I would do what I wanted to do," she said clearly. "I would do everything I wanted to do. I might teach and then marry and have my children. If I were gifted I would make that gift perfect, first, for it would be the only thing which would matter." She paused and then in a lower tone she added, "I wouldn't let anything keep me from doing what I wanted to do—what I needed to do to be the person I was made to be."

She was talking in Chinese and her syllables came in clear-cut distinctness in the still room. Suddenly I-mei spoke. Her face was white. "I've always wanted to be a woman doctor because Chinese women suffer so, fearing men. I know now I must be that. . . . It will be very hard."

94

There were quick little flutters of movement and another girl said. "I-mei is the best student in the class. She is the one to be a doctor " Everywhere there were nods of approval and whispers of "yes-yes "

The small group broke up and the girls wandered off in couples. their arms around each other and their faces thoughtful. Pearl was left with a tall awkward girl with high cheek bones They were talking of kindergarten work. "I love little children," the girl said and blushed and laughed, "but I don't want to bear them! There is no end to the bearing of children and one's life is swallowed up in it! I have seen it often Besides there are too many already."

The warmest, friendliest part of Pearl's life was the life in the Methodist school, that winter just before she was seventeen Of this experience in the school, Pearl wrote many years later from New York, "I had lots of fun at the Methodist girls' school and was really chummy with the girls. . . . One of the old girls came to see me last week. . . . We jabbered away exactly the same as we always have!"

Her preparation for college was nearly completed and she studied as she pleased, reading widely as books came within her reach and studying Chinese with a Chinese teacher. Carie saw her absorption in the Chinese girls and it made her uneasy She had never in all these years accepted the Chinese people as people. loving many of them as she did and being forever moved by their suffering and by her conscience which oppressed her with a mission to save their souls. So now she did not comprehend how to Pearl they were simply people as any other people. and so intensely interesting.

Andrew's furlough was not due until a year from that summer. Pearl would be eighteen and then she would return to America to enter college. For the intervening time Carie came suddenly to decision. There was an American boarding school in Shanghai. Here Pearl could make sure of her studies and take her entrance examinations.

At the beginning of the spring term, after Easter, Pearl went to Shanghai.

During these several years Pearl had cherished a dream and the dream was of going to Wellesley College. There was the standard of the school which was the highest she knew. There was the fact that it was in the North, where there was not the finishing school tradition of the South. There was the fact that the women whom Pearl admired most had come from there. And she knew she could earn part of her expenses there. Of this dream she had dared speak only once and then Carie had said, astonished.

"But Wellesley! That's a northern college and northern women are so mannish '"

Pearl said no more but she waited and watched and she knew that more decisive than the reason Carie had given was the fact that Andrew could not afford to send her there even though she helped herself.

When gradually Randolph-Macon Woman's College in Lynchburg, Virginia, came to be talked of, Pearl thought, "At least it has the highest standard of any woman's college in the South."

When she went to Shanghai it was with the intention of preparing to enter this southern college.

Andrew took Pearl to the Shanghai school.

Her first impression was of a dark hall, a parlor dismal with heavy furniture and too little sunshine for the struggling plants near the windows, windows over-curtained in pongee, bare staircases, stifled laughter from upstairs. The principal was a New Englander, a Puritan in China. She was sternly handsome and there was no warmth in her voice or eyes, and the hand she held out for Pearl to shake was long and thin and pallid.

But Pearl followed her upstairs into the small dormitory, and to a room which she was to share that spring with Ruth and Florence Longden. She unpacked the dresses Carie had had made for her and hung them carefully in the closet, wishing that there was none there to watch her.

She was tall and still too slender. Her hair was braided in a single braid and rolled at the nape of her neck and tied there with a large bow of ribbon. She was pale except for vivid lips and her brows were black in contrast to the fairness of her hair. Her eyes were always grave except when she smiled or when some inner thought lit them with sparkling amusement.

In a short time the teachers found that Pearl was already prepared for college. They assigned her lessons beyond what she was required to do for they recognized a mind straining to absorb. One of her teachers looking back writes, "She had an aversion to mathematics which she found difficult. I always put that down to lack of interest,

96

not inability to grasp it. . . . She seemed reserved and shy, wanting I think to be friendly, but not knowing how. . . . She was skilful at expressing herself in writing . . . I appreciated her literary ability (I always enjoyed teaching bright pupils). She was remarkably mature in her thinking. . . . I remember years later her quick friendly smile when I met her. . . . I believe that friendly attitude is one of my clearest pictures of her—a somewhat shy, but friendly smile."

Another schoolmate of that time writes of Pearl, "I remember her as very dignified and reserved for her years, friendly with the other students but intimate with none. . . . She seemed more intimate with the teachers than with her classmates. This was partly because she was taking her final high school work alone, preparing to enter college in the United States. . . . She spent a great deal of time in her room, reading and writing poetry and prose. She said she read Lewis Carroll's *Alice in Wonderland* at least once a year for its deeper insight. She had a keen sense of humor, and a merry twinkle in her eyes. When Pearl had a story to read in our Friday Literary Club, she was given the whole time, and she wrote a real novel with chapters. I remember that the whole room looked forward to hearing the interesting novel."

Another schoolmate writes, "I can recall that in our courses in literature and composition we realized that Pearl had far more ability than the rest of us. She could write wonderful descriptions and thrilling narratives. We frequently wished that she would write our compositions for us."

Here Pearl came to be acquainted with Ray Parker whose family lived in Shanghai, one China friend whom she was to see again in college, and one, too, whom she was to glimpse through the years.

But Pearl was not happy in that Puritan school. The classes pleased her but the atmosphere was deadly to one who loved freedom and normal everyday life. Discipline was strict and the pleasure there might have been in time to talk quietly with other girls, and coming truly to know them, was cut off by rigid rules. Everything was close routine.

Worse than this was the pressure of the religious atmosphere. There were long emotional prayers and constantly she was asked whether or not she was converted. She grew angry and disgusted, used as she was to the healthy way in which the Chinese enjoyed life

But she did not pretend to be stirred by the religion around her. She went steadily on her way and let it flow as turbulently as it would.

97

She found two ways of adapting herself. First she gave herself entirely to what interested her, and this was her study. The other was in seeing the unusual types of girls around her.

Each girl in that school came from some peculiar environment. Meifen was there. She was the only child of a long widowed mother. In her there was built none of the robustness of shared home, shared possessions and shared hardships. She had had no brothers nor sisters to remember, nor had she the heritage of a mother with irrepressible cheer which nothing could subdue. Pearl suddenly felt herself hearty and strong compared with this girl, delicate and over religious. In those months at school together their long friendship grew stronger than ever before and went on through many years until difference of thought separated the two when they were women.

There was a Eurasian girl. The school took a few of these who were American citizens because of their father's nationality. This girl had a creamy skin, snapping black eyes, a merry heart, and ways of thinking which made her forever western though she looked Chinese. She was aggressive, fearless, unreligious, objective. Pearl's best conversations were with her and through her she came to know a great deal of the life of a mixed home. Some things were done in the American way and some in the Chinese. "I nearly *starve* at school" the girl confided. "After good Chinese food these plain boiled vegetables and bread puddings make me ill. Come home with me and I'll see that you have some decent meals."

Pearl laughed and said, "But I know what decent meals are! Both American and Chinese!"

The Chinese mother, Pearl discovered, was a good woman, from a solid merchant's family. It was odd to see this Chinese woman with her daughter, such a slight girl and so totally un-Chinese in behavior. When they came back to school it was with boxes of small seeded cakes, candies, and dried spiced pork.

There was Shanghai. It was full of many different people, more, Pearl did not realize until later, than perhaps any other city of the world. There were suave Chinese gentlemen, more suave and sophisticated by far than any who frequented Andrew's study; fine Chinese ladies sitting with dignity in their rickshas; babies tumbling everywhere; poor girls in flowered cotton jackets, an occasional country man bewildered by the trolleys which went without reason since nothing either propelled or pulled them, asking in a loud voice what the magic was; red-skinned Englishmen keeping themselves carefully

98

aloof; blondined white women. There were East Indians and Russians and Germans and French and Japanese. There were Eurasians dressed in Chinese clothes but keeping their faces averted as if hoping that no one would see their foreign eyes in their yellow faces, or else ostentatiously British, in careful British clothes, pretending with heavy British accent that they were not Chinese.

Shanghai itself was half-breed. One part of it lay snugly Chinese, walled in and almost untouched by white men. Another part was European with parks and broad streets and French names for its avenues. Here were *cafés* and *patisseries* and Parisian hat shops. Another part was mainly British. This was the International Settlement and it was so called because here all but the French, supposedly, shared in control. The British were the first-comers and their presence dominated the Bund, deep, tree-shaded, permanent and backed by important British firms; Nanking Road, narrow and winding but displaying the goods of the best known companies of China; Bubbling Well Road; the Race Course, and the new section, Hongkew. Spreading slowly in this new part where the school stood were Japanese business houses. The clack-clack of *geta* on the damp macadam streets early in the morning was a familiar sound.

Pearl saw the city from the windows of the school, or as all the pupils walked for exercise in the streets themselves, or when they rode in trolleys to the parks. It was a city that had not yet become itself. It could not be mellowed like London, anchored in history like Chinkiang, stirred and melted together like New York. Here the French were still French, the American were American, the Chinese were Chinese, and most of all the British were British.

There was beauty as the sunlight poured into narrow streets hung with banners and lanterns and piled with fruits and fish and teeming with somberly dressed old people and brilliantly dressed children and all the others who went busily along their way. There was ugliness, too—poverty and sickness and hideous suffering. But it was life.

XIV THE LAST EXAMINATIONS were over
and Pearl went home to Chinkiang.
Now there were only a few crowded weeks before the long journey
to America. The bungalow was full of signs of travel. The trunks
were down from the attic, the suitcases sunning on the side porch,
and clothing in all states of repair and incompletion.

As they packed Carie and Andrew argued. Pearl writes, "Carie
felt she wanted to give her (Pearl) some parting gift at this time of
oncoming separation, something to satisfy the child's love of beauty
and adventure. After some thought she decided that this gift would
be to return to America through Europe." There was gayety in her
voice one day when she said, "We are not going home by the Pacific,
but across Siberia! You'll see Russia and Europe and England!"

Pearl thought instantly, "England—Charles Dickens' country,
London, the country roads winding between their hedges, cottages
tucked against low rolling hills!"

"Mother, how lovely!" she said aloud and Carie saw her deep
pleasure in her face.

Wang Amah had to be left again when the time for starting came.
It was the last time Pearl was to see her. She was very old and feeble
now, yet it was her pleasure to work painstakingly at making everything ready for the journey. Her withered old hands washed and
pressed and darned and sewed on fine edgings. She tottered in and
out, mumbling sometimes to herself, and often saying for no one to
hear, that her body could not again endure this departure of her
mistress.

The day came when they left her standing in the shade of a huge
oiled paper umbrella on the deck of the hulk from which their
steamer for Hankow started. Her cheeks were wet with tears which
she did not try to keep back. The outlines of the city of Chinkiang
and its background of hills and pagodas, and Golden Island, near
which they passed, slipped slowly by. They were steaming up the
river.

Hankow was hot and confused, much less foreign than Shanghai,
much less beautiful than Chinkiang with its circle of hills and temples. But soon they were on the train moving northward toward
Peking and a part of China which none of them had ever seen.

The second day they were in a country arid and bare, among tall
and angular people who talked a new dialect and were fond of garlic

and sodden breads. Here there was none of the greenness of central and south China. The hair of the women, instead of being ebony and smooth, was wind-blown and browned by sunburn, and their skins were harsh from the constant blown dust.

There was a day in Peking, a day crowded with palaces and marble bridges and blue-tiled temples. Pearl saw a China more ancient and beautiful and rich in art than she had ever seen before. There was time to no more than catch its flavor but once the flavor was sampled she knew she must some time have more. Scenes of sunlight on turquoise temple roofs, of shadow in a quiet temple court, of white marble glistening beneath the azure sky could never leave her.

Then they were on the train again in barren country leading northward to Mukden and Harbin. Here was a different world again and there was no beauty here unless one could find it in a bulbous minaret on a Greek Catholic church, or in the features of a broad-templed woman nursing a rosy-cheeked baby at her breast. Everything seemed bare and dusty and harsh and strangely mixed, Chinese and Russian, with nothing clearly itself.

And now ten days of travel stretched across Russia. It seemed sometimes that the train was the only moving object in all the immense space of almost uninhabited land. It seemed to creep over the wide expanses of field and pastureland. It halted only for the sheer necessity of taking on coal or water at a lonely station where a few peasants gathered, staring and talking among themselves.

Those days spent in crossing Siberia are strongly connected with the memory of Andrew, cooped up in the small compartment of the train which was their share of space. Pearl writes of it, "He who needed space and privacy was reduced to nothing of either.

"There was not even a lavatory, and we were compelled to do all our washing in turn out of a small enamelled basin we had brought along, and the water was very scarce and to be had only at stations and then by rushing out with a can and buying it.

"There was one dreadful morning when Faith forgot to empty the basin after she had used it, and Andrew, always absent-minded and now in deepest gloom over his situation, sat down in it and ruined his only pair of trousers. He had not recovered from this when he found a cup half full of water, and wanting to use the cup, he threw the contents out of the window. He was too near-sighted to see that the glass was up, and the water flew back at him, wetting his front very thoroughly. Carie laughed. It was too much. He sat down. 'There is nothing to laugh at,' he said severely, and for the rest of the day he stared gloomily at the flat Russian landscape and muttered over and over, 'I don't see anything to this country—there's nothing to make a fuss over, here' "

But later when they stopped more often in great cities, Pearl remembers, Andrew "wandered inevitably to the churches, and stood there by the hour, watching the hordes of people come in, poor and ragged and miserable, most of them, but a few of them rich, too, and poor and rich all bending to kiss the relics of cloth or bone or skin left from some dead saint ... 'They have the Bible,' he said. 'They could get at the truth if they would But it's an easy way—to live in sin and go and gabble to a priest and kiss a bone and call it salvation!' "

Carie was absorbed in what she saw. Pearl writes,

"She saw here the essentials of a grave and dangerous human situation and was appalled by the differences between the few rich and educated and the millions of the common people, living in a manner almost bestial. She kept saying, 'These people are going to make a revolution one day that will shake the world. You can't have this sort of thing in a country and be safe.' "

Absorbed as she was in the human problem she saw before her, Carie did not miss the contrasts of nature through which they flew. There was waste and ugliness, but there were, too, birch forests still hiding drifts of snow, even though it was July, rushing streams, brilliant lights and shadows, enormous fields and pastures It was the forests she never forgot. Years later she still told of the birch trees, beautiful and graceful, and of the snow, clean and white in the shade.

To Faith, sitting tailor-fashion on her berth, it was a time of intense creative effort. Carie had armed her with scraps from her scrap bag and now with her sewing materials she copied every new style of dress and fitted it to a tiny china doll so that by the time they reached England she had a costume record of all the countries through which they had passed. And there was the small diary in which at Carie's suggestion she set down something of their itinerary.

To Pearl the trip across Russia was a sweep of landscape, bare, perhaps, except for a few half-barren trees and the distant point of a church with the town houses clustering around it, and against that landscape a Russian peasant and his wife and child, their hoes across their shoulders, their loose garments flying, their faces turned toward the train, watching as it passed them and left them standing like symbols in a mural. Her eyes were alight with interest and when the train drew into a station she could not see enough of the crowds of people. The hearty Russian fashion of kissing appalled Andrew. He watched the bearded dirty peasants greet each other with loud kisses and shuddered; it was worse than heathen, he said. But Pearl did not shudder It was the way the people did and there was something robust and warm in their heartiness.

After Russia came Germany and France and Switzerland.

Andrew had looked forward eagerly to Germany for he was of German descent. "Yet the very first day in Berlin," Pearl writes, "we saw a sight we had never yet seen—Andrew so incensed that he offered to fight a cabman! The fellow was a huge, burly, heavy German and he shook his fist under Andrew's nose in the railway station in the presence of innumerable people because he felt the tip inadequate, whereupon Andrew, who felt all tips were of the devil anyhow, doubled up his fists and pushed them into the fellow's fat jaw. We were so amazed we could not believe this was our Andrew. Carie screamed and held his arm and fumbled in her own bag for coins to placate the Teuton, and at last roaring throaty oaths, he went his way, and we led Andrew hastily to a hotel, taking care to hire the meekest looking porter in sight to transport our bags. Andrew went with us looking more ungodly than we would have believed it possible, giving as he went his opinion of the white race, which for the moment was even lower than usual. Indeed, I believe this incident more than anything else was responsible for Andrew's strong stand against the Germans in the World War, and his complete readiness to believe atrocity stories.

" 'That fellow!' he would mutter years after, 'the Germans are capable of anything!'—this in spite of his own early German ancestry and an innocent pride he always took in his proficiency in the German language."

It had been a dream of Carie's to spend a summer in Switzerland and now that dream came true. They took rooms in a little *chateau* kept for tourists by a widow who had once been rich. From their windows they could see the beautiful Lake Neufchatel, and beyond, the Alps. Below them were vineyards and orchards. When they went to walk there were enormous blackheart cherries to be bought in baskets, and not far away they came by little mountain trains to a place smelling of chocolate for miles around, and tasted it in the making and bought it fresh and entirely unlike the stale imported chocolate of China.

Carie divided her time between the beauty beyond the windows and the tales of the little widow. There was always someone telling her story to Carie.

But Pearl did not take these weeks in Switzerland as a holiday. At last she had the chance to study under those who could teach her French and German as their own tongue. She worked hard and the help of those few weeks she felt ever afterward.

The summer passed and at last they were in London!

The love for England, begun by her reading, which took her back again and again in later years, became rooted now. Here was the quiet dignity of churches and cathedrals, of residential streets, and parks, and here, too, the cluttered color of Piccadilly with its markets and bookshops.

Here were Dickens, and Samuel Johnson, and Thackeray! The time in London was one of the happiest in Pearl's life, for it was as though history were turned back and she were walking in another world, the world in which, in her imagination, through long hours in China, she had lived many times before. Only now it was real.

Too soon it was over. There was the crossing of the Atlantic, rough and unpleasant, and then southward once more to the old white house in Hillsboro.

Grandfather was gone. Carie, she saw, missed intolerably the little old arrogant figure. She saw, too, that Carie felt now a visitor in this place that had been more hers than any on earth. Yet here were the dear house, the flower garden, the orchard. Here were the sweeping meadows, the woods, the farms. Here the spired church and the white village houses. Here was Cornelius, more than ever like Hermanus, and Cousin Grace grown and in college, and Cousin Mamie busy at teaching. All, together, made up America and America she knew now was her home.

PART FOUR

XV   WHEN THEY came to Lynchburg, Virginia, there
was Edwin, married now and with a baby girl.
Carie took her grandchild and with her old love of babies held
her and talked to her and said how deeply blue her eyes were, and
how curly her hair. It was satisfying to see this oldest of her children
settled in a home of his own and doing well as editor of a newspaper.

To Pearl, Edwin was strange again for he was not the college
student of those days in Lexington, but a father and a man to whom
she must grow accustomed through the days when she would see
him often.

Her mind was set now toward college. What would it be like?

The campus of Randolph-Macon lay outside the southern town,
broad and open with a few trees and a dripping wistaria against the
main hall. But the buildings themselves were not inviting.

That day when she stepped into the guest hall, she was disappointed, expecting for some reason, perhaps because she was in
America and this a place of learning, to find grace and beauty. Instead the room was small, drab brown, and cut by entering doors.
Girls seemed to pass and cross in confusion and everywhere there
was the sound of soft southern talking and repressed peals of high
laughter. Glimpses gave the impression of cascades of curls and rip-

pling flounces. What she overheard was small talk of families and friends and occasionally of courses and the best teachers.

Her first sight of the whole body of students was at supper that night She had never seen so many American girls at one time before She seemed swallowed in the buzz of conversation and the clatter of dishes. Listening to what was said around her she came to the conclusion that she had better take no part in the talking. Life was all here for these, closed in and pleasant and comfortable, exciting only where there came some episode at school or a visit from a boy friend. She tried to think what she could do to be friendly, but there seemed to be nothing which would not be alien to what went on here. And she did not want to be set apart. She wanted to know these girls and what American life was. She could not be a stranger in her own land.

She ate silently, feeling eyes upon her. She wore a Chinese blue linen dress with a small neat white trimming. Her hair, very thick and fine, was combed smoothly in a knot at the base of her neck. She knew she must seem almost severe in comparison with the coils and puffs and ruffles of the others. But dress could not really matter. She could change that.

She looked up and a girl across the table caught her eye She was a small girl with dark eyes and fair hair. She had been waiting for this moment. Instantly she spoke.

"I am Emma Edmunds. I would like to introduce you to the other girls," she said. She, too, felt strange. Perhaps they could help each other.

"I am Pearl Sydenstricker," Pearl answered, smiling to hide the shyness which suddenly overcame her. "Just call me Pearl," she added quickly. Her name went round the table, the girls all giving their names and smiling at her. In spite of themselves their eyes were curious and Emma feeling at once drawn and aching to make things comfortable said again,

"We want to get acquainted Tell us about yourself."

"There isn't much to tell," Pearl said. "I've just come from China where I've always lived."

"China!" they all echoed. "Imagine!"

The girl on one side of her touched the material of her dress, "Then this is Chinese linen. I've heard about it. It's woven by hand, isn't it? My aunt made a trip to China and brought back the most beautiful embroideries and some of them were done on this very

106

material." Her soft eyes were large with the excitement of being so near to a person who had lived always in China "Are they really like we hear they are?" she went on. "1 mean, do they eat curious things, and wear pigtails and everything? I've never been able to dream people were like everyone says the Chinese are."

Pearl smiled."They are just people like we are," she said simply.

"I suppose they are," Emma said suddenly. "Everyone is when one is acquainted." She longed to break the curious circle, kindly though it was.

When they left the dining room it was Emma who went with her to the campus and walked arm in arm along the walks. They talked, discovering each other, and it was the beginning of a friendship which has lasted through the years.

And now here came someone running towards them, her auburn hair familiar. It was Ray Parker of the old Shanghai school. Instantly there was talk of China and common friends. Pearl was surrounded by Ray's eagerness to make all easy and friendly. But she was already a junior and so their ways never crossed in classes. It was only as they planned it that they were together.

Pearl roomed in West Hall with a quiet junior older than she. Emma roomed across the hall. But that quick friendship between Pearl and Emma made them closer to each other than to their roommates.

In West Hall the girls were soon acquainted with Pearl, but they longed to know her better. There was something which made her unlike them. At first they thought it was that she dressed simply, not as they did. But soon they knew that the difference lay deeper. Some part of her was remote from them and although they felt her always more friendly, there was a door through which they could not pass. One of the girls in a whispered conversation like those which so often took place between roommates after lights out, said. "There is just so much of her life that we don't know about. She can't help it, and we can't help it. It's that way."

Andrew unknowingly did not help that feeling of difference. Pearl tells of an incident she will always remember. She writes, "She (Pearl) sat a timid freshman among other freshmen in the college chapel, waiting in some anxiety. For Andrew had been asked to lead vespers, and among the new friends she had eagerly made, the best friends of her own race she had ever had, she was anxious that all impressions be of the best. She looked at Andrew with some misgiving as he came in, tranquil as ever, behind the college president. No man could move with greater dignity than he before a service he was to give Everybody looked at him and his daughter saw him with a new detachment, a very tall, slightly stooped figure, the noble head carried with native pride, his big profile pointed straight ahead. But then she saw only that his frock coat was the same old coat, rusty, and given a little at the seams and of an obsolete cut, and well she knew the scene there had been before he put it on.

"Carie said, 'Andrew, you are not going to preach at the college in that old gray suit!'"

"'Old! It's not old—it's a good suit—good enough for a preacher.'"

"'Andrew!' Carie's dark eyes went on speaking, fixed upon him. He looked away from her doggedly.

"'A preacher oughtn't to be all dressed up,' he muttered.

"Her eyes, pinning him, went on speaking.

"He went on, restlessly, 'I tell you I hate that old long-tailed coat! The armholes are tight.'

"'I've been wanting you to get a new one for years.'

"Carie's voice was dangerously mild.

"'What for?' Andrew demanded. 'It's perfectly good!'

"'Then why won't you wear it?'

"'Oh, pshaw!' he said and got up, beaten.

"There was a whisper beside his daughter in the chapel. A girlish voice said in a soft, innocent, southern drawl, 'He looks as though he'd be right long-winded!'

"There was a bitter moment and then Andrew's daughter said, her lips dry, 'He's my father.'

"There was a shock of silence. 'Oh, I *am* sorry!' the pretty voice said.

"'It doesn't matter,' said Andrew's daughter sternly. 'He *is* long-winded!' and sat there suffering, while Andrew preached on and on."

That first month in college was strangely torn between the pressure of adjustment to this new life, and the coming separation from Carie. Other girls were near home and talked already of Thanksgiving and Christmas holidays, and read letters which had taken only a few short days to arrive. When her family left it would be to cross the Pacific and she would not see them until four years had passed. There was beside her own incipient loneliness the fact that she guessed how Carie felt. To Carie the ocean was ever an almost

108

impassable barrier. Each time that she crossed it she wondered whether again her strength could stand it And now she knew herself less strong. Illness which before had touched her, sometimes gave sign that it only lay hidden When they went, then, and Pearl clung for an instant to Carie, it was with a sharp sense of loss.

But she turned her thought swiftly back to college. Three things she had to do. She must make her appearance like that of the other girls so that she would never be conspicuous. She must learn the small arts of entering into this life which was now to be hers. She must do her work.

The first she set herself to quickly. When classes were over she went to Edwin's house armed with materials bought in the town stores, and there, cutting and fitting and altering she made a new wardrobe. Edwin smiled at her swift determination. Now she was glad indeed that Carie had taught her sewing.

The second she slowly accomplished in all the minute ways of girls, running in and out of dormitory rooms, belonging to the little Chocolate Club which met sometimes in the evening for chatter and food. The girls saved sugar and milk from the dining hall and bought cocoa and cookies from the small store near by and made cocoa over the open gas jet of the lights which lit the rooms. Pearl taught herself to enter conversations, bringing in a touch from her life when it seemed appropriate, but never allowing herself to seem alien. For a time Laurie Cash, who belonged to the group, suffered agonies because being fair she secretly pencilled her eyebrows and she was afraid Pearl would not approve. But soon Laurie Cash, writes a classmate, "delighted to get a small group in her room and try by her antics, to make Pearl laugh, to chase her around and try to kiss her. She had bright red hair, used to knot it on top of her head and wiggle her scalp until it tumbled down. We would double up with hysterics, and Pearl always succumbed."

It was only sometimes, when she did not know it, as the girls passed her in the hall, that they saw a distant look in her eyes, and when she spoke it was as if from far away.

The third thing she need make no effort to succeed in. It was for this she had come to college. She was surprised to learn from conversations around her that some girls had come for other things, for the college life, for the standing a degree would give them. For her it was opportunity long looked for. In her home Andrew had considered study above all other pursuits. Carie, though less of a student, looked back to her days in Bellewood Seminary, an unusual opportunity for women in her time, as days rich in training and association. China had ever a reverence for learning. And to Pearl books were always as real as life itself.

Already she made a distinct impression upon her teachers. Her mathematics professor remembers the picture of her sitting at the end of a row in the first floor classroom, the way the light shone in from the high windows making her hair, before soft honey-color, shining gold. She remembers her as a reserved student, obviously not interested in this subject, yet doing the work required of her. It was not until later and in terms of beauty and poetry and prose that they came to friendship.

The professor of freshman English soon found this girl far surpassed the others in her preparation for the work. It was a reference to Tennyson that suddenly revealed it. The question was which one of his poems was written in dialect. "The Northern Farmer" came in a flash to Pearl and she said it. She remembered her little fat brown book of Tennyson One time her teacher asked her of her reading and it was then that she knew there was nothing she could teach this student. Often in that class when they went afield from the required grind of rules and composition and wandered for a little in the work of authors, a light came into Pearl's eyes. The others came to watch for it. At that instant she was completely herself. The professor marked her papers as best she could but says, "I ran out of adjectives. There was nothing I could do to help her for she knew all I could teach already."

Yet one of the delightful stories of the campus, passed from one generation of students to another to this very day, especially when examinations draw near, is that Pearl Sydenstricker failed freshman English. It is a college myth, for the records give her a standing comfortably above ninety.

She took college Latin since it was required of her. But she did not like it. Already she knew her majors were to be philosophy and psychology and in these fields and in literature she read quietly herself

One of the greatest pleasures of college was her discovery of the small college library. It stood between West Hall where she roomed and Main Hall where the classrooms were—a large square room with a gallery running around it and the light falling in from windows along the side. It was not impressive, but here were books. For the first time in her life she had plenty of books.

She wrote a short story for the college magazine that spring and it appeared in March. She called it "The Valley by the Sea." But she was not at all satisfied with it. She knew she was not yet herself in her writing The religious influence in her childhood, and a mysticism and romanticism bound her. But her form was good and the words flowed with beauty

Commencement week drew near and in the annual, the *Helianthus*, there was another story by her. It was "By the Hand of a Child." Still she was not satisfied. But she was more sure, not less, that her work was to be writing.

Now as the closing celebrations began she was to have a part. There was a hooding ceremony when seniors were hooded by their sophomore sisters. Ray Parker, that old friend from Shanghai school days, was hooded by Pearl, using a hood which was to become famous as the list of names inscribed in its lining grew, and as some of those names in themselves became famous.

XVII   AUNT MARIA, a Negro woman who had been with the college since its founding, stopped Pearl in the corridor of West Hall one morning, as she made her round of the rooms.

"They say you came from China," she said, her eyes wide with surprise. "That's a long way off. Did you mind the ocean crossing and were you seasick? My sister's boy, he's been on the ocean, and he says it rolls and tosses fit to kill."

She smoothed down her white apron and stood looking steadily at Pearl.

"I'm used to it," Pearl said, "and besides, this time I didn't come across the Pacific, but the Atlantic, and it isn't so wide."

It was her first direct contact with a Negro.

"Tell me," Aunt Maria asked, lowering her voice, "what are the Chinese really like? I've heard people say they are queer and eat things no one else would eat and such, but I sometimes wonder. Are they like we are—we colored folks—or are there Chinese ladies and Chinese gentlemen? You know I love this college. I've been here years and years, since the very beginning, and I've taken care of the college president when he was sick and sometimes I even forget myself and call him 'son.' But colored is different from white here in this country and there's never the same chance for both." Her face held deep bewilderment.

"In China there are teachers and students and ladies and gentlemen," Pearl said slowly. "We are the outsiders—the foreigners over there."

"You don't say!" The Negro was silent a moment and then she went on. "I've a friend and her boy got sent to school by a kind white man but it didn't make any difference He's a porter, but she thought that seeing as how he'd been to school———"

"Aunt Maria! Aunt Maria!" a girl's voice rang down the hall. "I'm waiting for that collar you said you'd press up for me! I'll be late to class if you don't hurry."

The old woman gave Pearl a quick glance as if to say, "You see how it is!" and went slowly down the hall.

Pearl turned in at the door of her own room and sat for a moment at her desk, thinking. Then she drew her books toward her and began to work

It was the beginning of her sophomore year. She was preparing her history assignment. It was pleasant, for men moved through the pages as in tremendous drama, movements came to birth, succeeded or failed, and peoples struggled for freedom. It was this that held her greatest interest, this story of peoples searching for ways of freedom. "When freedom is already their right simply because they are people," Pearl said one day in class. The professor looked at her hard for an instant This student surprised him by her questions. She had read more and thought more than the others, grasping the sweep of history as he longed to have it grasped. But sometimes, as now, the way she thought of things was disturbing.

As she studied that morning, a memory of Carie flashed back. It was the famine year again and Carie's eyes were black with anger. "No one ought to suffer for food," she was saying. "The food is here. It simply cannot be gotten from one place to another quickly enough and there are those who hoard it for the high price they can get." Her memory of her own anger of that day swept over her again Everyone had a right to all the goodness of the earth, she thought now, and an ache, a resolve, uncertain, indistinct settled upon her.

Three responsibilities in the college organization fell upon her

112

this autumn. One was that she was chosen a member of the student committee Another, she was made the treasurer of her class Third, she was made leader of the Student Volunteer Band This last she accepted only under pressure. It was her background that made it impossible for her to refuse it In spite of everything some of the girls still connected her with that missionary life. One of the girls writes of her in a connection of this kind· "My most vivid memory of a personal contact with her was when for the Y.W C A. I was canvassing the girls in my hall to ask that for a month they pledge to read their Bibles each day I was a new Christian·and this was the first bit of active Christian work I had undertaken in the college, and when I got to Pearl's room I remember standing outside for what seemed a long time before knocking. Although I had a great respect for missionaries and for their children I had also a bit of fear. When I asked her to sign the paper, I remember her cordiality, and evident sensing of my embarrassment, and her amusement. She replied that she always read her Bible, but that if it would help anyone else, she would be glad to sign the paper." To Pearl the Bible has ever been great literature.

Her sophomore year was much easier than her freshman. She roomed this year with a serious senior. But Pearl was used to the life now and entered freely into the gayety of it. A college mate writes, "We had a good time on the fourth floor of West Hall. Pearl in our midst represented maturity, wisdom, intellect, poise, and yet we never doubted her warm interest in us, even suspected her own desire to be silly with us sometimes "

Yet it was never purely gayety The same friend says, "I recall a Sunday night I was in my room writing home, and Pearl tapped at the door and came in for a little visit. I put her in the letter, the interesting girl from China, and the incident seems to mark the beginning of my deep interest in International Relations. For most of us that was the background against which we came to sketch her future, social and religious work on a world-wide scale."

Competition between classes was strong that year and sister classes joined together against each other even more than was usual. The sister classes were divided into the Odds and the Evens depending upon the number of the year of graduation. Thus Pearl was an Even.

It was in this connection that she took part in one of the most long-drawn-out and exciting of college fights. Pearl became well acquainted with the class president One night Dorothy called a secret meeting Pearl was there. A classmate writes, "Our mascot, a white horse named Senator had died, and the freshmen had discovered the fact and cremated him with derisive ceremonies. Dorothy locked us into the room until a plan could be produced to restore our blasted honor. At that meeting the Even ghost was cooked up."

It became a tradition, that horse ghost, and he appeared always at the great events of the Odds and spoke disturbingly from sheeted depths

Pearl's class under the leadership of its president had other original ideas. It took pride in leaving the old traditions and setting up its own. When the time drew near for the great class event of the year, the freshman-junior party, initiative went wild. A classmate writes, "She (Pearl) took part in one of the most dastardly class tricks. The freshmen were giving the juniors a deep sea party. The lower part of the gym was the under-sea country; the balcony was the seaside, and it was festooned with fishing nets. Pearl, chosen because she looked so ill-suited to such a role, and was not known to the freshmen as a fighting sophomore and so might better pass unnoticed, was dressed as an aged fisherman and sent right in the front door with a pack of fish on her back. We had paid $2 for 200 fish some days before and they had been gently ripening in a convenient cellar. Pearl entered softly and dropped a fish in every net while the party was riding high. It became higher still, soon."

But beneath the flurries and excitements of college life in which she took full part, the stream of her own life ran evenly and strong. There was her ever-increasing use of the library. She writes, "The times I seem to remember as happiest were in the college library when I read for myself. This I did with great voracity, tracking down one subject after another and reading everything I could find. This I suppose was my real education. I remember more of what I learned thus than I do of teaching. By my junior year I was considering this my chief work, with the lessons to be squeezed in on the side as I could."

Again she says, "Another bright spot was my Sunday afternoons when I used to go to an orphanage near by to play with the children. (Students in the sociology classes sometimes went to the Methodist orphanage to help with the children and observe.) ... Then there were two old lady dressmakers who lived near the campus and did odd sewing for the girls, and I used to listen to them talk. And

114

there was a Negro family. . . . I remember clearly the effect of beauty of the natural scenery on me. The campus and buildings now are beautiful but then were not. But the James River ran not far away and Emma and I used to spend afternoons rowing on the river, and I enjoyed that and the blue hills and the autumn coloring. . . . I do enjoy nature so deeply, not being introspective, and am happy or at least entertained and occupied by next to nothing or anything that happens to be around. . . . I do get impatient at being restricted . . and when I feel that, I just break away at all costs, I have to feel free or I had rather not live. That was the way I was in college, too."

Because Pearl had roomed for two years with girls older than herself, suddenly now she longed for a change. About a month before school closed, she asked Laurie Cash to room with her the next year. The year looked promising in school interest for Pearl had been chosen president of the junior class. This she knew was a scholastic honor. She knew, too, that it meant that she had not failed in winning her place among the girls.

XVII DURING THE SUMMERS Pearl grew better acquainted with Edwin for his home was hers. But she was busy with tutoring high school students, and with a share in the care of her small niece and now with a tiny nephew. The tutoring was drudgery which she did solely for the income it brought her. The care of the children was pleasure for more and more she loved children. Her little niece shared a room with her and she took delight in making her pretty dresses and curling her dark hair and telling her stories and singing to her.

Edwin often watched her at it and sometimes said,

"They take to you as if you were made for it, Pearl."

There were evenings when they had time to talk in the darkness of the porch. These were the times when Edwin told of his work and hopes for a change in it. He was studying quietly, fitting himself for a new field in statistics. Sometimes he asked Pearl,

"When you have graduated, are you going back to China?"

Always she said, "Yes, but not at once. I must get better acquainted with America. I must see more of it. I want to see people in other parts of the country." But beyond that she could have nothing definite She did not speak of her inner certainty that she was to write. Yet there grew up between brother and sister a companionship which although still partly inarticulate, was to deepen with the years.

The junior year started off well Her roommate writes, "We started off this year 'in high.' Our room was a popular place Pearl seemed to blossom as president of her class. She had a good deal of business, the usual campus politics, to attend to. I had several class offices. . . . We both felt that we were liked by our fellow students, and we both had had to win that for ourselves. Pearl bloomed under it. She was invited to join a secret society—the AM SAM—the first secret society and the best. Usually the ones invited to join it were the best students and outstanding in every way. I was so happy for her. Then the Kappa Delta sorority rushed her."

Pearl had long hesitated over this step of joining a sorority. She had not been sure that she wanted to throw herself into a group of society girls. It was expensive, too. She writes of it, "I joined after some hesitation the most 'society' sorority with the purpose of getting to know that kind of girl. . . . I liked them all well enough . . . and they liked me except that I could never remember any of the sorority rules and would not be bothered to 'rush' anybody. I think on the whole they did not know what to make of me."

The AM SAM secret society took in only twelve girls at a time. Pearl says, "It was supposed to be a great honor since scholastic and general requirements were high. The girls were above average and my best friends were among them."

The little AM SAM house stood at the end of a narrow path beyond the athletic field, a small long house where the girls met, sat around a fire in the evenings—even though the chimney smoked—and talked sometimes merrily, sometimes seriously. It came nearest being a totally congenial group for Pearl in college.

Many speaking of Pearl in her junior year in college remember her as having a thoroughly good time. She was accepted everywhere where the girls knew her and many report, "We came to know her that year and often we said among ourselves, 'We did not know she was like this.' "

Her roommate writes, "I have often laughed about the way we fixed up our room. Neither of us had much to spend, but we purchased two couch covers and a screen to cover the washstand. As a

116

special note of elegance, we bought a little hanging bookshelf which we hung over my bed. On this we put what I was pleased to call the 'ancestral china,' some really rare pieces of blue china—a tea pot. plates and cups and saucers. It looked lovely, we thought, but my bed was in the outside corner, double windows on each side. Every time the door opened and closed, the draught and the closing combined to make a suction that drew one or more of the pieces of china down on my nose. It got so that every time the door opened, I ducked. By the end of the year all that was left were a cup or two and the tea pot. I used to tell Pearl that she put them over my head so that she wouldn't have any responsibility in the matter but could just act noble and say, 'Oh, it doesn't matter in the least,' to me."

But ever Emma was her close individual friend. Perhaps this friendship lasted because they did not always agree and accepted their disagreement. Pearl writes, "The truth of it was I had friends of all sorts and none very close. Emma was my closest friend ... Most of the girls at R.M.W.C. were from wealthy families.... Emma didn't have money and she was economical and helped me to be. Emma was really a sort of rock for me—very prudent, sensible, a wonderful student, not creative or brilliant, just intelligent and hard-working. She was always conservative. Later in life we had a quarrel on this subject.... I told her she had to take me as I was or let me go.... It is the proof of her real stature that from that day, though she has expressed herself frankly, she has done it without making me feel that she demanded anything or criticised me, or would think less of me for not agreeing with her, and so we have remained friends.... I have a feeling that whatever I do she will give me credit for doing it because I think it is right, and that, even though she does not agree, is the main thing with her."

But Pearl's real interest lay in her own quiet preparation. Her discoveries in the library went on and she came away always refreshed and delighted. She wrote, and her short story was awarded the prize as the best of the year.... Although she was not on the staff of the college magazine, the *Tattler,* responsibility for some parts of its work seems to have fallen upon her for a classmate writes, "Late one evening Pearl came to my room with the news that the class history was not satisfactory and that a class history in verse had to be written before morning. Pearl had already arranged for light privileges and would bring in any possible poets to aid with the job. Nobody thought of asking Pearl to stay with it!"

117

An article written by one of the professors appeared in the *Tattler* which resulted in the formation of a small and very exclusive modern literature club. There were only eight or nine members in all, and these from the junior and senior classes. But in her junior year Pearl was not a member.

That spring two representatives were chosen to attend the student conference of the Y.W.C.A. at Bryn Mawr. Pearl was one of them. Her roommate writes of the preparation for that event, "Such a scurrying around as we had. We were getting through college on a shoestring and of course we wanted our representatives to put the best foot foremost. Everyone who was the correct size put her wardrobe at the disposal of the two girls. I don't recall that I had anything that either would have. At any rate those two girls went to the conference with the cream of the wardrobe of Randolph-Macon. One girl contributed a particularly good dress so of course that went along. Unfortunately the back looked very much like the front. Pearl wore it to a tea and discovered all too late that she had put it on hind part before."

The election of the junior to attend this conference usually meant that that person was to be president of the student government for the next year. Pearl was, however, the logical choice for Y.W C.A. president. Another person could probably have managed to let it be known, without room for criticism, that she preferred the presidency of the student government. But Pearl, when asked, answered honestly that since she had for so long been connected with religious work she would really rather be student president. This candid answer stirred up the ardent Y.W.C.A. girls. There was a split in the girls and some jealousy over the membership in the Kappa Delta sorority. The outcome was that Pearl was elected to neither position, although that choice of student president was decided by one vote. After all these years one girl writes, "Pearl would have made one of the great student presidents."

Pearl's junior year was her roommate's senior year. In looking back Laurie Cash writes, "I told Pearl that if, in my next reincarnation, I was to room with a genius, I hope she 'will roll her eyes in a fine frenzy,' throw a shoe at me, or do something to warn me. To me she was so utterly normal, so full of fun and life, so like the rest of us, that I didn't dream of the heights to which she would ascend. Many people have asked me to appear before their book clubs to give them some personal touches and comments. I always simply have to admit that to me she seemed to be a fine wholesome friend Pearl says that I was always so head over heels in work that I didn't pay much attention to what she was doing, that she always did like to write and was constantly writing for the school magazine and the annual. The only peculiarity I seem to remember was that when we invited her for a special treat, whether for breakfast, dinner or supper, or in between, she always ordered ice cream. Calmly she would eat it for breakfast, saying, 'I always keep thinking that when I go back to China, that's one thing I won't have. It's all made of canned milk there and I can't stand canned milk!' "

One day Pearl and a classmate went to a moving picture. "Pearl and I were downtown together, when we passed a movie advertising pictures from China. She had to go in and we sat through some awful stuff until China came on the screen. Suddenly Pearl cried, 'There's Father!' Right down to the camera's eye marched a divine long black coated man who looked not unlike Pearl in her graver moments. Suddenly he saw the camera and registered the most beautiful consternation. He wheeled and fled, his coat tails level in the winds of indignation. Pearl was delighted and we had to sit through the vile feature picture a second time to enjoy her father's star appearance."

Pearl's and Carie's letters crossed each other regularly. Pearl's letters were read and re-read and brought much satisfaction but raised many questions in Carie's mind, especially now that she was constantly less well and more often not her cheery self. To Faith, now in Shanghai at school, they were a great excitement, for all the events of college were exciting and her elder sister having part in them made that excitement greater still.

Carie's letters told always of the small details of the life in Chinkiang, and Pearl, knowing that life, could picture it except when there suddenly came news that the home was to be moved from the old bungalow to a neighboring hill. She saw that Carie did not want to move from the hill, but it had been decided that that place was to be made into a school. Carie was rooted in the square house where the family had now lived for many years, and in the garden with its great old trees and flower borders and hedges. She complained that the hill to which they were to move was low and narrow, and that the odor of the fertilizer used on the vegetable beds in the valleys rose unbearably strong. and that at her age she could never again build up a home with any of the beauty of the old one.

Pearl could not imagine that narrow hill nor the new brick house which rose upon it. But she could see Carie only too vividly, her white hair blowing, her hands soiled with the red clay she wrote of with such hopelessness. Still it was not like Carie to complain—was she not well? A little seed of anxiety sowed itself and thrust down a torturing root.

Then there came a letter telling of the death of Wang Amah. She died quietly one night and Carie bought a good coffin and had her laid in it. She was dead, but strong and clear was the memory of Wang Amah in her crackling starched jacket, smelling faintly of yellow soap, holding her first as a little girl and telling her stories; Wang Amah as she wept for Clyde; Wang Amah as an old woman, pottering about the last washing and ironing of her things before she came to America. Years later Pearl looked back and wrote, "We know quite well and to this day that she left her share in us, her white children. Part of her went into us, as mothers are part of their children. so that now and forever her country is like our own to us, loved and understood, her people our own kin. And some essence of the gods in whom she believed lingers in our hearts still, and keeps us. when we think of our old nurse, too large for disbelief, too humble for any scorn."

As class president it fell to Pearl to make the class oration from the ghost horse, Senator, which was the class tradition. A classmate writes, "I suppose she tried it out in advance and found that she did not have the voice for it. I was drafted to serve as foghorn. . . . Pearl was to give me the gist of the speech as we walked along. Pearl led the astral brute and instructed him in hurried whispers. It was difficult to hear as well as to speak through the sheety bosom and I make a howling break—and got a good kick in the shins. It seems very strange that Pearl was no speaker in her college days."

When summer came, with sudden hunger for her own Pearl went to Hillsboro and then to Highland County to visit Carie's people. Cousin Grace had a gay house party. In the mountains Pearl slept in Cousin Eugenia's room, for Eugenia was away at nursing school in Richmond. Pearl wrote in a letter to her, "Your room is lovely and breezy reminding me of Kuling." The beauty of the mountains threw a spell of loveliness and she read and rested and thought deeply of the senior year ahead.

120

XVIII   Edwin had an opportunity in the new kind of work for which he had been preparing himself. If he accepted it, it would mean his being in Washington a great deal. Pearl saw suddenly that he hoped that she would live in his home and take his place in his absence. There were the children, and for them she decided to do this.

It meant sacrifices. Laurie Cash had graduated. After three years Pearl and Emma had planned to room together. To be out of the dormitory in her senior year meant that she would miss certain irreplaceable parts of the life. It meant that time would be lost going and coming even though now Edwin's family lived near the college in a bungalow on the spur of a hill.

Very swiftly the college offices fell upon her. She was president of the Franklin Literary society, president of the Senior Club, and then not only member but president of the small Modern Literature Club formed the year before.

Each year the seniors presented an original play. This had to be written and planned for far in advance. Very early in the year an idea came to Pearl. She hunted up a classmate, the one with whom she had given the speech from the ghost of Senator. This classmate writes, "I had never tried a play and I could not visualize it. Pearl was all on fire with it, however, and there was an established precedent for doing the impossible, so I found myself enmeshed. . . . The story was to be the story of a girl with no money and no connections, dressed in absurd clothes, who was to burst the chrysalis as a sound success. It was to be a realistic picture of the Randolph-Macon life. Pearl was to do all the serious scenes; I was to supply the light and slangy conversation. I went over to her brother's house and had supper to study over the plan. I don't remember that I ever drafted a line but Pearl was busy on it. She felt that there were many things that ought to be said to Randolph-Macon. We were to take the lid off. Brave and bitter. Pearl really put a great deal of thought and feeling into it.

"We presented it to the class and it was very dubiously received. Many objected that we seemed to say there were snobs at Randolph-Macon. . . . Finally it was voted to take our play . . . then reconsidered. In the end the original play was voted down and the 'Bird Sanctuary' was given, I think Pearl was disappointed. . . . She had seen the characters with real intensity. It is interesting to speculate what writing and producing an amateur play might have done to or for Pearl's genius."

Pearl was writing other things that year. The *Tattler* was publishing a series of translations from Greek and Latin and French poetry and they were well done. It occurred to a friend of Pearl's that a translation from the Chinese would be a pleasant and stirring surprise. She went to Pearl and in a few days Pearl brought two poems. This girl writes, "There was one odd thing about the verses. Pearl had rhyme but the meter just wasn't there. I asked why she hadn't written them in meter, and she said she had never had meter called to her attention. She asked for a lesson and we sat right down and patched up the lines and scanned several other examples. The result was an overnight miracle She wrote a literally beautiful poem and dropped it in the *Tattler* box unsigned, because, she said, she didn't know whether it was any good or not. That poem took first prize in the poetry that year."

In the March issue of the *Tattler* magazine she had a short story, "The Hour of Worship."

Pearl thought again in terms of poetry and the next two issues of the *Tattler* held poems of hers—the April issue a lilting lullaby of China, "An Eastern Lullaby," and the May issue a more serious, dignified work, "Song of the Sun," from which are the lines,

> . . . . *The light of evening stars gleams white,*
> *And now the nightingale's silver song*
> *Is weaving spells 'round the drowsy Earth;*
> *The twilight deepens again to night;*
>   *Night o'er the hills of Tang—*
>   *Night o'er the heart of me!*
> *And hopeless shadows are stealing long*
> *And silent over the distant lea;*
> *O, heart of mine, though the stars shine on,*
> *What matters it when the sun is gone?*

In the early summer Pearl was sent as a student delegate to the World's Student Volunteer Convention in Richmond, Virginia She stayed with a friend and saw her cousin Eugenia when she could have freedom from her work. Eugenia remembers, smilingly, that when the offering was taken at the closing meeting, Pearl found she had forgotten to bring her pocketbook and borrowed from hers. Eugenia noticed that she chose the largest coin and to her it was typical of Pearl's tendency to do things in a thorough way.

When graduation came Cousin Eugenia and Edwin were the only relatives present to see Pearl graduate. Laurie Cash came for the events She says. "Pearl asked me to spend the night with her over at her brother's. We talked until five in the morning and we settled all the questions of the world. She was going back to China if she did not decide to stay in America for a time before she went. 'I know the Chinese people, their ways, their customs, their needs,' she said. 'The missionaries who go out have the best intentions in the world, but they must spend three years learning the language. They know little of the people. China will never be won to Christianity except through those who love and understand her!' . . . How right she was, even though she could hardly guess, because I believe that she, more than any other person, has interpreted China to the world and has made us proud to call her our friend."

Eugenia writes, "I'll never forget watching Pearl move up the line of graduates to receive her diploma. To Edwin and to me, of course, she seemed the only one. We were in about the middle of the auditorium, and Edwin pointed her out and we watched as she received the diploma and changed her tassel. After it was over she seemed to reach us in an incredibly short time. We congratulated her, and she and Edwin exchanged some joking remarks about the sheepskin. She seemed very happy, but quiet and calm, smiling, and somewhat queenly in her cap and gown."

And then college was over. Eugenia stayed on a few days with Pearl who was responsible for clearing up the sorority house and putting things away. Eugenia looked at the skeleton which was the sorority mascot. Pearl tweaked its coccyx with a gleam of mischief in her eye, and then began to stow away pillows and pennants and dishes preparatory to locking up the house, remarking lightly and half-jokingly that she hoped it was done the way everyone wanted it done, but that if anyone had any objections to it, she didn't care a copper cash.

In a kind of farewell, and yet not farewell, for she had been asked to return to college to assist in the teaching of psychology and philosophy, and she did not know yet whether to accept or not, she led her cousin to see the old familiar buildings. She saw professors still

123

walking back and forth, their arms loaded with books and papers, and a few girls not yet gone home. It was an ending, a beginning.

Her teachers look back to Pearl's years at Randolph-Macon and agree that it was a time of waiting. The time for her blooming had not come. One says, "She was competent, ready for action, mature. College had nothing to give her. When she began to write it was a great freeing, a release of all that had been waiting. She became more simple, ample, magnificent."

Another, her professor of philosophy, writes, "In her novels I can see a quality that arrested my attention in my personal acquaintance with Pearl Buck as a young undergraduate student at Randolph-Macon College. She was a rather small and personable young lady, not so different from many others in the classes, but she had something striking in the eyes which I have remembered about her to this day. Those eyes were such as gave one the impression not just of animation though that was not lacking, but of contemplative detachment in following the subject. It was as if the soul behind the eyes was looking and registering successive impressions as they came into the drama of the discussions I see this now in looking back, as a preview imitation of that objectivity and realistic turn of mind which appears in all her great novels from *The Good Earth* to *Dragon Seed*."

Another professor, although never Pearl's instructor, saw her often as she passed along the campus and she made a definite impression upon him, an impression deeper and more certain as corroborated by the contacts of later years. Words carved on the side of the Pepysian Library of Magdalene College of Cambridge University come to his mind as perfectly expressing his feeling about her. They are words from Cicero's *De Republica* and they read, *"mens cuiusque is est quisque"*—the mind of man, that is the man.

The wife of the professor whom she had been invited to assist lived that senior year in West Hall. Looking back she writes, "She attracted me at once with her air of being well-bred, up-headed, beautifully normal."

124

PART FIVE

XIX   PEARL HAD not had enough of America. She wanted to see other places and to know other people. The college offered her an opportunity to stay in America and to follow the interests of her majors. She had studied psychology under Professor Crooks for two years and an invitation to assist him after she graduated was one hard to reject.

When autumn came she was back on the Randolph-Macon campus. Dr. Crooks was immensely pleased, for "he hoped for a real career for her in the line of his own interests. He wanted her to work in the department for awhile and then get a scholarship in a big university and so on."

Pearl enjoyed it thoroughly. She was free to do as she pleased and to study as she liked. But there, were times when she longed to be near Carie. She had a feeling that all was not well with her and sometimes in the night she awoke with cold fear and questioned her decision to stay away from China.

The autumn's work had just well begun, the first frosts tinged the leaves, the nuts were nearly ripe for gathering in the woods and there was talk of the Thanksgiving holidays, when a letter told her of Carie's illness Her first impulse was to leave everything and start instantly for China. Carie had no child with her now since

Faith was in Shanghai at school. Yet Pearl knew it was wise to await further news. If she went when it was not necessary it would displease Carie more than help her.

She waited, then, but the joy had gone out of her work. She walked again in the woods and watched an early fall of snow— beautiful snow which tinkled on the dry leaves as it fell. Because she might be leaving the beauty soon, she loved it the more. Somehow in the years ahead she must come to know her own country. She must see its great extent, the prairies and mountains and rolling grasslands.

She worked and waited Sometimes Professor Crooks knowing the decision which lay ahead watched her, troubled, and sometimes he was outright in saying she was a valuable assistant and that he had a dream for her. Once he murmured, "Your conscience is too sensitive "

But another letter came and Pearl knew there was only one thing to do. Carie was really ill. She must start at once for she could wait no longer. Yet she could not leave her work here untaken care of. She turned to her old friend Emma. Again that friendship was proven, for Emma took her place and she set her date for sailing.

The day the ship drew in to Shanghai was bleak and chilly as only the damp air of the Yangtze Valley can be chilly There on the small bobbing tender which had come to meet the ship, too large to go in to the Bund, was her father. Pearl looked at him and realized suddenly that in all the time that so many things had been happening to her, nothing had happened to him nor could anything ever happen to him in the sense of change because his life was fixed on the foundation of his work. Nothing else which swept near him, even in his home, would ever shake that unalterable inward security of his.

But she pushed her thinking quickly aside and went toward him, for she saw with a twinge of pain as well as amusement that he did not recognize her. It brought back the many times when he had failed to recognize even Carie when they had arranged to meet after church when he preached, if she wore so much as a new hat. "I don't like to stare, especially at a woman," he always excused himself.

"Father !" Pearl said and took his arm and began to guide him gently in the direction of the small saloon. There was nothing to do

126

Pearl when she was in college

A canal scene in Shanghai

A street in Shanghai

now but to find a seat and wait to be taken to the wharf where there would be the confusion of trunks and bags and customs

"Why, yes, yes, of course," Andrew said and glanced quickly out of the corner of his eye at this young woman who had appropriated him. "I didn't know what to look for.... I-I don't believe I would have recognized you."

Pearl laughed and brought him to a corner where they could sit down She must know about Carie at once. She began to question carefully only to discover that in this, too, Andrew was vague and able to say only that Carie had been unwell for a very long time, "never taking proper care of herself," and that now she seemed worse. But he could not tell how seriously ill she was because she was always making light of it.

Between the lines of his words, Pearl saw something of the truth. She fell into uneasy silence and sat watching the people around her.

There was the usual Shanghai crowd. It used to seem so sophisticated and fashionable, but now it looked drab and homemade. The people freshly here from America, many of them shipboard friends of hers, greeted her warmly as they passed, and were lost in a confusion of others of all nationalities. The little tender began to chug and head toward Shanghai. Through the door leading to the narrow deck she saw the yellow Whangpoo. There were the familiar sampans and fishing boats, even the familiar stench of water laden with the offal of a great city. In that moment nostalgia swept her, nostalgia for America, good American fields and woods.

Yet, even then as she thought of America with longing. curiosity came to her. Much had happened in China since she was here before. There had been the Revolution. The newspapers had been full of the overthrow of the Manchu government and the election of Sun Yat-sen as president of the new republic. Three years ago that had happened, and now she wanted to now what the change meant to the people. Carie had written of the poor Manchu officials' wives in those days when all over the country they were hunted. Pearl writes of the impression Carie gave her of it: "Carie had been back in her house (after the trip from America when Pearl remained) scarcely a few months before the American consul advised all Americans to withdraw to the coast lest in the general stir and lack of control lawless persons attack white people.... On the morning when they all were to leave, Carie felt unwell ... and declared she could not go.

127

They were left behind and the next day Carie recovered and trium-
phantly unpacked and settled herself to see the Revolution through
... She hated above all things the appearance of running from
danger.

"The heaviest fighting took place in Nanking, some miles up the
river, but in her bed Carie could hear the deep reverberations of
modern cannon the Chinese had learned from the West to use. Once
she heard the sharp crack of rifles near the house and with her usual
recklessness dashed to the window to see what it was ..

"There, hiding in the bamboos outside the compound walls, she
saw crouching figures. She hurried into her clothes and swiftly she
went downstairs, saying nothing to anyone. Outside she found the
refugees were women, Manchu women, beautifully dressed in long
silk gowns, their hair dressed high and their feet unbound after the
fashion of Manchu women. Some of them wore Chinese garments
as a disguise, but their high cheek bones and their big feet betrayed
them. It came to her in a flash that they were the wives and daughters of Manchu officials in the city, now at the mercy of the dynastic
change. It was ever the custom in China that when a dynasty fell the
incoming rulers killed off all surviving members of the old ruling
class, and these poor creatures suffered the same fate. Carie
beckoned to one tentatively to come into her house to hide, but the
woman shrank away into the long grass terrified, and wringing her
hands in impotence, the one thing she could not bear, Carie went
back. True it was that she could do them no good; she might even
bring down more harm on them if as a foreigner she tried to help.

"On that day none can tell how many Manchu women and children and men were wantonly massacred there and all over China.
Carie sat in the room with Faith and they shut their eyes and tried
not to hear the sounds around them . Carie could never forget the
pity of those ladies, delicately nurtured and sheltered all their lives,
hunted now like deer and lying among the bamboos dead, their satin
gowns spotted with blood. ... But when those days were over and
the Chinese republic had established itself in form, at least, she
turned hopefully to the new future. 'Maybe they will clean things up
a little now,' she said "

Of Andrew at this time Pearl writes, "Andrew was so weary of
the corruption of the Chinese officials with whom he often had to
deal that he would have welcomed any force, even to an earthquake

and their being swallowed up ... Indeed, his estimation was low of any nation willing to set a woman to rule. 'Jezebel' he called the Empress Dowager, and would recount with relish the end of that queen. when having been thrown from her high tower she was devoured by dogs. . . . He allied himself with the young men's revolution.

"Yet it was somewhat dismaying to discover that in spite of Sun Yat-sen's being a Christian, there was a strong anti-Christian feeling in the revolution. But Andrew had complete faith in God. 'Tares in the wheat' he said."

But already Pearl had read enough to make her wonder whether changes brought by the Revolution were fundamental What could change the Chinese people? Would not their life go on in the old ways? She watched all the small details of the villages and towns as they rode to Chinkiang. As the train went, nothing seemed different. She must look more closely as the days passed.

And then they came to Chinkiang. They drew into the small dusty station. How well she remembered the first train that came there! The station stood on the flat below Golden Island The hills rising all around—how bare they were after American hills! The country folk leaning over the enclosing fences, shouting their wares of pickled eggs and steamed breads and water chestnuts, seemed suddenly to draw her back into the heart of China Everything was so familiar—scene, odors, and talk.

A little group of friends stood waiting for Pearl. They were nearly all Chinese, old schoolmates now grown up and married, her Chinese foster sister and her children. But Pearl was searching the platform for the dear figure of her mother. Carie had not been able to come to Shanghai. But if she were well enough, she would be here at the station.

Suddenly a little apart from the others, Pearl saw a small American woman in a gray dress with a touch of pink at the neck. Could that be Mother, so slender, so white-haired? She rushed forward with her arms outstretched, and Carie ran toward her.

"Mother!" Pearl cried, "Oh, Mother, Mother!"

Then she was terrified at the smallness, the thinness, of the little figure in her arms. "Oh, Mother," she said in deep anxiety, "how little you are!"

The dark indomitable eyes looked up with their old gaiety. "Daughter," Carie said, "how big *you* are!"

129

They clung to each other for an instant. They knew, in that flash of time, how alike they were.

Pearl set herself to two tasks. The first was her care of Carie. The second, her study of the Chinese language which she must perfect in order to carry on what Carie had been doing. The care of Carie was arduous. In her illness she was often impatient, impatient not so much with Pearl as with the weakness of her "old body." It seemed that nothing Pearl could do would please her. Pearl spent long hours at it—a careful bath, a long massage with olive oil—how thin the poor body was, which had once been so sturdy and strong! Doctors were changed, new treatments tried, but Carie still lay weak and wasting. She worried about what was not being done and Pearl tried to keep up the church classes and played the little wheezy organ at the services.

Her only escape was the old one, walks through the hills and valleys. She saw clearly with mature eyes that no revolution could change China. The people were the people of the villages and here government was as it had been for centuries. Life was planting and reaping, laughing and quarreling, giving birth and dying. But the fact that this was so gave her a rooted feeling. Here was the reason for the long unbroken history of China—the common people.

To other Americans in Chinkiang Pearl came as a fresh breeze from their homeland. One young missionary mother remembers an evening when a small welcome party was given for Pearl. To please them all they urged her to sing one of the new songs. She stood between the open fire and the piano. She wore a black velvet dress, one she had made herself though no one knew it then, her bronze hair piled high on her head, and her voice filling the quiet room with a melody not new, not old, but full of the legend of their homeland. "She was beautiful," this friend says.

The first summer Pearl was back Carie had to be taken to Kuling on a stretcher. It was a hard trip up the steep mountain paths. A British doctor attended her in the mountains. One morning he stood looking down at her poor wasted body and sudden moisture stood in his eyes. But Carie's eyes were not moist. They were black with determination.

"I've decided not to die," she announced. "I'm just not going to be beaten by this old body of mine. I'm not old. I'm young yet and there are lots of things I want to do. I'm going to take care of myself and enjoy life from now on."

But that summer was full of poignant moments Carie lying on the long chair on the porch told her children how selfish she was going to be when she got well. She pictured the delightful old lady she would be some day, with well-kept hands and soft lace shawls and the mildest of tempers. Her daughters laughed, then came near crying, and knew even more that were she so, they would be bereft indeed, for she would be a stranger to them.

Slowly, slowly she grew better, until when the first tinge of autumn came she decided upon her course. She must not leave the mountains yet. Pearl and Faith must stay with her until she could take complete care of herself, and then a good servant couple that she knew was to stay with her. Relief and satisfaction showed in her face.

A few others stayed in the mountains. There was a young American couple who lived near in a pretty house they had designed themselves They were cheerful and hearty and kind to Carie. Pearl came to be acquainted with them. The woman writes, "I knew Pearl first that winter she was in Kuling with her mother, fresh back from college. It must have been very lonely for her to go from college to such an isolated life in Kuling. But she held her mother in such tender love that I know it must also have been one of her greatest satisfactions to have been with her. We were young folks, too, only a little older, and also lonely in the Kuling hills. It was natural that we saw a great deal of Pearl. . . . The hours we spent together indoors and out were always fun because of a sense of real compatibility. Soon we were hearing stories of Pearl's mother so that by the time I first saw her when she began to feel better, I felt as if I already knew her. I loved her on the spot and the affection deepened as I came to know her better. She was always so much fun to visit with, as if she were our own age, and we never felt a barrier because she was older. There was just an added respect for a courageous soul that had made the most out of life under hard conditions."

When the first frosts tinged the leaves and brought a beauty much less vivid than the colors in America but still suggestive of it, Carie left her bed and began to walk a little. Soon she was creeping into the garden, and then she was taking a short walk along the pebbly road, and then she announced that she was well enough to be left.

They left her then, with misgivings, Pearl to go to the loneliness of the house on the hill and Andrew more silent than ever, and Faith to go back to her school in Shanghai, full of new impressions of America, of pretty clothes, of her big sister "just back from home."

Letters from Carie told of her growing steadily better, of going to see other invalids less well than herself, of longer walks, of the first snow, of coasting with the children, of the entrancing beauty all around her. She sent a little snapshot. There she was bundled and sitting on a bobsled, children in front and behind, her eyes shining as they ever did when she was happy. Pearl knew then that Carie was finding delight in the winter in the mountains. Besides this there was something more and this Pearl could not guess to save her. Carie had a secret and it sang through her letters in unwritten words. When they came next summer they would see what it was.

Carie's secret was kept until the day that the coolies set down the chairs on the mountain road beside where the house had been. For the little old house was gone. In its place stood a neat stone bungalow with a pretty corner porch, steps leading up in either direction, a long living room with a broad window opening into the trees of the lower lot, a large bedroom, two smaller ones, two baths, a pantry and a kitchen. The old yard was almost the same and by some miracle scarcely a fern seemed to have been disturbed. Carie had rebuilt the Kuling house.

She told Pearl then of how the American couple in the house near by had helped in the plans. "They had so many nice ideas," she said, her eyes sparkling. Pearl writes, "She had worked hard to have it ready, even to the white muslin curtains in the windows and fresh mats on the floor and flowers everywhere. It was the home of her heart, her picture of America that she had borne ever in her heart and made actual in this transplanted spot How she loved it!

"And, indeed, it was a lovesome place, the little clean stone house set in a small terraced lawn along the treetops that grew on the slope of the hill. Through the trees one caught a glimpse of the opposite mountain and through the gap in the farther hills there was the blue vista of the distant plains. Inside, the cottage was as simple as poverty itself but how fresh and clean and how swept with winds and mists! I believe that she could bear sometimes to think that she might never see America again."

Here in the new little house Carie was herself again. She looked nearly like the fine old lady she said she would be She was thin but well and her eyes shone as she went from one room to another pointing out that there had been just room for a closet here and just space for a window seat there, and how she herself had chosen the white rocks from the stream beds for the lovely stone fireplace set in the main wall of the living room. "I liked the ones with a tinge of pink," she said, ' because they are warmer looking," and her short tapered hand seemed to caress a rock in its place. "I put the picture of your college campus here, Pearl," she said pointing to a space above the mantel, "because I thought you would like it and because it is a pretty picture with all the trees."

The girls had a feeling that the old house must be just around the corner even yet. In sheer amazement they asked Carie, "How *did* you do it? It takes so long to get a house built in China. And where did you get the money?"

"Oh, I managed it," Carie said and the dimples at the corners of her mouth drew in in the way they did when she was determined. "I *had* to have something to do!" she went on.

XX F AITH REMEMBERS still the day she knew that Pearl was to be married. The news came with shock and a poignant sense of loss. To the younger sister home had been brightened and touched with new freshness and cheer by the older sister's return. During Carie's illness Pearl had been the rock upon which she had leaned and the center about which all had moved. She had taken Carie's place for Faith during those uncertain days.

It was the year after the re-building of the Kuling house and Faith had only one more year before she finished high school in Shanghai. She was well on her way to her own life and yet suddenly she was bereft when she knew that Pearl was to leave the Chinkiang home. For of course it meant Pearl's going away. What Pearl wrote her in long sisterly letters about nothing being changed did not help it. Things would be changed however much Pearl intended to keep them as they were. She was going to set up her own home in a city north of the river.

Pearl married John Lossing Buck, a young specialist in agriculture, on a June afternoon in 1917. The wedding was out in the garden at home. It was a vivid summer day. The yard was beautiful. Friends were there. Carie wore a soft gray dress touched with pale pink and her white hair curled softly around her face. Faith saw that she was carefully cheerful and in an instant when they were alone her mother's arm went around her as if to reassure her that there was no loss. After the simple ceremony there was punch and cake. Andrew made a few jokes as he did when in genial mood. But Faith did not speak for the simple reason that she could not. She gazed at her sister and thought how lovely she looked in her white dress.

That night the younger girl went to her room and wept with a bitterness she still remembers, entirely unaware of her colossal selfishness. She could not know then that beginning with the very next year when she went to America, alien and suffering agonies of shyness, it was to be Pearl who would soften every step of the way by sending money to augment what she had from home, by writing with complete knowledge of the adjustment to be made. Nor could she foresee that in later years Pearl would be the one to share both what she herself possessed, her home, and what she had learned of ways to meet the strange accidents of life, so that the younger sister never bore any hardship completely alone, certain of that most precious of all things, which is understanding. . . . But then the wedding day only made the younger girl aware of what her sister already meant to her and it seemed a portent of the years ahead.

The little Chinese city of Nanhsuchow where Pearl made her new home lay about half-way between Nanking and Peking.

It was a small, mud-walled town, dry and dusty and barren of the beautiful foliage of the Yangtze Valley. She looked with dismay at the small garden, dead now with the coming of autumn, wondering whether even in spring one could encourage a single blade of grass to grow or a flower to bloom. The house was set almost under the city wall which rose like a rampart, its surface broken only here and there by bunches of coarse grass or by a vine which by some miracle found moisture enough to encourage its meandering way. But spring would come, and so she had the coolie carry in manure from a farm where a farmer was willing to sell it from his stable, and had the

Fishermen near Nanhsuchow, the scene of most of *The Good Earth*
(Photo: Presbyterian Board of Foreign Missions)

Chang Amah, who cared
for Pearl's children in
China

Lu Amah, who saved the
lives of Pearl and her
family in 1927

A page from the original manuscript of Pearl Buck's first American novel, *This Proud Heart*. This page corresponds in part to the passage quoted in the text

flower beds dug deeply so that they might lie fallow and be ready for planting when the winter was over.

Then she turned her thoughts to the house, a small Chinese house. Something was fundamentally wrong with the house and she decided it was the plain whitewashed walls. Marion, a friend who was at that time a new missionary there, writes of Pearl's determination to change this. "When she went into the house the walls were whitewashed and Pearl decided they must have some color. The painter arrived with what was supposed to be a deep cream but which turned out to be a sickly mustard yellow. The effect of that color on walls with the golden oak of the woodwork was just too much, but the painter insisted there was nothing he could do about it. It was then that Pearl's practical mind went to work. There beside the house was a pile of brown clay soil which the workmen had recently dug up. 'Bring that dirt over,' she said to the astounded painter. He obeyed, wondering what it was all about. 'Put some of it into the color wash,' she said firmly. He protested violently that it was something that was never done. 'It will be now,' said Pearl. She had to stir the mixture herself, but the first stroke of the brush on the wall proved how very right she was, for out of that mixture of mud and mustard came forth a lovely rich tan which gave warmth and color to that house for years to come."

This friend lived in Pearl's home those first few months while major changes were made in the rooms she was to occupy. She saw the making of Pearl's home and found help and reassurance in the fact that Pearl was accustomed to all the things so strange to her as a new missionary. She writes again of those days "Pearl is having Chinese paint put on the floors. The smell is enough to knock you over, and it quite sickened me when I was told it was made of dried pig's blood, but Pearl says it is only tree juice and I have been able to endure it better ever since. In the meantime and for two weeks more we cannot use the living room or study. I am separated from Pearl by a great gulf but we call back and forth from the windows and I frequent Pearl's bathroom door and she mine so that I am not a bit lonely."

When the floors and walls were done Pearl was ready to decorate her house. She made curtains of rich Chinese colors, and cushions, and hung pictures, some old, some new. She laid rugs of straw made in China, and bought pots of chrysanthemums to brighten all with their brilliant warmth. She arranged her own kitchen and taught the

135

cook how she would have things Her hands moved with deft surety to the fashioning of a well-seasoned dish. Her friend of those days writes again, "How I did envy her the way she could go into the kitchen and gossip with the servants. She was one of the best listeners I ever knew. . . . She could draw out torrents of conversation by a few questions and came back convulsed with mirth at the tales she had been hearing, or indignant at the injustice done someone, or grieving at the results of poverty or neglect."

Pearl instinctively made friends with everyone, whoever they were, and soon she was looked upon as interpreter and go-between in difficulties of all sorts. Because China was her home the Chinese soon knew that she could understand in a way no other more recently come could possibly manage to do.

Part of the life that autumn was to attend the friendly feasts given to the newcomers to the mission station. Marion writes, "This has been a great week of Chinese feasts. The first one came at the home of the 'richest family.' They had never invited the Americans to a meal there before but they certainly are friendly folk . . They were all standing out in the courtyard when we arrived about five-thirty, all in their best bibs and tuckers. . . . Materially you see some of the best side of a Chinese home there in that mansion The rooms were all clean and neat and everything showed signs of wealth from the cloth on the table to the ivory chopsticks we ate with. I had a fierce time with them, too, they were so heavy. . . . Everything tasted so good to me that night, but the sea slugs I put down one after another proved too much for me. I found even a charcoal tablet failed to quell the disturbance after I got home . . . After the feast was over we were asked to go into the exceedingly narrow inner room. . . . It was really the most interesting part of the evening, and we found they were just dying to know what we had on under our skirts. We displayed our petticoats for them, and I was sure they were going right on in their examinations when Pearl told them we wore k'oudzes (trousers) too. Then they said wouldn't we please sing to them. They had heard the lovely song the school girls sing."

In November of that year Pearl's "boy" or indoor male servant was married. Marion writes of the event: "The wedding was quite a thriller for the boy determined to have a Christian wedding. We found out at the last moment that the bride was a slave and we felt

136

that that didn't bode much future happiness for the groom. Our fears were amply justified. The gorgeous wedding chair would not go through the churchyard gate, and when the bride was asked to get out she refused, saying very firmly that she was not an enquirer or a church member nor had she been baptized. Therefore it was clear that she was not going to be married in a church, and she forewarned them, and she would not stir a step. . . . The poor groom spent some moments in agony with his face pressed against the window near which he stood waiting, while Pearl patiently played the wedding march. The boy is a good simple pious soul. If he were in America he would never miss Christian Endeavor or Sunday School and the boys would give him an unflattering nickname. Alas, the girl he has chosen is just about the kind such a person would get stuck with at home, for she is a very gay, bold sou' and probably a very bad lot in the bargain. After they were married Lao Djeu (the boy) told her they would have a blessing at their meals, whereat she said she would eat no blessed food. He further told her he was going to love her and treat her like a Christian and never beat her, at which she replied that if he didn't beat her it was because he was afraid of her. The boy spent the day upon his bed in tears, and came to Pearl in a lachrymose condition to find out what to do. Pearl wanted to say 'beat her,' but restrained herself . . . At last Pearl decided to advise a beating, but the wife scratched him and the poor boy went around for days with lacerated hands which he bound up with jelly labels for court plaster. Pearl says it is quite unique to see 'Quince jelly' plainly stated on the back of his hand as he passes the tray at lunch."

Part of the work of the mission station was to have meetings for women. Ordinarily this was a talk on a Bible text to which the women listened apathetically. When it was Pearl's time to lead, Marion says, "She fastened on the blackboard a cover from a woman's magazine which pictured the head of an attractive child. That, of course, drew the attention of the women, and I realized for the first time since I had had anything to do with them, that they were listening. It was a novel experience, for Pearl was putting into a form and language familiar to them some ideas of how they should treat their children. They weren't just playthings to be laughed at and indulged and punished with severity if they annoyed, she said I can still remember how she quoted some of their favorite sayings about children, for example, 'That boy is only five and he can curse like a grown man!' She proceeded to pour out some withering remarks about the mother who used that sort of child training. I sat in front where I could see the response of the women to that talk and for the first time I began to believe that foreigners using the Chinese language could make a real indentation on the peasant mind."

Then there was the work with the Sunday School. "True to her interest in children, Pearl's first contribution to the work at Nanhsuchow was to start a Sunday School to keep the children occupied while their mothers went to church. We had always seen the difficulties—no building, no equipment, no trained teachers. Pearl swept them all aside with her characteristic ability to get a thing done when it needed doing. No building? Then have an outdoor Sunday School. We had plenty of land and infrequent rainfall during the school year Equipment? Little bamboo chairs were cheap enough, and we could make tables out of boards on benches. Teachers? What about putting the oldest class in the girls' school to work? They had had plenty done for them. Let them give out a little. The result was that by the end of that year there was a flourishing Sunday School."

At Christmas that first year after Pearl made her own home, Carie and Faith came to visit her. They found the little house inviting, pretty in every detail, an open fire for warmth, meals served up with the art of a French chef, an endless stream of Chinese people who came in to talk over everything. For already there had begun the emanation of friendship and good counsel and shared troubles and shared joys that was always to mark any house where Pearl lived.

During those years in this town and home, her life grew and broadened and deepened, not only through what she herself did and experienced but through what she saw of the Chinese. Here the only life was the life of the Chinese. Of this time Pearl says, "These years were among the richest as well as the hardest of my life. Part of the time we were the only white people in that town and countryside, and at no time were there more than six of us. But my life has always been among the Chinese people and I came into the closest and most intimate knowledge of their lives. As a married woman I had more freedom than I had ever had to come and go among them, and the Chinese women would talk to me as woman to woman and

138

friend to friend. Some of my best and closest friends were made among those years and I have them still.

"Outwardly the life was exciting enough. We had a famine with all that means; we had battles between bandits attacking the city, and bullets flew as thick as flocks of birds over our little Chinese house which clung to the inside of the city wall. Sometimes we went into the country, into places where white women had never been, and I furnished topics for conversation for weeks, I am sure."

But this does not tell what a bandit attack is like. It does not describe the smothering stillness which falls on a Chinese town when word is brought by runners from the outlying country that the *tu-fei* are coming. Nor does it make you see that hurried, secret rush to hide every valuable thing from the shelves of shopkeepers, smoked meats and delicacies from the food shops, rice and wheat in the grain stores. It does not give the feeling of fear for daughters and babies nor the quick concealment of these in lofts, beneath heaps of fuel, or wherever they may pass safely the searching of men out for plunder. Most of all, it does not bring the clutching in the pit of the stomach which is fear of human violence. These all come and stay through interminable nights, when not the flicker of a light is seen in the narrow streets and every house is tightly barred and not even the blind beggars roam twanging their three-stringed violins and singing of the sages as they often do when the people have gone in for the night. . . . Now there is only silence and the town seems a town deserted.

In the morning there may be news—a farmer running in to say that last night the attack was there or there, that the rich merchant Li of the village of Cloudy Mountain was taken for ransom; that the daughter of Ting, the tax collector, was carried away; that all the rice from the secret hiding place of the Wang rice shops was discovered. But luckily the bandits are moving away towards another place rather than toward this. Little by little a few things are laid out on the shop shelves. A woman asks for flowered muslin and the clerk is gone a long time fetching it but when he has cut off a length he leaves it on the counter as a sign that business is being done. Doors creak open a little way, heads are thrust out. A few country men bring in their produce, for bandits or not they must eat, and the cabbages cannot be kept longer without spoiling.

If the news of the bandits is less good, silence lasts through the day, and there are only faint voices behind closed doors. When again dusk falls the fear is there stronger and more sickening than before. They are coming this way—twenty miles away, ten miles away, five miles away. Already someone has rushed in breathless to say that the homestead of the Fu family has been attacked They are coming, then! What was that? ... On another day it might be taken for a distant firecracker or a belated hunter out with his ancient blunderbuss after ducks which are settling for the night. But now the sound is the sound of fighting. The local militia is on guard. They have thirty guns but only fifteen will "shoot to sound." Some have only staves and hoes and bamboo poles. There is a *ping* as a bullet lodges itself in the tile roof of a temple and a thud as another buries itself in the city wall. The dogs begin to bark excitedly in the empty streets and a child shrieks in terror. There are bangings on wooden gates, screams, loud voices, the noise of heavy articles being moved, shouts, crashes—and then the low tones of bargaining What is the price the bandits ask? The rich men of the town will make it up between them after hours of haggling. It will be the price of peace and safety and business going on again—their living.

In the compound there is darkness and quiet. The noise of the attack comes clearly over the wall. The bullets whiz over the roofs and strike the city wall beyond. The old gateman at the compound gate stands belligerently waiting for the battering on his gate. His living depends upon the white man, his living and that of half his family employed in one way or another by the foreigners. If he lets these men in all is lost for him—besides, these are good people. Did they not save his son when he was ill to death last summer? Did not a woman show his wife how to make the flesh grow back on her wasted baby? And will they not bury him when he is dead, decently and honorably in the Christian burying ground? He will not let them in! The gate is strong.

The shattering blow comes. He stands hands on his hips, feet wide apart, his sparse beard thrust out by the set of his old toothless jaw. "They'll not get in!" he mutters again and again.

The hinges hold against the next blow and the next. A voice shouts, "*K'ai'*—open!" Another says in a lower tone, "Foreigners in there." Foreigners bring high ransom. The old man shouts. "They knew you were coming They've gone long ago! There's nothing here but furniture that you can't carry away. It is on my body Go! Go! Talk to the merchants before the foreigners send their forces to attack!"

There is more muttering, incredulous whispering. The gateman hears the word "Yang" Yang? Why, he is another bandit leader. There is to be another attack—a counterattack! Ha, these men cannot afford to stay! They had better go while they can, take what has been bargained for. He laughs a little, hoarsely, hawks and spits in relief. "Let them fight it out between themselves. They forget us!"

There is the sound of fighting outside the city walls When the sun comes up the flat beyond the town is empty except for half a dozen dead who lie there gray in the morning light. Inside the walls the shopkeepers take out their wares again, women come out to fetch hot water from the hot water shops, children run to play in the streets. Once more the bandits have gone.

The summer after Pearl made her own home, Andrew took a short furlough in America. Carie could not think of the sea, but there was Faith to be taken to college. It was the last year of the Great War. After eight months Andrew was back. Pearl says of that trip, "He was not one to be able to relate at any great length his own experience, but bit by bit Carie extracted from him parts of a picture which her keen mind was able to fit together, a picture of a country awry and beside itself—and it was her own country!"

And now Pearl thought to make home more than ever home. Long ago as a little girl she had said, as she held the chubby baby Mary Lawton on her lap, "I am going to have a million babies when I grow up." Now Pearl knew she was to start her family. All the enthusiasms which had gone into her schooling and then into her care of Carie and then into the making of her first home, turned now to the coming child.

That winter of 1919 it was decided that Pearl should be in Nanking where there was specialized medical care. She went there and of those days a Nanking friend writes. "The winter that Pearl and I lived together there while waiting for our babies was a happy one. Her baby and mine were born six days apart."

On a day in March Pearl held her baby in her arms. A few days later she wrote of her to her sister, then in America. That letter is not yet forgotten, for it was like a magnificat of motherhood—joy and tenderness and sheer ecstasy. Already Pearl's heart reached out for the little children around whom her home was to be centered. The past, beginning with her love for Clyde, for Mary Lawton, for

141

her younger sister, for her own nephew and niece, for the children of the orphanage, for Chinese babies everywhere led to the present with tremendous power. Indeed, she knew now more than ever that she "could never have enough of babies."

She did not know yet that she was not to be well and that her own condition made it important that she have a serious operation as soon as she was strong enough to journey to America. Her whole thought was of her baby girl.

When the child was three months old there was then the long, terrible journey, dangerous for Pearl. One of her older friends in Nanking helped in the closing of the house which they left and stood on the upper veranda to see them start. "I saw them leave and begin the long trip to America, the little baby in her basket," she writes. "I will always remember the cheerful courage of Pearl's mother as she, saw them go "

At last when they reached America and plans were made for Pearl to go to the hospital for the operation which she knew now would endanger her life, her thought was still of the child. There was no one to whom she could entrust her most precious possession except to Faith. So Faith came and took care of the baby all the weeks that Pearl was away.

And then it was over. The day came when she saw the baby again, asked of her gain in weight, found it not what it should have been, and knew the cause instantly, as if by intuition. Always she had had an uncanny ability with babies, taking sometimes a small, scrawny Chinese baby and in a few weeks changing it into a bouncing fellow, or by advice and supervision helping the mother to improve it herself.

But now as she held her own baby in her arms, it was with a great hunger and sadness, and a secret pain which she showed no one. She knew now that no matter how well she was to be, she could bear no other child. So had ended her dream of a large family, she thought. But she had this one child. She need not think beyond this now. She was alive. She was to be strong again soon. The child would be the center of her home. She might have had no child, she told herself. Infinitely thankful, she set her face again toward China.

142

XXI   Pearl's second home was in Nanking, a gray brick house set in a rambling garden which at one corner fell away to a wood of bamboos From the house and the higher part of the garden one could see the majestic tip of Purple Mountain which rose to the south. This garden became under her care a place where something was always blooming in summer and where even in winter there was the beauty of red berries on holly trees and "heavenly bamboo." One corner became a rose garden where roses as beautiful as those of America grew profusely. A grape arbor led to it and here grapes, a fruit rare and dangerous if bought in China since there was no thorough way of cleansing them, flourished and were served often at her table. Behind the house was a vegetable garden.

Many friends remember Pearl's Nanking garden. One writes, "Often I see her sitting on the ground in the garden in Nanking, a Chinese trowel in her hand, weeding or transplanting with firm, economical motions of her hands. She wears a pink smock. She is strong and vigorous. Her handling of the soil has almost a peasant quality and speaks of kinship with the earth. . . . I see the setting she made for herself in the perfect garden with its trees and shrubs and flowers, all so beautifully related to each other, the irregularity of line and contours making that walled-in compound so satisfying to the heart. The garden was perfect and spoke of Pearl, and yet it led as perfectly to Purple Mountain as it rose far away beyond the hollyhocks of the gray wall, framed between dark arborvitae and grave trees. . . . One other special memory I have of Pearl's house has to do with the garden. It is of vases of mixed flowers from that garden, each perfectly placed. I never could miss a visit to each one, in the dining room, in the hall and living room. I think she expresses herself through flowers as she does through writing."

Another writes, "Time spent among her flowers was not work for her but rest and recreation. Indeed her love of nature and of music are distinctive characteristics. Every time we had a free day we would hire one of the never-to-be-forgotten carriages, pack a picnic lunch and launch forth to some spot of beauty."

The house itself was a large one, two-storied and with a small, half-finished attic. The living room, large as it was, grew larger while she lived in this home. Porches were taken into it, the south side was pushed out until it became almost an enclosure of a fragment of outdoors, it was so full of sunshine and light and flowers. The colors in the room were rich and warm, for she is passionately fond of color—deep apricot and brilliant Chinese blue and a touch of jade green and the black of ebony. The furniture was made up of odd bits bought in old Chinese shops, but each piece was right for its place, adding to the grace and comfort of the room. It seemed there could be no room more attractive, more beautiful, and yet more lived-in than that room. For it *was* lived in People came there and went away to their work each carrying with him something of warmth and adaptation which would stand him in good stead in the hard years ahead.

Several friends still remember this Nanking home with delight. One writes, "I shall always associate with Pearl the artistic and distinctive interior of her home while she was my neighbor. It was furnished with Chinese furniture and fabrics bought mostly on the Chinese street in Nanking out of a modest missionary salary. She has always had the knack of bringing out the beauty of simple things."

Another writes, "The atmosphere of peace and charm that she created was a constant marvel.... Often I would exclaim over an exquisite bowl or table of rich wood and find that she had bought it for a mere pittance.... Always in those days she had a large household.... Never a week passed that there were not overnight guests.... Almost every day guests were invited to lunch, to tea, to dinner—professors and their wives, Chinese students, friends. How gracious her hospitality by her open fire!... One winter she longed for new draperies but they were too expensive. Finally in a little Chinese shop she found some silk that had been on the shelves a long time and had faded. Since she knew the wearing qualities of Chinese silk, she bought this at a great reduction and re-dyed it herself; and her draperies that winter were the envy of all her friends."

But she longed for a room of her own where she could work undisturbed. She was reading as always, and she was writing. This longing was the beginning of the story of her attic room which became her study where she wrote her first novels. A low dormer window looked toward the mountains. Here were her desk and typewriter and books and paper. Here she kept no order except the order of her work. Sometimes a bowl of gorgeous flowers, for flowers were as necessary to her as breathing, stood in a clutter of manuscripts, while dust lay heavy on a chair. No servant intruded

144

without her express command. This was the place of work and came more and more to be the place where she lived.

A dear friend of hers writes, "Her study I shall always remember as a place where my spirit felt completely at home Here, too, as in the garden, Purple Mountain was the completion. In the third story under the irregular ceiling, I remember the books, the good Chinese desk, the comfortable chairs and there, through the low open window, beyond the garden below and the roofs of Chinese houses, I see rising the long line of the city wall and the changeless and ever-changing mountain. There is no room in Nanking I remember as that, and the perfect tea and sandwiches there, and such good talk."

Soon after Pearl came back from America this time and made her home in Nanking, she saw that Carie's illness had returned. It had taken a new form and she was not prostrated as before but she grew thinner and soon showed signs of extreme anemia. Pearl saw with alarm each time she made a visit to Chinkiang, which was only a short distance from her own home in Nanking, that things grew worse rather than better. She begged Carie to visit her and rest, and she did, luxuriating as she had never in all her life done before, and going back with memories of Pearl's home which she was to recall time after time.

But she grew steadily worse, and one day she was not able to walk upstairs to her own room. Word was sent to Nanking and Pearl came instantly, prepared to stay. The doctor was called and the report was not good. Carie read the anxiety in Pearl's eyes.

"I'm not going to die," she said, although feebly through sheer lack of strength. "There are too many things I've not done yet. You must go home and take care of your baby." She paused, then she said, and Pearl saw that her thoughts had completely left herself, "I'm so glad she was a little girl."

The summer came again and once more Pearl took Carie to the mountains. Again Carie determined to set about curing herself in the cool, clear air.

Then suddenly those who watched her knew that the fight was over. The young, brave spirit of the woman looked with anger and disgust upon the old body which lay worn out unable to revive itself again. She knew that she must die.

That autumn when the first cold tinged the mountains she longed

145

for her home on the hill, so they took her carefully back again, wasted now with the last stages of her illness. The poison of the disease had crept through her body and every sense seemed dulled. She slept as if in stupor.

And yet when she knew that Faith was on her way from her college in America, hurried by letters which awaited her at every port, she suddenly rallied to think of the house. It must not be a dull, drab, worn place full of the atmosphere of dying, for the girl coming back from America. There must be cheer here, and beauty. With her own hand she wrote a letter and addressed it to Shanghai and enclosed a check to buy a new rug, a victrola, some good records and some curtains. She could not know what anguish that letter would give her young daughter a week later when it was handed to her, seeing as she did the old valiant spirit, unable to accept its passing.

On the day before Faith came she demanded a stick of chewing gum and it was ordered for her from the compradore. No one could guess why she could make such a request until the next day. Then when she was told that Faith had come she put it quickly in her mouth, and was chewing vigorously when the door opened and the girl came in.

"Well, here you see your old mother!" she cried gaily, as casual as though she had seen Faith the day before instead of three years before. "I hear chewing gum is the thing in America these days." Everyone laughed and the moment all had dreaded was past.

And then it truly seemed as though Carie forgot separation. Her bed was moved to the window and she lay looking out. Once she said half-dreamily, "I have had after all so many of the good things of life. I have had little children at my breast. I have had good earth to garden in, ruffled curtains blowing in at my windows, hills to look at, and valleys and skies, books and music, and people to do for. I've had a lot of good in my life. I'd like to go on living, but this time I would give my life to America."

This was the last time that she spoke of her life. Of her death she said only, "Do not sing sad hymns over me. I want the Glory Song. I hate to die. My life is unfinished. I was going to live to be a hundred. But if I must die, I'll die with joy and triumph."

On an autumn day she was laid to rest in the same graveyard where Clyde lay. The brave words of the song she wanted sung went

146

out like a challenge to death. The prayer made by a Chinese pastor was the prayer of a man moved to depths beyond his own knowing. The glory did not leave his face.

This first great loss was to Pearl a defeat for, like Carie, she had fought for life, knowing that death was threatening too soon. And now another defeat was waiting.

That was a hard year—how hard she has told no one. The home in Chinkiang was broken. Faith was young and desperate with loneliness, Andrew distraught with Carie gone. The wise thing seemed to be to close the house and auction all except what could be used to furnish a room for Andrew in Pearl's house. Faith should enter the Chinese language school in Nanking to prepare herself for teaching.

It was only when it was arranged that Andrew might continue his field work from Nanking, as well as teach in the seminary there, that he was willing for a moment to consider the change. And it was only by much contriving, infinite resourcefulness, and great kindness that the whole thing was accomplished.

Of that contriving and of the resourcefulness and kindness Pearl writes, "It happened that part of the fruit of Andrew's life had been helping to build a theological seminary. That passion of his for a literate and educated clergy had gone beyond his training class for his own helpers into the planning and building of a school where young men might go and be trained. . . . To this institution, then, one of Carie's children turned speculative eyes. It would make a good place for Andrew to work in his old age. . . . Best of all he would be under her own roof where she could take care of him. . . . He had grown too thin and his ruddiness had gone and left a sort of transparent whiteness out of which his eyes looked too blue and unearthly. But first she must get a place for him.

"It was a task she loathed. She would never have begged for herself—Carie was in her. But she was put to it for Andrew. So she went, in as matter-of-fact a way as she could. . . . She returned again and again . . . and the time-worn method of women had its reward. . . . The church dignitary said at last, 'Of course we had planned a sort of correspondence course—'

"She seized on it. 'The very thing!'

"Andrew was to have ten more years to live. He began them happily by disliking at once the room Carie's daughter had given him

147

in her house. She had gone to great pains about that room. First she had chosen the biggest and best room, the one that faced the mountain and the pagoda, into which the sunshine poured cheer. She had furnished it with home things—the rug from Carie's living room, his own chair, the clock he had wound regularly for forty years, his books in the bookcase—and she made curtains for the windows, very simple white ones, knowing Andrew. She was proud of that room. She ushered him into it.

" 'The whole house is yours, Father, but this is your special room.'

"But it soon appeared that Andrew was uncomfortable. He ranged about the house looking at various rooms.

" 'That room of mine,' he complained, 'it's too big—too much stuff in it—it looks too luxurious.'

" 'You shall have the room you want,' she said.

"He chose a small room over the kitchen and his things were moved into it. Once more Carie's daughter hung the curtains and pictures and spread the rug. Andrew was out when the moving was done, and he made no comment when he came back. But that evening after he had gone up to bed they heard noises prolonged into the night. Carie's daughter went to the door.

" 'Are you all right?' she called through.

" 'Yes,' he answered serenely.

"She tried the door handle, but it was locked, so after a moment there seemed to be nothing to do but to go away.

"The next morning when she went in after he had gone to his day's work, she could not believe what she saw. The floor was bare and the curtains were gone and there were no pictures—not even the picture of Carie she had hung on the wall. And the cushion she had put in the back of his chair to soften its wooden hardness was gone, and the extra mattress she had put to soften the hardness of the single iron bed he had insisted upon buying for himself was gone. She looked under the bed and found the rug and the mattress and in the closet were the curtains and pictures. The room was a cell, and the sunshine streamed in mercilessly to show it bare and hideous. But Andrew had arranged it to suit his heart. . . . He had his own monastic way to the end. . . .

"He was perfectly happy. He came home in the evening exultant with the day, for he loved his work in the seminary. . . . When he had everything ready, the new school was announced and immediately met with remarkable success. In the course of ten years Andrew was to see the student roll mount into hundreds and upon it were men from every country in the Orient and some of the South Sea Islands and a few among Chinese in the United States. Andrew was especially proud of that. . . ."

Thus Pearl's home in Nanking came now to include Andrew, and for a time, Faith. There were still others who lived there, and there was the usual flow of guests who stopped in Nanking sometimes en route to inland places and sometimes to see the sights in a city famous in history.

Now Pearl set about the writing of a record of Carie's life. It was her purpose that her child, too young to have known her grandmother, should through this one day come to know her. Quietly and unknown to anyone Pearl wrote it simply from a small diary Carie had always kept, and from what she remembered of what Carie had told her, and from the events she herself had had part in. When it was finished she laid it away. It was not until many years later that she bethought herself of it. Time had softened the sharpness of Carie's death and it seemed only right that others should share the humor, the pathos, the beauty of the woman who had been her mother. Near the closing lines she wrote, "I do not think one of us would have called her a saintly woman. She was far too practical, far too vivid and passionate, too full of humor and change and temper for that. She was the most human person we have ever known, the most complex in her swift compassion, in her gusts of merriment and in her utter impatiences; she was best friend and companion to us. . . . Young in spirit to the end, indomitable, swift in generosity, eager after the fine things of life and yet able to live ardently if necessary in poverty, idealistic with the true idealism that is never satisfied with mere idealism not translated into actuality— she was the very breath of America made flesh and spirit."

Meantime, Pearl kept her busy household running smoothly. She was a hostess full of wit and good solid advice, and besides she was a cook whose meals were envied.

But now underneath and weaving through the fabric of her full life there came a gnawing, aching fear. All was not well with her child She watched the little girl, compared her with other children. She followed every instruction, spent hours in careful treatment, talked with others who had had similar cases. Nothing helped. She suspected that her child, the only one which her body could ever

149

bear, was to be an invalid all her life. There was to be a great struggle. She did not yet even consider defeat.

In January her old college friend, Emma, and her husband, arrived in China to take up their work there. Emma writes, "Never shall I forget that cold afternoon when we landed in the Nanking station and spied in the noisy Chinese throng Pearl's well-loved face. That was before Nanking boasted any taxis, and I wish that I could give you a picture of the carriage Pearl hired to take us into the city! That tiny moth-eaten horse and that over-burdened carriage; first its high driver's seat, then the low seats where we were, the top folded back and the trunks piled high on that. As we drove over the cobbled streets, through the big gate in the city wall, past the picturesque Drum Tower, beneath beautiful Purple Mountain that overlooks the ancient city, Pearl explained the sights and sounds, and introduced us to the oriental life so familiar to her."

Emma was astonished at all Pearl did. There was her home sheltering her father and her sister and the young missionaries studying in the language school. There was the special care of her child and the agony of it. There was the constant flow of guests. There was her experiment in using a Chinese woman rather than a man for cook and this raised a thousand small difficulties as over the assignment of the tips or "squeeze money" belonging through years of custom to certain servants. Constantly she was called on to act as interpreter when the Language School students had dealings with the Chinese. And she was teaching English to classes of Chinese boys in two of the universities. And she was ever reading and ever thinking of her writing. Once Emma asked her how she had time for so much reading and Pearl said that she was a poor sleeper and that whenever she was awake she always reached for a book.

More and more her inward life was absorbed in her thinking of what took place in the Chinese student life under the increasing impact of the west. More and more she planned to know of the roots of the Chinese in literature She began to collect material on the Chinese novel and found it scarce indeed. There was a loneliness in her in spite of the fullness of her life for she saw with deep sadness that the line of her interest led away from that of the man she had married.

Then she began to write. In 1922 she sent an article to the *Atlantic Monthly* and it was accepted. It was about the younger generation of Chinese and she called it, "In China, Too." The editor of the *Forum* saw her article and wrote her asking her to write something for him. She sent a piece entitled "Beauty in China." In 1924 the *Nation* printed an article of hers—"The Chinese Student Mind."

In the summer of 1924 Faith was married in her home. The garden wedding had to be swiftly moved inside when rain threatened. Characteristically, as if by magic, the bamboo branches were cut, the hydrangeas moved in. Candles were grouped in the foliage and the whole end of the living room became massed beauty The simple wedding was carried on with grace even though plans had to be altered at the last moment.

The time for furlough had come. Pearl came to America to consult specialists about her child. And she entered Cornell University to study for her master's degree. A great pressure was upon her. She knew that could her child be cured, vast amounts of money would be needed; that could she not, there might be all her life to provide for. She had decided that she must have a higher degree so that she could get a position as a teacher, unless she could make money by writing For she must have money to pay for doctors and specialists and for everything possible for her child.

When she reached America there was something in her luggage which she could not guess was to lead her forward on her way. This was the first section of the story later published as *East Wind; West Wind*. Written in the lounge of the ship, in long hand and in odd moments, it was her first attempt to write anything longer than a sketch. She thought it was nothing and only upon insistence showed it to a friend who was forever urging her to write He made her promise to type it. She sent it to *Asia* magazine where it was accepted and appeared under the title, "A Chinese Woman Speaks "

XXII AT CORNELL UNIVERSITY Pearl set herself to her study. She settled herself in a small house which stood near the campus. She was interested to find that the enrolment included a large number of foreign students, but amazed to discover that these students were considered outsiders and rarely if ever were guests in homes of the faculty.

Pearl was simply studying for a degree. But it was known that she had published articles on China and for this reason she was invited to give talks to small groups. A friend from Ithaca writes, "It was then we realized she was different. She didn't just tell us about the Chinese; she made us feel acquainted with the Chinese people.... One time she asked how many of us had ever invited foreign students to visit in our homes. The reply was almost negative. Then she went on to tell us that our group, situated as it was just in the shadow of the Cornell campus where there were nearly three hundred students from foreign countries, were missing a great opportunity by not inviting these boys and girls to our homes. They needed the home contact; she knew how lonesome one can get away at school for four years without the opportunity of getting home for vacation.... And we, in turn, needed the contact with different parts of the world which these students could give us in a much more personal way than any study books we might be reading. Of course read the books, but also know the people.... It would do more toward world friendship than we might realize since many of these students went back to become leaders in their native lands She said, 'Inviting these students to your homes and being real friends, not curious observers, to them will mean more for Christian missions than putting a twenty dollar bill on the collection plate every Sunday. There is nothing so hard for the missionary to bear as to send Christian students to this country and have them go back hating Christianity because of their treatment in so-called Christian America.'"

After years this same friend writes, "Thank her for me for the lecture she gave us smug Americans on opening our homes to foreign students. Our family has enjoyed a number of lovely friendships on account of her advice."

On another occasion the question of racial inter-marriage came up in a group of women. At this time Pearl said that she did not feel the time was ripe for international marriages because of the differing backgrounds, 'But,' she said, 'God didn't make different races; climate and living conditions did that.' She felt strongly that a person could not be really Christian and have racial prejudice.

One of the English department professors under whom Pearl studied writes, "I recall that she was apparently somewhat surprised and disappointed to find how little people she met knew about China and that she expressed strong disapproval of the then popular saying among students that they were willing to 'try anything once ' In China young people accepted from the counsel of their elders which things were to be tried and which avoided. I remember also her telling with a twinkle how a Chinese boy in one of her classes in Nanking had written in an English theme, 'Jesus is very much like his father. Indeed, he is a chip off the old block.' "

Pearl's professors soon found her an unusual graduate student because she was intellectually mature, and because of the quality of her writing. Her dissertation was on the English essayists, and she won the Laura Messenger Prize in History (although herself in the English Department) on the subject "China and the West " Never before had this prize been won by a student outside the History Department. This study was so soundly built that she was able to use a large part of the historical matter seven years later, in an address before the American Academy of Political and Social Science, at Philadelphia.

Busy as she was, she had now to meet her greatest sorrow. She knew certainly now after months of waiting and hoping that her child would never be well. This fact she had to accept and she accepted it with the courage of her nature. There is no hopelessness in her.

There came an upsurging of that instinctive strength which is hers. It had come before in her awareness of wrongs in life—suffering in famines, sufferings through oppressions and racial misunderstandings. She was one to have a family. Thwarted by accident, she set about the building of that family in spite of it. She put bitterness aside. She would have children, if not in one way then another, and so in the words she was to use later to her younger children, she thought, "Some babies are born to a mother and some are chosen by a mother out of all the world of babies."

When the year of study was over, she chose a baby girl, then, from a small orphanage, one known to her, and prepared for the long journey back to China. The baby was one upon whom her eyes fell instantly and whom she knew at once she wanted from among all the others. She was a small child, with a head of golden ringlets, huge brown eyes and a rosebud mouth. She was so small still that she must travel in a market basket and there must be all the clutter of

153

bottles and diapers. But these details were nothing. The difficulties of traveling with an invalid child as well as an infant were nothing.

She had now a new center for her family and her old enthusiasm and absorption came back stronger than ever. Once she had taken the child, she forgot that she had not borne her. Her motherhood at once surrounded the baby and she watched every new development with excitement, delighted as she always has been in the growth of any human being near her.

She reached Nanking again in a sort of triumph and watched while her Chinese nurse gazed at the new baby. The amah looked and exclaimed at the child's beauty, but her hand was clinging to the older girl and she kept saying with the devotion of a Chinese woman for the child she cared for, "But mistress, she is better. She will be all right after awhile " Never once in the years to come was that woman to agree in the truth Pearl knew, even though she, too, knew the truth. That very obstinacy had a certain strength in which at times was comfort.

Now Pearl set about the enriching of her first child's life. She made it full and developed every capacity the child had. It was not easy. Hours every day went into the painstaking work of teaching and training with results so small that only Pearl could see them. After twenty years she says, "The experience made me patient with dull people. Before I had always been impatient with anyone who did not grasp an idea quickly. Now I came to know that people cannot help being as they are." Again thinking deeply she said with a warm half-sad smile, "Of course that sorrow changed me as any great inevitable sorrow changes anyone. A part of one is gone and never comes back to the full hopefulness that existed before. Those who have had such experience can always be picked out because this is so." Once she wrote to Emma, "Sometime I want to write a book about what suffering does to people."

Almost at once she was thinking of her child objectively and she could do more for her and be of greater help to many others, because of this strength in her. She re-established her home in Nanking. Andrew settled again into the routine of his life and the children lived according to their ways.

She began that year the study and translation of one of China's most famous novels, *Shui Hu Chuan,* a volume comprising over twelve hundred pages when it was completed, and telling the adventures of one hundred and eight major characters with an even

154

larger number of minor ones. In her preface to the book which was later published under the title *All Men Are Brothers* she says, "I think it is one of the most magnificent pageants ever made of any people. Before your eyes on the pages of this book march the people of China—all the people, men and women and children, priests, scholars, robbers, courtesans, soldiers, emperors, captains, kings, princes, governors, gaolers, vendors, prisoners—the whole past passes by. They are a host vivid and living beyond belief. . . . When you have finished the book to its triumphant end, you will find that, without your knowing it, there will remain in your mind certain unforgettable men and women whose lives you have lived with them, across the seas and centuries."

And now a New York publisher wrote asking her to enlarge that first fiction story of hers which had been published in *Asia* magazine. She thought it over carefully but decided that the framework of the story was not strong enough to bear the enlarging But she could do something else. She could write a sequel and offer the two parts together. She made this proposal only to hear after long months that the publisher did not find it acceptable. She laid the manuscript away then. A year or more later she took it out again and sent it to a literary agent in New York to see if he could find a publisher for it, and thought no more about it. What lay ahead could not be clear yet, but she knew she must make provisions for her child and she hoped that it might be through her own interest in writing.

She could be absorbed in a Chinese novel written centuries before and she could be absorbed in her children and she could fashion a garden always lovely, and deftly make a salad, for like Carie she never trusted raw food to servants, feeling them inclined to be careless with their hands, and she could sew assiduously to dress her older child so as to make her at her best, and she could read every book as it came out, spend a little time in the dusk of every evening walking among the hills with Andrew, lonely as he grew older, and she could throw open her home for endless entertainment of guests who came for a cool dinner on the lawn in summer, or for an evening by the fireside in winter, or could meet those who came from a distance with a carriage at the riverside and show them the Old Ming Tombs or picnic at Purple Mountain or Lotus Lake, and yet have time and energy to write.

155

Her articles began to appear more and more widely, linking the significance of China with the significances of the world. She was still teaching, too, in a Chinese state university and in the University of Nanking and here she found rich human interest, deep questioning, amalgamating of East and West. And moreover she was now writing steadily on a long manuscript, one which she thought was to be her first novel.

When the day was over and at last she went to bed, it was to read. And if in the night she awoke it was to read again.

During these years Andrew grew old, in spite of himself. He never admitted more than a little weariness. Pearl writes of this time: "But it could be seen that his body became insufficient for his soul's reach. . . . He came home unexpectedly one sunny October afternoon, and his daughter saw that he was desperately ill. He staggered up the stone steps to the front door, and the sunlight seemed to shine straight through him as though he were a ghost already. . . . The doctor said that Andrew must go to the hospital. . . . But it was no good. Once there, he insisted on watching his schedule, he rang his bell every few minutes to remind the nurse that he was a very ill man and that his medicine was due at such and such a time—he kept his watch in his hand. As soon as he was fully conscious he insisted upon being taken home. That was the time he said, 'I have a daughter who has nothing to do but take care of me,' and he raised such a storm that he had to be sent home then and there, though he was too sick to sit up . . . So Carie's daughter took care of him and he grew well again at last But he was never quite so well. The illness had frightened him. He sat in an easy chair in a sunny corner of the garden one day with a blanket over his knees and Carie's daughter came to bring him a cup of broth.

"He raised solemn blue eyes to hers and said suddenly,

" 'I'm nearly seventy-five years old!'

"She looked at him and saw a childish terror in his eyes. Her heart flew to him, but she resisted the impulse to gather him up like a child for comfort. He would have been miserably embarrassed at such demonstration. Instead, she tucked in his blanket and said, 'What's seventy-five? Your family is long lived on both sides. Besides, you're well again, and it's a glorious morning and I've been

156

thinking you ought to revise your book on Chinese idioms. There isn't anything to take its place if you let it go out of print.'

" 'That's true,' he exclaimed, pleased. 'I've been thinking I ought to do it.' "

Those years of her home were rich ones for her and for all who came to her house. There was a quality there which the pen cannot quite set down in black and white. It was a mixture of charm and wholesomeness and heartiness and solidity and humor and sanity. There was color there in what the eye saw, and there was abundance, not in the sense of what money could purchase, but in the sense of what the mind thought and the hunger for beauty craved and the need of human nature sought. There was abundance to satisfy what one went there searching for, perhaps even unconsciously.

A Nanking friend writes of the Chinese who lived in Pearl's enclosed garden in those days: "The household next door to me was so interesting with its settlement of Chinese families. . . . That part of the household was as Chinese as the world beyond the walls. I can see the women squatting, sewing or weeding or drying their cabbages; the children playing about or doing their little chores It seemed a very happy place in spite of the occasional quarrels—an example of what simple Chinese life at its best might be." The friend remembers an incident: "The ricksha man who lived behind our house had a fourth child, a little skeleton of a baby I liked them all so much I wondered if I should not give them special food for it, but I didn't because I knew they were unspeakably poor and could not really provide for the other three and I thought it would probably be better if the last little one did not live. When I came back after that summer spent away, he showed me with such pride a sweet, fat little baby and told me that Pearl had fed her all through the summer with milk she had prepared herself. I think I have never felt more touched or ashamed."

Many came to Pearl wanting advice and help. There were foreigners and Chinese—students and teachers and missionaries and servants and beggars. Like her mother, everyone could talk to her and even though she might lay open a fault, they saw the truth of what she said and so were not angered but helped.

Among those who came were refugees from north of the river when times were bad there, as they seemed to be almost every alternate year. They were sometimes people who had remembered Pearl from the years of her home in Nanhsuchow. One of them was a

157

woman who trudged down with her baby on her back—a poor bound-footed thing whose husband had left her and who in her desperation came to find Pearl. Pearl helped her get a place to live and through her friends provided the woman with sewing enough to keep herself One day the baby was terribly burned and Pearl herself dressed the wounds for weeks and saved the baby's life This woman, Lu Sao-tze, probably saved the lives of Pearl and all her family in the time which lay just ahead.

XXIII

THE EVENTS which led to the showing of Lu Sao-tze's depth of gratefulness are not simple. For a change of government was coming.

It was the year 1927, the time of the Nationalist Movement in China. Because of the likelihood of conflicts between the Nationalist soldiers and the others then in control, all westerners from the interior of China had been warned to leave their places and go to the coast where they could more easily be protected. Some went as far as Shanghai or Manila, but some stopped along the way, and a good many of them in Nanking where it was thought they would be safe or where at least they could go to the coast at the last moment. Pearl's household then consisted of her father, her sister and her husband and small son, who had come from the interior, as well as herself and her own immediate family.

As winter passed, conditions grew worse rather than better and Nanking became restless. The American consul urged those not immediately necessary to the carrying on of definite work to leave But a morale had developed in the group of westerners in Nanking. They were in sympathy with the Nationalist aims, and besides this, they could not bring themselves to leave their Chinese friends and run from what might be a dangerous situation. They decided to stay where they were expecting inconveniences but nothing worse. Yet, even were it to be worse, Pearl, like Carie, could not bear to run from danger, nor could she bear to miss the change that might be coming among her Chinese friends.

As the southern, or Nationalist, soldiers approached the city, the Government troops met them in battle outside the city. Terror swept

158

the Chinese inside the walls, for there was real danger of looting whenever a change of military control took place Pearl opened her house to her Chinese friends and their families and they came in to occupy the attic room, the children's room, the basement. The guest rooms were already filled by her family. Her children were crowded into her own room.

It was a strange night, that one before the entrance of the on-coming soldiers. The battle was over The city had fallen. In the streets everything was utterly silent with that fearful stillness which falls on a Chinese city whenever there is fear. In Pearl's house there was silence, too, except for whispers and for quiet movements. Her faithful servants went about packing some of the things she most cared for, hiding them in water jars, burying them in the garden after darkness had fallen.

In the morning of that raw March day breakfast was served as usual for the family. They had scarcely begun to eat when like an apparition a Chinese man stood at the entrance to the front hall. His face had the sickly pallor of terror. His hands were shaking and he seemed scarcely able to speak It was a neighbor tailor whom years later she made the central figure in one of her best known stories, "The Frill."

"Run, run!" he was saying. "They are killing the foreigners. They have shot Dr. Williams just a little way from here!"

He was wringing his hands in desperation, looking at the table full of people eating calmly as though nothing threatened. The servants rushed forward and pulled Andrew and the children from their seats. They helped them on with their wraps which hung in the hall, and then pushed them out of the door toward the walk leading to their own quarters at the back of the house.

But the tiny quarters near the entrance were hopeless as a hiding place This Pearl and those with her saw at once in awful indecision. But already there were the sounds of shots and of wild, excited voices—it was dangerous to hesitate. Where could they hide?

Then, at that instant when there seemed to be no road to take, the small side gate of the garden creaked on its hinges and someone came running down the stone-flagged path toward the servants' quarters It was Lu Sao-tze. Her sun-browned hair was uncombed, her jacket half-fastened, her face gray.

"Come, come! Come with me!" she cried breathlessly. "I have a room where they will never find you. There are other children in the house. Their noise will hide the noise of your children." With that she took Pearl's hand and the hand of her older child and began to drag them. "Quickly, quickly!" she said. "They are coming this way."

The little group went out through the gate and started along the path which led through the fields. Already there was banging and howling at the main gate. The street which they could barely see because of intervening trees seemed in mad disorder. They went as swiftly as they possibly could, holding themselves low to avoid flying bullets.

They came to the mud-walled house where Lu Sao-tze had one rented room. She pushed them into the first room, whispered something swiftly to the man standing there, and then led them into her own inner room at the back of the house. It was a small room, not more than ten feet square, windowless except for a single pane of glass set in the wall. The furniture was only a board bed, a table and a long bench. It seemed completely dark after the brilliant sunshine of outdoors. The woman smoothed her quilt for them to sit on, pulled forward an empty box, and then urged them not to speak because a single word overheard might give away their foreignness.

It was the beginning of a strange day. Later Pearl wrote of it to Emma from Japan. "We hid in a Chinese house all that terrible day in Nanking and I never saw the home again after running out of it that morning in the midst of breakfast. Faith and her family were with us and we spent the day—thirteen hours—in a tiny near windowless room, listening to the shooting and yelling and burning of the houses around us. Our house was not burned. I wish it had been for it is full of filthy soldiers, and their horses are stalled in our beloved garden. Well, of course we thought every moment would be our last, but the soldiers did not find us and that night we were rescued by two Chinese friends. Our Chinese faculty and the students were simply wonderful. So were many Chinese. Every foreigner had the same story to tell of being saved by some Chinese. Foreigners were stood up to be shot time and again and every time Chinese leaped forward and shielded them with their own bodies. Even at that I do not believe that the devotion of our friends could have saved us, if the (U S.) gunboats had not fired off shells. About five in the afternoon, when things were at their wildest, and we had given ourselves up for lost, since we were just about to be discovered and killed, those great guns went off, and within fifteen minutes the

160

crazy shouting and yelling ceased. Then our Chinese friends found it easy to get the leaders to call off the soldiers and then hunt us up and get all foreigners assembled in Bailie Hall (one of the University of Nanking buildings) under a guard. . . . I feel that when we go back the experience will bind us so closely that no small differences can ever make us doubt each other's loyalty. . . . All this makes our personal losses (all possessions) sink into insignificance. I have had very bad times of homesickness for the home that is gone, and many of my beloved pictures and books haunt me with the thought that I shall never see them again, but if they serve China thereby, why, my loss is gain, somehow!"

Comparing notes afterwards in the place of refuge to which they were taken, Pearl and Faith found that each had been planning how first to see her children killed before her own life was taken. Worse than death would be the realization that the children were in the hands of those maddened men.

Yet during those desperate hours there were incidents of unforgettable humor which they laugh at still. Often Pearl's servants came opening the door cautiously to bring in some object they imagined she especially cherished. Once it was a bedspread filled with aluminum pots and pans which Pearl had brought from America. These must be precious! Again it was a gold watch which her brother-in-law had forgotten beneath his pillow. Again it was a mirror slung on the back of a woman servant. The sight of her slipping sideways into the narrow room brought a burst of stifled laughter to the lips of everyone even though no one felt like laughing.

Pearl does not tell in her letter another incident. After the bombardment it grew dusk, then dark. The little group waited. The rescue had not begun. Then it was that the door was opened cautiously. An old friend, a Chinese professor in the university, motioned a coolie to bring in bedding rolls which he had spread on dry straw on the floor; then he himself set bowls of steaming rice upon the table. "You must eat and keep your strength," he said, "especially your father."

"But you must not take this risk," Pearl protested. "It may be your life for our comfort."

"It does not matter," he said. "Sleep if you can," he added. "The bedding is clean for it is my own." He was gone as quickly as he had come. They tried to eat because it was true they must. Andrew under pressure lay down and rested a little Shells had silenced the looters But none in the room knew what to expect.

Without warning, about nine o'clock the door of the room was thrown open again. A Chinese officer stood there. He motioned them out. They went, Andrew with that dogged expression he always had in the face of physical hardship, then the others, each thinking that now, this, was that moment of death for which they had been waiting all day.

They marched behind the officer across the fields they had seen that morning. Now they were littered with cushions, with pictures they remembered seeing on the walls of their friends, with broken dishes. The night sky was lit by a house burning near by.

They came to Bailie Hall and walked between two lines of soldiers who stood with bayonets fixed to guard their entrance. They went upstairs to what they were told was the place of refuge. Here were their foreign friends, more than a hundred of them.

What a strange group it was that night and what stories there were to tell! Some were wounded, many were scarcely clothed, and all had lost everything they owned. Even yet they could not tell whether this was merely a prelude to mass killing. How could they suddenly become rescuers, the men who had brought them here when they were the ones who had killed and looted all day?

Only if these men feared enough the power of the foreign warships at the river seven miles away, would they keep from killing these who were in their power.

But the warships were there, and as they learned afterwards, the American admiral steadfastly demanded the release of the prisoners, threatening to bombard the city if they were not delivered. There was delay after delay. The deadline was several times postponed, until finally the Admiral would postpone it no longer. He was almost ready to order the guns to open fire again when suddenly the first of the prisoners was seen approaching the river. All were taken aboard the ships and then to Shanghai.

Of this incident, soon to be known as the "Nanking Incident," Pearl said later, "I have had that strange and terrible experience of facing death because of my color. At that time nothing I might have done could have saved me. I could not hide my race. The only reason I was not killed was because some of those in that other race knew *me*, under my skin, and risked their own lives for me and mine."

Pearl found herself in Shanghai with her family. No one of them

162

had any possessions except the much-soiled clothes he wore. First, then was to get money and food and clothes.

She did not say anything of another loss. No one guessed that she must be thinking of an immense amount of work gone for nothing. Much later she wrote, "Incidentally, my manuscript for a novel, which I had just finished, was scattered to the four winds with everything else in the house. I console myself by thinking it probably was not any good. At any rate, it was a lot of work gone for naught." What was gone was the manuscript that might have been her first novel. She never tried to write it anew but went on to the next work she had in mind.

China promised to be unsettled for a long time. Many Americans returned to America to take early furloughs or to stay. Pearl could not so easily leave a people about to meet a great change. She wanted to see it, for she intended to live among those people again, and she determined to stay as near as she could to China.

She thought then of Japan. It was soon to be summer. Here her family might find a place and watch from there the developments in China. They found a tiny Japanese cottage in a valley near Unzen.

XXIV

THAT SUMMER Pearl had a chance to see the Japanese people more closely than ever before. In the little cottage almost hidden among the trees of a narrow valley near Unzen she came to know the mists and shadows which in Japan are in some indescribable way more beautiful than in any other country; the rocks and twisted pine trees; the precipitous paths and graceful bridges; the country people who came in the early morning bringing their baskets of fresh vegetables and fruits from the lower farmlands, the women with their fish and lobsters. She could not speak their language yet in some way she came in that short time to make herself somewhat understood and in her own way learned much of them.

Far above the valley where she lived towered the high mountains. One of these, Fugendake, was famous for its contrasts of beating, blistering sunshine and its crevasses deep in ice and snow. There was a wind cave where eternal breezes blew with uncanny strength. There was the flagged road which led through a fairy wood with giant ferns and beautiful flowers.

Unzen itself was famous for its hot springs. The water gurgled and boiled out of the rocks and the people held baskets of eggs submerged and then offered them for sale, hard-boiled. There were bath houses where men and women bathed together with the complete lack of self-consciousness which was so unlike the Chinese. There was a market place with colored banners and open shops. There were the tiny chinaware shops with their fascinating dishes and teapots and bowls. And everywhere was the Japanese sense of beauty expressed in the simplest detail. Where anywhere else cloth printed with a gray lobster and a trailing end of green seaweed would seem ridiculous, here it was graceful and entrancing. The tiny homes were open to the street and their arches and paper partitions and their low polished tables and their single vase of flowers and their artistic scrolls were like a kaleidoscopic view of Japan itself. There was the Japanese artist who climbed the valley and displayed his water colors of woodland and mountains, a sort of art which one did not find in China, for it was the East and West combined to interpret Japan.

The little cottage was crowded, for Pearl's sister and her family were there as well as her own. The paper partitions grew damp and the paper blew off in the night leaving the entire house one room. Her small nephew, born in Japan only that summer, howled. It rained, it poured. The older children played in the mud for there was nothing else they could play in since the world was mud except for the tiny house.

Yet Pearl managed meals with the help of one faithful Chinese woman servant who had come with her. Somehow fish was broiled over the charcoal stove which was all that the cottage afforded, and pies and biscuits, miraculously good and tender, were made in the galvanized oven set perilously on the stove. Even the cottage was attractive when, after an evening of pasting, the partitions were whole again and flowers gathered in the woods gave grace and color.

During this time Pearl was still working and writing. Her mind was busy and she enjoyed the contrasts of Japan and China. Much of that summer was to come to its expression in a book written years later. She seemed to understand Japan because of her quick appreciation of the people she saw. Later she planned and took a journey all through Japan, going third class on the trains and stopping at

164

small inns that she might see what she always calls "the real people."

Her Nanking neighbor has memories of that summer in Japan for she and her family, too, lived in a cottage in the narrow valley near Pearl. She writes, "Pearl and her family reached Unzen before we did. The people with whom she stayed in Nagasaki (en route) marvelled that in spite of her weariness after the bad experience and the worse sea trip from Shanghai, her patience with the children and her consideration for others were unaltered."

This friend adds: "There are two or three special memories of that summer in the mists under the cryptomeria trees. There is Pearl's account of the first night there when no others had come to live in the glen and she was roused by shouts of the Japanese soldiers or police come to investigate the source of the smoke from her fire rising through the trees; her account of seeing an eye gazing in through a knot-hole as she took her bath and her joy in applying the soapy sponge instantly to that knot-hole; her fascinating account of visiting Japanese Cornell agricultural men who were old friends on a trip she took through the country. That summer her little adopted girl was the most enchanting creature with her tight fair curls and dark eyes. Her amah assured me in an aside that if her mistress would use some vaseline and a good stiff brush the child's hair need not look like that!" Of this child this friend writes further, stirred by this incident, "I always feel that I have never seen the creative power of love more perfectly displayed than in the way Pearl loved this little girl into life and health and beauty. . . . I have never seen more absolute, self-giving devotion."

Again she writes of Unzen: "It was in Unzen that I first realized how remarkably Pearl wrote. She gave me a rather long story to read, the end not very good, but the first part showing the same masterful treatment of China and Chinese life that was later to take everyone's breath."

Then autumn came. The Nationalists were moving steadily toward Peking. Nanking was quiet, and yet foreigners were advised to go no further than Shanghai. Pearl took a house in the French Concession —a large house to accommodate her family, that of her sister, and of another member of the faculty in the University of Nanking. But here she was in China again and she waited impatiently for the time she could return to Nanking to re-build her wrecked home.

It was a year before she could go back. Of the return to Nanking, she wrote Emma, "We are back in the same house. It was badly wrecked—living room floor burned out, windows torn out, horses stabled downstairs, etc, but we came back in July and got it into some sort of order. It is clean, and straight, and homelike again—upstairs makeshifts, for of course we cannot refurnish it at once—but we decided we must have one room like home, so the living room is much as it was. Two of my three pieces of over-stuffed furniture my servants saved, as well as some other things. They were wonderfully faithful to us, as were many others. What kept those two days from being impossible to bear was the devoted faithfulness of servants, neighbors, students and faculty around us, between us and those soldiers, whose faces I cannot forget as long as I live. It is wonderfully interesting if one can keep a working sense of humor. If one can take everything as part of a game, it is fascinating to watch things grow—change, anyway. Many of our friends and former students are in the government. We get lots of chances to mingle with the official class and see the wheels go 'round.

"Meanwhile I plant cabbage and spinach and larkspur in my poor demolished garden without being at all certain that I shall ever pick them. But I may—who knows?"

She found time, too, to remember old friends. She wandered through the ravaged yard of the Dr. Williams who was shot early that morning of their day of hiding. The beautiful violet border was trampled and all but destroyed. Mrs. Williams writes, "She dug up all the roots that were left and took them to the little foreign cemetery and planted them on my husband's grave."

In the year after the return to Nanking, 1929, it was necessary to make a hurried trip to America for the sake of the elder child. After Pearl reached there a cable was forwarded to her. She looked at it astonished.

It had gone to China and back. It was from the New York literary agency to whom she had sent the little book she had written so long ago that she had forgotten it. It said that a publisher had made an offer for the book, and it asked her to cable her agreement. The day the cable reached her she was only a short distance from New York. She had herself so forgotten the whole matter of the book that she had failed to tell her agent of her change of continent! She says,

"When I could, therefore, I went to New York and to the John Day offices and found that the title I had given the book was not liked. We compromised on the subtitle. I found also that in my effort to write English that would be usual enough to be acceptable to English-speaking people, I had used a number of trite phrases which I had remembered from the English books I had read. In Chinese it is good literary style to use certain well-known phrases previously used by great writers. Therefore I went over the manuscript deleting the phrases I had so painfully put in.

"But it was worth the effort chiefly because it gave me confidence to go on writing, since now I had found a publisher who could be interested in what I wrote, even though, I, knowing nothing else well, could write only about China."

Before that first little book appeared in May, 1930, Pearl was back in Nanking.

Those months in America, that journey back, and the next two years were the hardest she had known When she set sail for China this time it was with only her younger child. She had left her first child in the United States where she might have the special care she needed

She will never entirely recover from that separation. As she wrote to her sister, "The distance between America and China is too great, time is too long, too much can happen to a child who can never fully make any other know the small agonies of its heart." . . . But she had set herself to the inevitable separation, and when she reached Nanking she forced her mind upon two things—her adopted daughter, now a child of five, and her writing. Meantime, *East Wind; West Wind,* her first book, began to be praised by critics who knew China and by others who knew good writing.

Pearl, hearing of the increasing sales of her book, wrote Faith, "Of course I know this is due to little groups of Nanking and China friends scattered all over the country who are being kind enough to help push the sales."

The attic room came to hear the steady click of her typewriter whenever she could possibly be there. A manuscript heaped itself upon her desk. No one in her family, no one in Nanking knew anything about it.

In 1930 Pearl finished the writing of her novel. The manuscript was sent to the publisher who had accepted *East Wind; West Wind.* She wrote to Emma, "I have finished my second book and sent it but I do not yet know what favor it has found with my publishers.

Personally I think it better than *East Wind; West Wind* but I am not a good judge of my own work, I am afraid."

She received one day the next autumn a cable from America which said that her manuscript had been accepted with great enthusiasm The letter which followed she could bear to show no one. It was too embarrassing and she could not half believe it. Among other things her publisher said, "You have written a book of permanent importance, one that will rank with the great novels of the soil that have come out of other lands. . . . The structure is perfect and the beauty of the style is only one of its great merits. . . . Congratulations on a magnificent piece of work! . . . By your choice of incidents you have somehow succeeded in making us feel that we are seeing almost the whole life of the plain people of China in all its details from birth to death." She wrote to her sister, "It gives me a wonderful feeling, primarily of relief, for I feel I can write—I haven't been sure—and that I can provide for my child's life as well as interpret some quality of China that I love. The book will probably be called, *The Good Earth*." Her publisher had suggested this title.

The years of her childhood, and those years in Nanhsuchow, living with the country people, had stood her in good stead, for it was of them she had written now.

Near the end of January Pearl was cabled the news that her book had been chosen by the Book-of-the-Month Club for March of that year. The letter which she sent in reply caused amusement and disbelief in the publishing circles of New York, where it was widely quoted. It read:

"Dear Mr. Walsh:

Your two cablegrams arrived when I was just coming home from a month in the country, going about from place to place on a sort of trip of adventure, and so I was delayed two days in getting them.

Of course it is very good news that the Book-of-the-Month Club likes my book. I do not know exactly what it means, since I do not belong to this club, but I looked up an advertisement of theirs in the *Atlantic Monthly* and see a very imposing list of names there of well-known authors, and so I appreciate the fact that it must mean something for them to like my book well enough to put it on their list. . . . . I am getting rather absorbed these days in the shaping up of the next book. As usual, I cannot think of a title for it and shall probably have to lean on my publishers again!"

The publisher's staff said it could not be that there was such a person in the world! A writer who wrote so calmly of the choice of her book by the Book-of-the-Month Club! It was simply impossible that she could be so naïve! People were not like that. The publisher's staff teased him by saying that this was a pose and that he had better be prepared to deal with it when she arrived in America.

Pearl had no idea of the excitement her manuscript had caused. Dorothy Canfield Fisher, one of the committee to judge on books for the Book-of-the-Month Club, tells of the event. She says that usually she starts out loaded with manuscripts to read on the train going from her home in Vermont to New York City where the monthly meeting of the committee is held. On this occasion she remembers that she had left the long manuscript about China until the end, working on the principle of reading the most interesting ones first. Besides, a peep within these pages gave her the impression that this one was about Chinese agriculture, a seemingly impossible subject for Americans. Therefore when she was well settled on the train she undertook the reading of Pearl's tome, "rather dreading it," she says.

She read steadily from the moment she began until two o'clock the next morning. Then it came to her that this book must be chosen for the first available month. She rushed to the Book-of-the-Month Club offices the next morning, far too early, and scrawled a note to bring it to the attention of the others on the committee the instant they arrived.

The book, when it appeared, stood on the best-seller list for twenty-one months It was the story which for the first time made the Chinese people real to the peoples of the west.

The success of *The Good Earth* became known to Pearl in Nanking and she began to be told that she was becoming a famous writer. She wrote to Emma and to Faith, "I don't care for being well-known. My keenest pleasure is in producing a unified work of art, if I can ... I am my father's daughter in that I don't give a penny for praise or blame." Again she said, "Well, I am definitely committed to the career of a novelist. I *love* the act of creation, but hate the fuss afterward."

Through the excitement and the pleasure ran a stream of satisfaction too deep and strong for any to know. This was the knowledge that if she did not judge wrongly now she could plan for the security of her child at school in America. With deep thankfulness she set herself to the year which was to be the last before she went home to the child herself. Her mind was busy with the plans she had.

But now at the end of the summer there came sudden news that Andrew lay desperately ill in the little Kuling house. It had become his custom to spend the summer with Faith there. In the night his old malady had returned and he had grown ill and, reticent as always, called no one When the next morning he did not come out promptly for breakfast, dressed as always immaculately, his white hair combed with precision, they opened his door and found him ill indeed.

It had been a season of floods and the great plains below the mountains were like a sea so that much of the distance usually crossed, in the old days by sedan chairs, and in the later by rattling buses, could now be crossed by nothing but sampans. Not even the rare planes which sometimes flew in this direction had landing place. When Pearl received the telegram about Andrew's illness, it seemed that there was no way by which she could go to him. And then, as though Fate was determined to intervene, she became ill herself and was not able to go.

Andrew never truly rallied. Although he lived on for a week reinforced by saline injections and by the best care that could be had, it was clear that at seventy-nine he could not rally.

There was a day when for the first time it occurred to him that he might be dying. Then he told Faith to write a check for a certain Chinese student who would soon be registering in the theological seminary in Nanking. "He will need the money and I have promised it to him," he said weakly. With difficulty he signed his name and asked that the check be sent at once. His daughter saw that its withdrawal would come near to using the total left to his credit in the bank. His last cent was to go to the help of the Chinese.

On another day he asked to have a certain passage in the Bible read, a passage about Paul's missionary effort, telling of the success of the Word and the triumph of Christ. After that he fell into a sleep from which he did not wake. The only sign of his death was a deep, freeing groan, as if at last he cast off the shackles of physical living

When the casket was closed the Greek Testament was laid in beside his wrinkled old hand, for there it belonged And then he was carried beneath a blanket of ferns and wild white flowers to the little foreign cemetery high on the end of a knoll overlooking the plains of the Yangtze, where his life had been spent.

But all this had to be written to Pearl, and in a deep sense of regret that she could not have been there, she read of what had happened.

She wrote Faith a long letter of loss and appreciation of what their father had been, of sorrow that at the end she could not even have been with him. One passage reads, "When your letters came I felt impelled to come up to my attic room for awhile and read the certain passages I had heard him read and speak of with such conviction. I am beginning to realize what it means to have a truly *good* man as a father. Goodness is not common. It is what the Chinese keep mentioning—'He was so *good*'."

Years later she was to write a book about her father, seeing him with poignant clarity Of his death she wrote, 'The body was so little part of him that its final stillness seemed nothing of importance. He was half out of it anyway and death was only a slipping out of it altogether and being at last as he always was, a spirit. We buried the pearly shell on the mountain top There is nothing between that spot and the sky—no tree, no human habitation. The rocks are beneath, the swirling mists about it, and the winds blow and the sun and the stars shine down, and there is no human voice to be heard anywhere."

Ten years Andrew had lived in Pearl's house, and she had done her best to make that home his home. She had grown up in the Chinese tradition of reverence for age, and she had tried in all the ways she knew to make his old age happy, and to keep from him anything which might distress him. Although she could not share his faith in his creed, she never allowed any talk in his presence, by students or guests or family, which might disturb his faith. "He must die in the faith in which he has lived," she always said.

And now she was more glad than ever of a promise she had made to him, to have published the final and complete revision of the New Testament which lay ready. This she had done at once. The book over which he had worked so long was printed in an especially good format with funds which she supplied. Thus Andrew's work was finished—that translation of the book which to him was the Word of God. In every way he knew, he had striven to make it available to all.

Pearl went steadily on with her writing, this time a longer novel, sequel to *The Good Earth*, which she entitled *Sons*, and which she has often said is her favorite among her books about China.

As was usual there were many guests that autumn. This year, 1931, a year of great floods, came Colonel Lindbergh and Mrs. Lindbergh. Colonel Lindbergh gave his services to the National Flood Relief, surveying with his plane the worst areas, and making maps. Pearl wrote Emma, "We dined with them last night at the Consulate and had a chance to become acquainted. The Colonel is absorbed in his subject, caring for little else He either talks aviation or is silent, but mostly talks aviation! . . . His wife I thought perfectly charming. She is very small, one of the smallest women I ever saw, and with a face that is increasingly pretty, because her prettiness is not obvious at first. She has lovely eyes and hair and a very winning simple manner. Both of them seem very young. But Lindbergh impressed me as the type of mind that will always be young because it is so limited to its own line, while she will probably unfold more and more. . . ."

It was this November that Pearl had to speak before a large group of women in Shanghai. It was an appointment that was postponed three times for various reasons. But at last she went. She wrote Faith of the event, with her keen sense of humor. "I simply rushed down for the day and gave my speech before the greatest mob of women I have ever seen. I was aghast and quite terrified, and found the only way I could bear them was to stare at a stucco decoration on the wall above their heads and address that. After the meeting tons of women came up and I do not remember one of them—no, I do remember two, one large slangy creature who roared out, 'Say, I bet you could sell that speech and get good money for it.' Another gushing creature who panted and said with most maudlin sentimentality, 'Oh where is the hand that wrote *The Good Earth?* Oh, let me clasp that hand!'

"It was so repulsive that I replied with the utmost frigidity that I used a typewriter and two fingers.

172

"It was all very funny and convinced me once and for all that it is no life for me—publicity, I mean It leaves me quite cold. It is no temptation to take advantage of having written a 'best-seller.' In other words, I am the same old thing." Then she went on of another matter connected with that trip. "By the by, while I was in Shanghai I bought me one of those little hats that you hang on your right eyebrow and bolster on your right ear. I thought I would look silly in it, but found to my amazement that they are extremely becoming. I like it because it solves the perpetual difficulty of my hair It sets high on the head and is quite remote from my bun."

That winter of 1931 and 1932 was a disturbed one. There were rumors of Communist attacks and of Japanese invasions. After a bad week Pearl and many of her friends went on short notice to Peking. She had long wanted to renew that old acquaintance begun when she was a girl, and now that opportunity had come. She was making good use of the time "I am having to give a series of lectures, long-promised, to the Language School here. Next I am getting in some study of certain books not to be found elsewhere in the world. Next, I am seeing Peking. The palaces, the old paintings, the carving—it would take a lifetime to know it all. Peking is not overrated, at least. . . . I think the thing I love most about this city is the old palaces—miles and miles of them. I love wandering about through them. There are wonderful vistas through them. . . . I have met a lot of people here, and the most interesting to me have been the Chinese who are writing or doing things of some sort" . . . .

After she reached Nanking again in early spring, Peking was still with her. She wrote again, "I met there a very interesting circle of modern Chinese writers—they were very modern and very much a circle Peking is, I suppose *the* literary center of China today These people were most wonderfully cordial and kind to me. I was much impressed with their ability and sincerity, although at the same time I felt them living remote from life. . . . The thing that stands out to me as the most beautiful out of the thousand and ten thousand beautiful things, is the Valley of the Thirteen Kings, or the Old Ming Tombs. I think I have never seen so noble or beautiful a scene. The old crumbling buildings are set in a semi-circle of strange, barren mountains—a somber, wild, fierce landscape, the mountains warped and black and craggy against the brilliant sky—the vast old silent buildings. There are thirteen tombs in the semicircle."

At the same time she mentioned a small mission study book which she had written. It was *The Young Revolutionist.* She said, "It is making a peck of trouble because people think it is a new novel " She mentioned, too, her translation of the long Chinese novel on which she had been working for years. "It has been a *job* and I think will satisfy forever any instincts or desires I may have to translate anything again. The thing will be to get it published, next, and yet I don't want it abridged."

With the first signs of spring, there came the thought that soon she would be returning to America Her first thought was of her child. She wrote, "I am in sort of a fever to get back, now that I have the money ready and waiting. I want to get a cottage built at the school and everything as safe and right for her as can now be made."

Knowing that now she had the money she needed and the ability to make more was in another way a bitter knowledge. The memory of Carie was still strong in her mind. She could not forget how Carie had loved beauty and certain things which she had never had. Deep in her heart Pearl had always planned that one day she would give her mother all she wanted, to satisfy fully that starved part of her nature The time when she could have done this had come, but Carie was gone It was too late. Years later Pearl still spoke of this moment, when she knew she had the power to give, but could not.

But she could do everything humanly possible not only for her own child but for all others like her. By stimulating research in this field she would perhaps bring improvement to many. She did not think further than this. She did not foresee that through her hunger to share with her mother who was gone, and with all the other ill children of the world, she was, for their sakes, to share with many. In later years she was to say openly to others dear to her, "I couldn't do it for Mother. Let me do it for you It is only so that anything that comes my way has meaning "

In that spring of 1932, before she sailed, she was awarded the Pulitzer Prize for *The Good Earth.* The success of the book swept on meantime in China and in many other lands, and in the end it was translated into more than a score of languages.

But as of every great work, there was criticism as well as praise and of this Pearl's good friend, Emma told her, and told her, as well, of her longing to defend her. Pearl wrote, "Whoever said it was a coarse book is perfectly right—it *is* a coarse book, from their

174

point of view. If they met Wang Lung they would consider him an extremely coarse old fellow, and so he is in their eyes.... They would be completely horrified by the almost animal way in which he takes his life . Wang Lung is in the medieval age. His class in China must be judged, not by Christian, or even American standards, but by the standards of Elizabethan times. You see if I had not made him coarse, he wouldn't have been Wang Lung, but some imaginary creature that never was on land or sea!... This doesn't mean that I do not admire this very quality in the common Chinese —I admire it immensely. I like their extremely matter-of-fact attitude toward all the natural functions of life. I think it sane and wholesome.... When one writes of a Wang Lung he must come true, and to do this I can only write as I see him.... If I write about a coarse person, he will come coarse, I am afraid! Only it's not coarse to me. People are people, and each individual sacred in his individuality, and I cannot tamper with him and make him this or that. I can only make him as he is in my understanding of him.... So, my dear, don't try to defend me any more. If my work can't stand on its own legs, let it fall!"

When there came further news from America, she wrote her sister, "I had a cable from my agent last week that the dramatization of *The Good Earth* would reach me about May eighth. The Theatre Guild has taken it and will produce it in New York in October.... I am awfully pleased that the Theater Guild has taken it, because they will do it as well as it can be done.... I shan't go to the first night. I couldn't stand the suspense of people liking it or not."

Then, thinking of all that was coming about she wrote, "In spite of all this fuss, the only realities in my life are what they have ever been, my invalid child and my home here, those of my sister and my brother. And then my very few intimate friends. All the rest seems external and in its final analysis unimportant. My agent and my publisher keep writing me letters and sending me cablegrams warning me of what they feel I do not comprehend awaits me in America. My publisher wants to meet me with a secretarial staff as I come from the steamer to 'protect' me from newspaper reporters. I wrote him I didn't know when I would be coming or at what port I would be landing, being by nature a casual and unstable person—which as you know is the bitter truth!. .I don't know when I will really start or where I shall land but I do know I shall go straight to my child."

On a summer evening she boarded a train in Nanking with her family. "I shall avoid all publicity stuff and slip into America unnoticed," she had written someone that day. Her sister remembers how she looked that night when she left for she had come to Nanking to see her off. Pearl wore a soft green silk suit and becoming hat. She was a little heavier than in years before but her hair had the same changing glints and her bearing the same repose. She was not excited for she was as ever herself

She carried a small Chinese suitcase In the confusion of boarding the train it was mislaid for an instant. "Oh," she said laughing, "I mustn't lose that! It has my manuscript in it!" Her smile had that slight half-humorous, half-whimsical twisting of the lips that is characteristic of her to many. The manuscript was her translation of the Chinese novel, *Shui Hu Chuan*, completed at last.

PART SIX

XXV   ‖ T WAS nearly three years since Pearl had been in America. She arrived in July to find that her publisher had tried in every way he could to check the great wave of publicity that awaited her. It was his intention that she be quietly accepted rather than that she have to undergo that ordeal so dear to Americans—worship of a famed person.

Richard J. Walsh, the president of the John Day company, her publisher, planned to introduce her in New York not by the usual round of parties, but by a single dignified dinner. This was held at the Waldorf-Astoria in New York City, on August the third. On this occasion she so clearly showed her genuineness that those who before had said there could be none like her, and had suggested that she must be maintaining a pose, confessed, "We were wrong—she is genuine."

When at the end of the dinner she rose to speak—her first speech in America, and before a brilliant audience drawn from the New York literary world—she was to all outward appearances perfectly composed. She spoke simply, gratefully, for only a few moments, and then, choosing the words of a Chinese rather than her own, she read her translation of Shih Nai-an's preface to *All Men Are Brothers*, ending,

"How can I know what those that come after me and read my book will think of it? I do not even know if I myself afterwards can even read this book. Why therefore should I care?"

The beauty of the translation, and the modesty and humor of the closing lines, won at once the hearts of even the most cynical of New York critics.

A veteran of the publishing world, one who had discovered and introduced many of the writers of the previous generation, came to her publisher and said quietly, "She is a genius. I have known only a few."

One of her old college professors was there. She remembers that on that occasion she said, "It would be nice if I could claim that Randolph-Macon made Pearl Buck. But I can't honestly say that I believe it did. I can only say that I hope we did not hurt or hinder her. She was already completely self-sufficient."

That autumn the play of *The Good Earth* was to be performed. Owen Davis had written a stage arrangement from a portion of the book and the Theatre Guild was to present it. Pearl went often to rehearsals to help in the authenticity of the costumes, settings, and the interpretations of Chinese backgrounds. She went on the second night to see the performance, and sat in the balcony, for true to her word, she could not bring herself to go the first night.

One of the pleasures of the year was her meeting with Will Rogers. Long before this he had said of *The Good Earth*, "It is not only the greatest book about a people ever written but the best book of our generation "

Among the millions who were reading *The Good Earth* was an eminent Negro leader. Elmer Carter, editor at that time of *Opportunity,* says of the experience, "I didn't know anything about Pearl Buck, but I knew that anyone who could write such a book must understand the whole question of race. This was no sugar-coated philanthropy, it was basic understanding " He felt at once that there would be great value in personal contact between Pearl and a small group of selected Negro leaders. He decided to try to arrange such an occasion. His staff thought him mad and a dreamer. Nevertheless he wrote a letter to Pearl addressed in care of her publisher and was amazed to have her accept and agree to speak at a tea in Harlem in December.

The group met in the Harlem Y. W. C. A. "Instantly," he said, "we felt her a wonderful person. We saw that she was not political or economic in her leadership. She had a natural interest in people."

He said, "I was and am in a daze to understand how Pearl Buck imparts her feeling to other people. All Negroes have implicit faith in Miss Buck They have greater confidence in her than in any other white person in public life." This feeling began with the reading of *The Good Earth,* and that Harlem tea.

That winter was a full one. Edwin wrote Faith from New York, "Pearl dropped into my office the other day. It would delight you to see her. I have never seen her looking so pretty. She seems to have the world wrapped around her finger, and yet she is exactly the same. It hasn't touched her at all. I am just beginning to realize what a wonderful girl she is, and she has only begun. We spend delightful evenings together sometimes, seeing a play and talking no end. She is so sane and hearty, like a clean, cool breeze. . ."

Before the end of the year, 1932, *Sons,* which was a sequel to *The Good Earth,* was published. Dr. William Lyon Phelps described it as "one of the outstanding works of our time." It, too, was a best-seller. For the first time Chinese were becoming people to the ordinary Americans, and this was the real satisfaction which came to Pearl out of her success. She had succeeded in interpreting one people, one she knew, to another whom she knew less well but loved for her own.

In the spring of 1933 was published a collection of the short stories which she had written for many magazines. This was *The First Wife and Other Stories.* Later in the same year appeared the translation of *Shui Hu Chuan.* The work begun nearly five years before appeared as *All Men Are Brothers.* It was a tremendous undertaking and she had brought it to a magnificent conclusion. It stood as a monumental effort to disclose to the eyes of the English-speaking world the pageant of China

She was interested particularly in becoming acquainted with Chinese people in America. Nor had she for a moment forgotten those in China. There is an incident, for example, which was known to no one for a long time. She had a Chinese woman friend in Nanking who needed a job and money. Casting about to find both for her, Pearl discovered that in all the city of Nanking there was no public bath-house for women and children, though those for men were plentiful She secretly got a bath-house started and saw that this friend was given the work of running it, paying all the expenses herself and not allowing the friend to know. This went on for years even after the Japanese occupation of the city and the woman had no idea how it had been managed until years later when her husband discovered it.

In June Pearl was awarded an honorary degree by Yale University. The Randolph-Macon Alumnae Bulletin said of it, "Pearl Sydenstricker Buck is the only woman in the group of distinguished persons given honorary degrees by Yale University In presenting her for the honorary degree of Master of Arts, William Lyon Phelps spoke of her as the ablest living interpreter of Chinese character."

And now Randolph-Macon invited Pearl to speak at the commencement exercises. Her old friends urged and she decided to go. There would be reunion with many of her college mates. Two years before the college had elected her to alumnae membership in its chapter of Phi Beta Kappa. The next year the *Helianthus,* the college annual, had been dedicated to her. At the request of its editors she had written a special message for it. It read,

"Dear Randolph-Macon Girls,
"It has been many a year since I walked your college halls and the green lawns of the campus. Across those years, across the wide seas, what have I to say to you today?—I think only one thing; believe in life! Life is glorious I would not have missed any of it. I shall be in love with life to the very end. Bring zest to it and bring humor and purity of purpose and you will find that, pain, or pleasure, life is *good.*"

Now the Alumnae Bulletin said, "Pearl Buck is to speak at the Alumnae dinner in June. Her subject will be 'Women and International Relations' .... Mrs. Buck is much in demand Recently she gave before the University Club in Baltimore, an address on 'Chinese Humor' .... On April the nineteenth one on the same subject at Bryn Mawr .... and an address on Founders' Day in New York on 'The Background of Chinese Literature.'"

Then Pearl was back on the old college campus, more beautiful now than in the days that she was a student there.

A college mate writes of those few days with warm feeling after many years have passed, "That reunion is vivid to me. One of the other girls and I drove up from Richmond, had car trouble and arrived late, just as the crowd was going into Main Hall for the

Alumnae luncheon. We had been wondering along the way whether we could feel easy with our famous friend, and hurrying across the front campus ran right into her with Emma and some others There was an impulsive kiss, a quick look and then 'Why, Nannie, you haven't changed a bit!' It was as easy as that."

That evening Pearl's old China friend, Ray Parker, had a dinner for her, after which there was the Alumnae Address. The house was overflowing and Pearl saw everywhere her old college mates. She began her speech with seeming ease, although to this day speaking is hard for her. There was a twinkle in her eyes with her opening words "My subject which I must confess I chose myself, was to have been Women and International Relations. I chose it because it seemed to me a subject at once wise and serious and the sort of thing in which a group of college alumnae might be interested, or at least, in which they should be interested. Unfortunately, it was not a subject on which I had done much individual thinking, and when I began to do so, I found it became more and more vast and intangible. As a title it was superb. I could see a whole row of volumes written about it. But the more I looked at the row, the more I became convinced it would never be written by me and while that title might be extremely well chosen, it was for me nothing forever but a title. . . . The truth is, and I may as well be truthful, I don't know anything about Women and International Relations " With this she began her address on the Writing of Novels, a speech in which she was thoroughly at home and which delighted her listeners. Near the end she gave her creed of a novelist. "I believe only in life, tragic, gay, glorious, incomprehensible life. I believe in human beings and in the good and evil mingled in us all. I believe in art, that it is to be kept to its one holy use, which is to portray faithfully, as only the purest art can, life itself and life only "

She wore that evening a white lace dress Her hair glinted gold. With her face alight and the sparkle coming and going in her eyes, and her characteristic smile flickering in and out, she gave many the impression of a promise fulfilled.

The week-end was a whirl of engagements. Her friend writes again,

"I wish I could describe the psychological climax of that weekend, what happened to a group of persons who came out of real admiration and love, and soon felt the strength of a fine personality flowing into themselves. As it turned out it was not Pearl Buck, the author, who interested me most; it was the woman with the vitality and power from secret sources, whose greatness was sure. . . . Two of us who were rooming together talked about it. We made up our minds to ask her about it and found the opportunity. Pearl said that the sorrow about her child had been overpowering, and that when she had mastered that, no other happenings in life could confuse her "

Pearl wrote about this later · "I don't believe in an ivory tower. I don't believe in a withdrawal from people. . . . Yet one shouldn't be at the mercy of life but should take time and space to be one's self and live one's own inward life, full of what enriches. I can do all sorts of things on the fringe of my life, but I must have a quiet center. . . . After you have suffered, seen death, had loss, you aren't afraid any more. Those fears get out of your way. I don't believe in suffering for its own sake. I think you learn as much from happiness as from suffering But if you live you can't escape suffering; you find that you get through and it opens a door."

Her friend wrote again of the college reunion "It was fine to see her sincere interest in each person's accomplishment and her skillful manner of getting others to talk of themselves. She gave a dinner at the hotel for personal friends. Her beauty on that occasion was especially marked, in costume, voice and gesture, and from the head of the table she seemed to express a rare balance of East and West, in bodily composure and facial animation. I felt she was absorbed in each person who spoke, wondering about her, analyzing. . . I could tell of the inspiration experienced by many. . . . Pearl had time for each who had special difficulty or who was ill . . Pearl's friendship has run like a bright thread through the lives of some whose lives are incomplete or lonely or those who have had always to struggle with ill health."

There was opportunity to talk with old professors, to confess to her hunger for beauty in the college as it was when she was there. There was time for her professors to see her as she was and to feel delight in the fulfillment that had come.

Pearl found opportunity to make a few visits while she was in the South and drove over Droop Mountain to her old American home. She wrote in a letter, "I found the tiny village of Hillsboro, and the old white home where I was born. I remembered it as beautifully ordered and kept, with a great smooth lawn about it, and big maples. The lawn is weeds now, and all the maples are gone except one, but the house is still noble in its proportions—the biggest place around there still. But the village has gone down very much. It all made me rather sad "

She planned to return to China by way of Europe, more keen to see and interpret and experience than ever in her life before, but this keenness was the stronger because of its contrast with her inward sadness. Her separation from her older child was final now. That child could never again be a part of her home. She would see her again and again in America, and she knew she wanted to live in America to make this possible. She had done financially all that she had hoped to be able to do for her child. Nothing more could be done by anyone. Almost all the proceeds of her first great success had gone for that purpose—for the care of the child, for her medical help, for a house in which she would live, not alone, but with fifteen other children who had to be cared for in the same way. She wanted her child's life to count for something, even though the child herself could not take an active part in the world, and so she built not only the house, but a shallow outdoor swimming pool and a well-equipped playground for the children of that and other houses, and paid the salary of a play director. Finally, she started, and supported for years, a research by scientists which might help to prevent such illnesses in other children not yet born. That research has already borne fruit.

There was another reason for which Pearl wanted to live now in America. She knew that the kinship with her own country which her mother had built all through her childhood was growing stronger. In her heart she knew that she was American through and through.

She would always be interested in any people, as people, but America was of all the world her place because she was the branch of a tree rooted here She loved the clean soil of America, its freedom and challenge. Here, in time, she, too, would root herself.

In June 1933, nearly a year after she came to the United States, she sailed from Montreal for Liverpool. Her brother and his wife were with her. She had bought a car and learned to drive it during her year in America and she was taking the car to China. As she landed in England she decided to drive to London so that she might better see the countryside she loved. She drove with delight at what she saw, braving the differing rules of driving and the unfamiliar routes. She saw the Lake Country of Wordsworth, and crossed into Scotland to the country of Robert Burns and Thomas Carlyle.

Some months later she drove across the continent stopping here and there at places she wanted to see again. She wrote to Emma of the journey, "I enjoyed the beauty of the countries we visited and did a good deal of business with my various publishers. England remains the loveliest of all the countries still—so small and yet with every variety of landscape, from the grandeur of mountains and lakes in the north, to the lush, low meadows of Devonshire—whose clotted cream, I found, by the way, particularly obnoxious. I want to go back to England. Sweden was like Ohio, except Stockholm, which was lovely. Denmark was pretty and tidy; Holland flat and dull, uninteresting. . . . Italy. . . . beautiful, and France enchanting. The war areas we motored through and found still war areas—bleak and sad, young trees beginning to grow, and middle-aged people with their eyes tragic with memories they can never forget. The war memorials and cemeteries were frightful—cemeteries packed with white crosses, and great buildings with every inch of their walls covered with names of lads never found—the American forces. I was in one such building with a friend, and when we saw those thousands of names, each representing a lad who died and whose body even could not be found—and to what end such death?—we turned and ran, weeping. I never was so overcome by the horrible meaning of war. If anyone ever starts another, let him go first and look at those silent, speaking names. My heart aches when I think of them."

Pearl sailed from Italy for India, by way of the Red Sea It was the first time she had been in India. It left a deep impression of beauty and of suffering which was to come to her with poignancy in days ahead.

In October she arrived in Shanghai. The staff of *The China Critic,* a modern Chinese magazine, gave her a dinner. It is to be remembered because it was the first time that she met Lin Yutang.

For several years she had enjoyed Lin Yutang's keen and witty essays in both Chinese and English Now she met him for the first time He thanked her for writing about the ordinary people of China, and later in the evening remarked, "I think I will some time write a book and tell what I feel about my country." She seized upon the idea saying, "You must. No Chinese has yet written such a book " And she urged him then and later as their friendship grew, to write the book. When he finally made an outline for it, he sent it

184

to her, and she gave it to her own publisher, who eagerly accepted it. When Lin Yutang had written the book and it was published with the title, *My Country and My People*, she wrote an introduction for it in which she said, "Suddenly, as all great books appear, this book appears, fulfilling every demand made upon it. It is truthful and not ashamed of the truth; it is written proudly and humorously and with beauty; seriously and with gaiety."

That year was to be a year of journeying and of acquaintance with new peoples. She went again to India through Indo-China, Siam, and Burma, returning to China by way of the Dutch East Indies.

She was to come back from that long journey among many peoples confirmed in her hatred of imperialism. Even the best of empires, she was now convinced, was not good enough. Wherever she went she saw what seemed to her the incontestable proof of the evils of one people ruling another. She compared the peoples she saw under British, French, and Dutch empire, and saw the same fatal results in both the rulers and the ruled. Thereafter when she was asked to speak, she often spoke for the freedom of peoples to govern themselves and to develop as they could.

But now her decision to be near her invalid child, and her sad but clear certainty that the years had proven that her way led in a direction apart from that of her child's father, and her own hunger to be in America, all decided her to return once again to her own country.

XXVI   ON JUNE, 1934, she was in America again. She found that her latest book, *The Mother*, published while she was yet in China, was being well received. Several years later, in the citation for the Nobel prize, it was said of the character who was central in the book: "To this woman the writer does not even give a name for she needs none, being that woman whom all know—the mother. Chinese, yes; the woman is kin to both the farmer Wang Lung and his wife O-lan, and she has the characteristics of each. But she is also the universal mother, playing out on her little patch of land the part of any other mother, rearing her children, sinking her life into theirs and seeing them marry and move on to their own destinies. It is a tale of tense quiet and inexorable simplicity." Some have said of this book that it is her greatest work.

While in China another book had been finished. *The House Divided*, planned, too, around the figure of Wang Lung and his family, was published and well received. The imposing trilogy begun with *The Good Earth* and *Sons* was now complete. It was brought together within the covers of a single volume as *House of Earth* in 1935.

To many the name Pearl Buck suggests instantly this trilogy and more particularly *The Good Earth*. To others and to those who know her best her trilogy stands as an introduction to the entire body of her writing.

For now she began to feel a great curiosity about her own country and her own people. China was an old country, its people unified by thousands of years of living together as one race, and bound together by a single culture. America was new, its history short. There was no unity of race or cultural roots. And yet there was a unity, and it was the unity of people who believe in the freedom of the individual.

Pearl had opportunity to express her feeling on race in her own country in an unpremeditated way that February. She went to see an art exhibit in Harlem It was called An Art Commentary on Lynching. There were many there, chiefly Negroes, and all walked quietly about looking and commenting in undertones. A small group gathered about Pearl as if waiting for her reaction. Among them was Carl Van Vechten. He remembers that she suddenly began to speak as if too moved to be silent. Everyone listened electrified by her simple statement. She said, as she closed with that characteristic smile, touched now with feeling, that she was so violently opposed to the idea of lynching that if her own daughters had been attacked and the violators had begged her to save them from the mob, she would do so. Those who heard will never forget.

That March Randolph-Macon started a Rare Book Collection for its college library to be given by the New York Chapter of the Alumnae Association, and asked Pearl to give a message. It hangs there now in her writing. She said, "I have been asked this evening to tell you why I think a rare book collection is a valuable thing for a group of alumnae to give and support in their alma mater.... After many years away from college when I look into myself to discover what remains of those years I find it is atmosphere. Everything else is gone. . . . What remains is remembered beauty, beauty of atmosphere. At no time in life, I think, have you or I been so sensitive to beauty, physical and spiritual, as we were in college. . . . To contribute something, then for beauty's sake, is to contribute the greatest possible good to the new generations."

Pearl planted, that year, her home in America. It was to be in the beautiful rolling hills of Pennsylvania. Her eyes had already chosen a house, an old stone farmhouse set on a rise and looking out to the woods and far-spreading country and peaceful farms Here in this place she would build her home again. She must have a home, for she is a home-loving woman, and her heart is warm to her own family. And that home must be in the country. She has no love for a city.

That American home began when on June the eleventh, 1935, she was married for a second time, to Richard J. Walsh, the president of the John Day Company and editor of *Asia*. This was the publisher who had accepted her first book because it was so beautifully written and because it showed such promise of more to come, even though the subject was Chinese.

In November of that same year Pearl was awarded a very special honor. She spoke of it with a touch of embarrassment. "It is awarded," she said, "by a group of very profound scholars—elderly men. Why they should decide to give it to me—!" It was the Howells Medal, given only once in five years in recognition of the most distinguished work of American fiction published during that period. It had been awarded first to Mary E. Wilkins Freeman, and second to Willa Cather. In presenting it, Robert Grant said, "For the third time the medal is awarded to a woman, a choice acquiesced in by four Academicians serving as the Committee, three of whom are men, and approved by the majority of the American Academy of Arts and Letters. . . . It is to honor those who can write so convincingly of people, whether in the tragedy or comedy of human life. . . . that this memorial to William Dean Howells was endowed Because she has done this so unerringly, and with such an artistic sense of value, I am commissioned to bestow upon the author of *The Good Earth* the medal of gold for the five year period just ended."

187

In reply Pearl spoke of her appreciation of her own country. She said,

"I find here, surely more than in any other country of the world, opportunity for a writer, unknown and obscure, with no influence of any kind, without money or particular friends, to come into recognition, to find generous praise and welcome and many friends. . Mine is indeed a country of matchless opportunity for the artist. I cannot ask for more. When I remember the little distant poor room in which I began to write, and when I look about me today in your presence, I cannot but feel a great humility and gratitude for opportunity, so freely given, and so richly rewarded, in America."

As a writer in America, Pearl began that full, rich central portion of her life which was to make her known not only to the reader of books wherever he might be in the world, but to every man or woman who in the days ahead was to look up from his tangled path to listen to a voice that dared to speak the truth.

Pearl's roots began now to grow into the American soil. The old stone house in the Pennsylvania country was the spot she had chosen for the rooting. She loved the house from the instant she first saw it. High under the roof-peak were inscribed the initials of the first owners, set there a hundred years before.

The house was built of the warm brown and red stone of the fields. The doors and windows were fashioned in the original way, the latches of wrought iron, the walls thick. The floors were of the broad boards belonging to earlier times There was a fireplace in the "parlor." The old kitchen was there with its huge hearth. With deep delight she saw just how partitions could be taken out and stairways changed to throw two rooms into one and give the house space and grace, and the plaster ceilings be torn away to show the heavy hand-hewn beams.

None of the original feeling was to be changed. What modernization there was must be only for convenience Beside the narrow old porch she planted a trumpet vine which quickly grew to the chimneys. The space beyond could be broadened to a terrace with native flags. The gnarled pear tree must stay just where it was.

Here, upstairs, were to be three bedrooms, and there above the kitchen another. There must be more, for soon she would begin enlarging her family. She would choose more babies and this would be their home She had already planned their coming

From her windows and her terrace she looked out to the fields spreading as far as she could see. She felt especial affection for the big red barn with its white "hex" signs. Here there could be a garage and above it a playroom for her children and for the children of her friends.

Back of the house and away from the narrow country road which led between two villages was the woods. She wandered through it with her husband. American woods! She had once described the experience of being in an American woods thus:

"How can I put the excitement of it into words! No one had told me how paganly gorgeous it would be. Oh, of course they had said, 'The leaves turn in the fall, you know,' but how does that prepare one? I had thought of pale yellows and tans and faint rose reds. Instead I found myself in a living blaze of color—robust, violent, vivid beyond belief. I shall never forget one tall tree trunk wrapped about with a vine of flaming scarlet, standing outlined, a fiery sentinel against a dark rocky cliff."

This she had written when for the first time she saw an American woods in autumn. Now she wandered through woods of her own and watched the colors come, listened to the tinkle of the creek, searched for sassafras and red berries, paused beside a pool There where the stream ran from the woods into the meadows lying between her hillside and the adjoining house she would build a dam so her children could sail their boats. Higher, near the house she would dig a pool where in clean, cold water her children could learn to swim and so escape the fear of water she had always had since those days so long ago now, when the Yangtze had put it into her mind.

The old summer kitchen beyond the porch, built too, of brown stone, could be a study, far enough away from the house to escape disturbance, yet near enough to keep her close to the children. She would put a rose garden outside the windows. Over against the edge of the woods could be a flower border. She saw it already—a long line blazing with a succession of flowers, each in its season

It was done at last as she planned. The home became a part of the countryside, and people have come to accept it as such. She seldom leaves her own grounds and yet the neighbors are friendly to her, and she likes them.

Today, anyone trying to find the Walsh home may stop in the village nearest and ask if a man there can tell him where Pearl Buck lives. He is likely to push his cap back, scratch his head, look hard at the questioner, take two or three chews on his quid before he says, "Don't rightly know for sure, but I think it's down the road there past the filling station." This not being much help since it does not agree with the instructions sent in Pearl's own hand, the questioner holds the letter for the man to see, saying meantime, "No, that can't be it. She says to turn left at the store but I don't know which of the two left roads to take." The man has stepped down from the narrow porch by now and is grinning, "Well, I guess she ought to know where she lives, oughtn't she? As a matter of fact, it's that right one of those two left ones there. Just about a mile down."

So her friends let her live among them and try to give her the quiet she loves.

In January of that first winter in her American home, Pearl was elected a member of the National Institute of Arts and Letters.

In that year, too, *The Exile,* the book about her mother, was published. Two years later she was to receive the highest award in literature partly because of her biographical work. This was her first biography, written years before as a record for her child. She had tried only to draw a picture of her mother as she was. Now letters poured in thanking her for what she had done. Women said that this mother seemed to come to life and they shared her humor and sadness and the personal struggle which she had had with her own nature.

One Hillsboro neighbor of near Carie's own age read the book and looking back wrote, "I was seventeen and going to teach school when Miss Carie came home from a Kentucky boarding school. I with two other friends went to call on her.... She was happy as if the word has been coined for her; she seemed overflowing with life so that the world about her was the best of all places to be. We talked and sang together.... It was a delightful evening.... I never saw her again. When I married and returned, she was gone—a missionary's life, a noble choice, the very noblest of all. But I was sorry gay Miss Carie had to be so good.... Your mother's life as you show it in your book stands alone for beauty and for surely unexampled courage, like some fine epic. I have never read or heard

190

her equal. Anyone who has written, or who loves writing, feels with George Eliot, 'What good is like to this? To *do* worthy the writing and to *write* worthy the reading.' ... Did Comfort's (Pearl's) mother, before she died know that better than all missionaries, the people she lived among and compassioned would, by her daughter, be brought to the understanding and sympathy of her America?"

Pearl wrote Faith, "I'm getting floods of letters from people who *feel* Mother. It's a wonderful thing—perhaps she will' do more for people now than she was ever able to do. Always the letters are not for the book, but for *her*—that pleases me so."

Carie lived again. It was almost as though she had come back to America, back Home again.

But there was Andrew. Andrew and Carie were so different that it had been impossible to put them in the same book, and because of this some people thought she did not love him as well.

This determined her to write his story, too It must have been hard, that writing, for she was more her mother's daughter than her father's, and to write of Carie had been, although she would deny it, like writing of herself. But to write of Andrew she must see him entirely apart and understand the building of his reticent, lonely soul and its escape and fulfillment in the Work to which he knew his God had called him. She wrote with tenderness and understanding and beauty of the great, gaunt man who never saw himself or knew of the strange small incidents which had turned him toward the direction of his life. She called the book, *Fighting Angel*. It was a book like *The Exile* in its touch and beauty, but so unlike in the picture it drew that the reader could scarcely believe that these two could have lived out their lives together in the situation which was to one exile, and to the other the Land of Promise.

Later, Selma Lagerlöf, the great Swedish novelist and member of the Swedish Academy, told her that *Fighting Angel* was her favorite among the books, and had decided her vote in favor of awarding the Nobel prize to Pearl Buck.

In the winter of that first year in the new home, Pearl and her husband chose their first two babies. The babies were only five weeks old but instantly Pearl was caring for them with her old skill. She would have no nurse. She must enjoy these children. Herself she bathed them, mixed their formulas, fed them, put them in the sunshine for their sunbaths, and watched every new development with keen delight.

At once she was seeing their differences and their similarities. At once she could predict their personalities by the very set of their pursed lips or the timbre of their crying. They flourished, as all babies do for her. Soon they were in rompers and sitting and crawling The old love of babies was as strong as ever in her, stronger perhaps, because of that disappointment in her first child Now to see achievement in its due time was in itself enough to make her happy. When the weekly trip to New York was made they went, too, these tiny boys, tucked in baskets for the long drive. She would not leave them even for the few days in New York

That spring, the brother from whom she had been separated so much and yet with whom she had a strong, close understanding, died. It was a shock and loss she could not accept. Again and again she said, "He should not have died. There was no necessity for it for he was a young man and not yet in the prime of his work." With sorrowful regret she herself had his ashes brought and laid in the quiet village cemetery near her, and herself sorted and put his things in the little stone house near her own which he had bought one summer when they were together.

When, the next year in the spring, she and her husband chose two more babies, a boy and a girl, some remonstrated with her saying that already she had her gift and her work and that she could not possibly manage a large family as well. But she knew herself. She took this time a little boy with curly brown hair, and a little girl with wide pansy-blue eyes and dimples and a sweet face. In the little boy she found a secret pleasure because of his likeness to Edwin.

She had with her, then, her second daughter, now a girl of eleven, and her three baby boys, and her baby girl. Thus fully she satisfied her determination for a family. She wrote Faith with something of the feeling of that first letter about the birth of her baby, "I do love a lot of children around, all normal and hearty, if possible All my friends think I am insane, but a good many people have thought that of me at various times. It's only that I know what I want and go after it, and don't count the cost. If you go counting costs you never do anything or get anywhere, I do believe."

192

XXVII   During the next years she was to reach out to all that was of America. In the summer of 1936 she drove to Bethlehem, Pennsylvania, to hear the choral of Bach music given by working people. She had long planned to do this, interested in this program carried on for twenty-five years in this way. She wrote to her sister: "This is a yearly event and rather remarkable. . . . Eight hours of Bach music. . . . The Lutheran church, a huge affair, was packed, and the lawns outside full of people. The choruses were *beautiful*—three hundred voices. It was glorious weather and I felt the music was restful and refreshing."

And now she began to write of her own country. At first she wrote short stories and articles and novelettes. To many she seemed not herself in these because they had so allied her in their thinking with the Chinese people of whom she had written with such interpretive ability that they could not recognize that same touch when applied to another race. And yet they read what she wrote. She could not fill the demand for her writing, for now she was writing not only for the readers of books but for that much greater group—the readers of magazines.

To those who criticised her superficially for writing for popular magazines and so "debasing" her literary art, she gave an answer far from superficial. In an address delivered before the National Education Association in 1938, she said, in part,

"It would be easy for me to do what many others have done—simply shrug my shoulders at the mass of popular writing and say that it has nothing to do with literature. But I cannot. I keep going back to it. It is what most people read—then it must have its importance somewhere in relation to literature. One cannot dismiss lightly a magazine bought and read by three million people. . . . It is important. It is a serious thing for literature if three million read—not literature, but something which gives them greater satisfaction."

To Faith who heard comments on Pearl's writing of America, she wrote with characteristic downrightness, "The next time you hear anyone mention my 'new style' of writing, just tell them that my style from now on will vary with my subject. If I write of Chinese things, I will write in my usual Chinese style, which is really Chinese translated, and if I write of a western subject, it will be in western style. Also say that as many people don't like the Chinese style as do,

193

and a writer must just write as he pleases since people will always be divided ... The only safe thing is to pay no attention whatever and write as and what one pleases."

But the relation of popular writing to literature and whether or not in the passage of time its true place will become known, is not all of the answer. More fundamental is the simple fact that she also writes for those who are not the readers of books.

Underlying her interests and her writing and her other active life there was and there is one unchanging unity. It is the fulfillment of that feeling which came to her first as Carie's child All she does must work toward mutual understanding between the common peoples of the earth and toward justice for all. Through her first books she interpreted China to the West. Now the base of her interpretation was enlarging and deepening to include common people everywhere. As the subject matter of her writing broadened so also must her audience. More and more, then, in keeping with her purpose she wrote where she would be read, not only by the student and lover of books but by the workman and the clerk and the stenographer. With deliberate intent she wrote that everyone might read because she wants to write for people.

But now she was drawn sharply back to her writing of China by the presentation in January 1937, of a moving picture based on Owen Davis' play adapted from *The Good Earth*. The New York *Times* wrote, "It is an extraordinarily fine translation of a novel, taking a few liberties with the text, but none with its spirit or quality. The picture, like its stalwart original, is a superb drama of Man and the Soil, at once dignified, tragic, beautiful, ugly, and inspiring." The picture was Irving Thalberg's last production.

Pearl would not go to the preview but waited until she could go unnoticed. She wrote to Faith, "Well, we went in the crowd Wednesday evening, and had good gallery seats and saw no one we knew. The house was packed and the morning reviews were all enthusiastically for it. I must own to a little intensity of feeling as the thing began, remembering inevitably how I began in that attic study that difficult spring, when I had left my child so far away, to write that book. ... It was a far cry to sitting in the biggest Broadway theatre and seeing those people in a moving picture. ... As to the film I hardly know what to say because I can't make up my mind between

194

the obviously glaring faults of it, and the equally undeniable virtue. ...Luise Rainer does such a perfect performance that it is incredible that she isn't Chinese. It is so carefully worked out as to details that it is really authentic in setting in spite of some Hollywood garishness.... An honest, and I think on the whole successful, effort has been made to follow the spirit of the first half of the story— the last half is completely changed, as I told you. But the crowds seem crazy over it and the people relieved, if one is to believe their remarks, over the new happy ending and they all say, 'I'm glad O-Lan got back her pearls at last!' " It is still one of her favorite stories that as she left she heard a man say, "Well, I'd ruther see Mae West, myself."

Luise Rainer was to be remembered by many for her part as O-Lan. As Pearl said of her, "She lived her part."

There was shaping in Pearl's mind during this first year of her home in America, the plan for a book which was to be American. She had come to it slowly from the writing about Chinese, through writing about her parents, the two Americans she knew best, and now to America itself. So began one of her most poignant, sensitive, beautiful pieces of writing She called it, *This Proud Heart.*

It is the story of a heart. That heart was artist and woman and mother. In the book Susan is a sculptor In one passage it tells of when one day she was thinking of her life and of her husband and her little son and baby daughter:

"So their lives drifted in upon her and out again, and she was bound to all of them partly, and to none of them altogether She got up (from her work) and went home at last ... The house stood sturdy and accustomed and dear to the sight and she entered it gladly.

"But the instant she was there, in the midst of all the familiar and the warm possessions, her heart fluttered in her breast and something moved in her ... a creature confined in her and yet apart She was not restless at all, she was happy, for she had a nature made for happiness, being easily absorbed in every passing object. An unexpected yellow rose open on the vine over the porch was as absorbing to her as news in the paper last week of the award to David Barnes (her instructor) of five thousand dollars for his new Titan, Christopher Columbus, which the city of New York wanted to buy.

She was enchanted by these things as she was by the discovery of the North Pole, or as she would be by Marcia's first tooth. But she knew, not so much by knowledge as by instinct, that she could comprehend infinitely more happiness than she now had in everything, and that she was capable of a profounder peace than the peace of this life with which she was nevertheless quite content.

"Out of this instinct came a movement as blind and as inevitable as the instinct of a tree to branch, and of a branch to leap. Out of perfect happiness she began to need her own further growth. . . . Her very content forced her to creation again. And the beginning was her restlessness.

"She had not enough to do. However busy she was, she knew there was an energy in her still unused, a primary function unperformed. She began to feel beyond what her eyes saw in the shape of a tree whipped by the wind, in John building his block houses, in Jane (her maid) bent over pots, in Jane looking up to answer her at the door, in Jane half-startled, wiping her hands on her apron. Jane —Jane—Jane had no curves at all. Her body was cut as simply as a slab of granite—yet every line had been made, not born, but made by the inwardness of Jane—her straight, sad mouth, her stoic chin, her knotty hands, her thin, strong shoulders and flat big English feet.

"'Jane!' she cried one day at the kitchen door.

"Jane looked up, startled, and wiped her hands on her apron.

"'Mum?'

"'What are you doing, Jane?'

"'The pots and kettles, Mum!'

"'Then come upstairs!'

. . . "Just stay like that!' Susan said. For suddenly she saw the essential Jane.

. . . "She closed her eyes a moment. She need not hurry. She caught the deep, hard beat of her heart. Then she opened her eyes to see what she had done. There, life-size, roughly and crudely enough, but serenely true, her clay still wet and dark, stood Jane wiping her wet arms. But this was more than Jane. Here were all women like Jane . . And out of these socket-like eyes, out of the half-open, drawn mouth, from the whole drooping, fragile yet somehow unbreakable figure, Susan could hear a voice—asking why it had been born . . . This was Jane, thousands upon thousands, and Susan realizing her, went to the window toward the wood, and stared

196

out into its summer greenness There was sunshine everywhere, the street was brilliant in sunshine. Through the window she could hear. the creak of the hammock next door. Now the house was still Jane had taken Marcia up, she had fed John. But Susan stood by the window, weeping, her body a blaze of pain she could not comprehend, except that she was somehow weeping for Jane.

"She did not again want any Jane in flesh and blood to pose for her. It was not necessary. . . . Each day when she opened the attic door it was to open it to ecstasy and when she shut the attic door behind her, she shut it as upon that secret ecstasy. She was alive through all her being. And she told no one. There was no one to tell."

Women who read the story of Susan understood and loved her, and men who read it wondered sometimes why she must want to use all her gifts and not be content with husband and family. Susan herself answered that question when she said to Mark, her husband, "I want to be the best wife in the world, the best mother. I want to make a lot of lovely things in stone and bronze, perpetual things. I want to see the world and people—there isn't anything I don't want to do." To Faith, this was Pearl Years later Pearl said to her one day, "My great fault is that I can never give myself entirely to any one thing. I always seem to be concerned in several interests and I just have to be that way. I could not possibly choose one. The trouble is that I always have too many things I am interested in and live too many lives."

And ever she was interested in more and more.

She went in August of that year to Coney Island. She wrote in a letter, "I was really stunned with the immensity and the horror of the place and the vacuity of the faces. I looked into hundreds of faces and saw no old faces that were mellow or philosophical and no young ones that held any promise. The faces are what impressed me most— and the fact that almost no one was smiling or really gay. We got home at three o'clock in the morning and we are a little ragged. We do not do such things often!"

A girl told her one day bitterly that she herself was not gifted enough to excel in any one thing. This set Pearl to thinking and with a touch of self-imposed introspection, for it never comes naturally to her, she wrote Faith, telling of the conversation. "I realize how little I have bothered my head over myself in anything There has always been something I had to do—or felt I had to do, and

I've never stopped to think whether I could or not—I just did. So this girl's difficulties have been new and interesting to me. She feels nothing is worth-while at twenty! Thank God I inherit from Mother a tremendous capacity for interest in anything and everything." Later she confessed that it was perhaps a fault of hers that she always feels responsibility for those around her. She said, "I seem to have an imaginary responsibility for all the people I come into contact with. I love going among people but I cannot stand too much of it because in spite of myself I 'take them on' and it is a strain on me."

A new field was opening before her during these days of rooting in America and that was the radio. She made one speech over the air that autumn which brought women buzzing about her. It was on Women and Art. She said, "My point was simple enough, that I believed one reason women have not excelled in art is because they are not used to disciplined labor. Their refuge has been in a sense the home where they may work in an unsupervised fashion, without competition or concentration. . . . If a woman is gifted, the lack of necessity still allows her to be fitful and unconcentrated in development. So—about ninety-nine per cent of the country seems to think I am a traitor to womankind." It was the beginning of a more and more definite thinking on her part as to women and their place in the world, a thinking which was to result in more speeches and articles and one of her most forceful collections of thought on a single subject.

Her interest in American people, men and women, continued more strongly than ever. It was the time of a wave of publications on charm, making friends, influence. She wrote privately with her usual naturalness, "Personally I think this striving for charm and success and influence over people and all this self-help stuff is too silly for words. I think one has simply to be what one is. Giving up, sacrificing time to achieve, is, I think, nonsense. It will never succeed, anyway. The thing is to do what one enjoys doing—if it is a little of everything, it is just as worthy as a lot of one thing—the main thing being to be one's self and not impose an outside ambition on one's self and be wretched because one does not achieve it."

Chief of her interest was always her children. One day a child specialist came to see them. With great pride in her children, Pearl looked forward to her visit. With humor Pearl writes of the occasion: "She arrived a little earlier than anticipated, in the late afternoon, and I was at the dentist's. But it seems the two older boys chose the moment of her arrival to escape their nurse, go into the kitchen and come into the living room, beaming, to greet her, one with a large corkscrew, and the other with a paring knife! I am sure she leaped to the conclusion that they were neglected children. I'll probably see the story in a book of hers some day—mother a writer, father a publisher, children running around with knives! Can't you see it!"

The next summer, 1938, they took a trip through the West. Pearl had anticipated this journey through parts of the United States new to her for a long time. This was part of her dream of seeing America, dating from college days. They drove in leisure through Iowa, Kansas, the Dakotas, Wyoming, and back by the South. She wrote to her sister who was then living in the West, "After we left you yesterday we went through the most beautiful flower-covered plains we have yet seen. We went among rocks and low hills with the Black Hills as backdrop. In Wyoming the road was fine and the sky a murderous black. It looked dangerous and sinister over the strange wavy plains. It was a terrific thunderstorm and the wildest rain we have ever driven in. We found ourselves in a miniature Bad Lands, just at the storm's height, with streaks of lightning and cracks of thunder and all the eerie shapes around. I felt as if I were in a melodrama with too much piled on in the way of storm and scenery. Hollywood could not have done better. We drove out of it, and the evening light was beautiful on the immense distances."

On the way home they went far out of their way to visit Mark Twain's birthplace in Missouri. She wrote back to Faith, "Main Street runs cobbled and wide straight into the Mississippi and we were so fortunate as to see moored to the shore an old steamboat with a back wheel, the sort Mark Twain used to work on. . . . We spent one night in a little hotel in a small Kansas village. There the tub leaked and we came down to find the proprietor and all the guests mournfully watching a stream of water flow down a chandelier into a bucket surrounded with newspaper. The proprietor said, 'We expect this on Saturday night, but this ain't but Thursday,' looking at us reproachfully."

Even the early fall hats in New York were a revelation of American personality, that autumn. She said, "Everybody in town is wearing the silliest hats I have ever seen. I say everybody—I mean the young girls and the fly-away women. . . . Hairdressers to get business are trying to bring in a new vogue of high hair fixing. The only sort of hat that goes on this is the so-called 'doll's hat,' a saucer affixed over the left eye. Picture to yourself this on every sort of silly face. . . . Earrings, by the way, are much worn. And as the hair is being brushed straight up in the back, the back fringe, which you remember as the aggravation of Mother's life, is again aggravating the young girls."

It was a happy year and she could not foresee what lay ahead by way of greater happiness. But nothing could change the deep current of herself, not even happiness She wrote late in the fall, "I can't think of anything I lack except more years of life ahead. But life has been life wherever it was and I have tried to do the best I could with whatever happened to me." Many things had happened to her and more were to happen but she was the same.

XXVIII   On November 10, 1938, the Associated Press reported from Stockholm, Sweden, "The 1938 Nobel Prize for literature today was awarded to Pearl Buck, American author of *The Good Earth* and other novels dealing with China."

Pearl, taken completely by surprise said at once, "That's ridiculous, the report must be a mistake." Later, as she thought more of it, she said in an interview she felt that Theodore Dreiser merited the honor rather than she. "I don't know him and he doesn't know me, but I feel diffident in accepting the award just the same." She actually did not believe the news, or comment on it publicly, until her husband had called up Stockholm on the trans-Atlantic telephone, and had her Swedish publisher confirm it.

On the Sunday night after the great news she sat by her open fire in her country home, the babies asleep, to write of it to her sister. She said simply, in the usual tone of her letters,

"I want to tell you about it. It was so totally unexpected that I can't tell you *how* unexpected it was. That I should ever get the Nobel Prize was never in the range of my mind. . . . I went up to New York Wednesday evening. Thursday morning I had about made

up my mind to drive back early, because the country is so lovely now.
. But I was stern with myself, deciding that I mustn't because it
would destroy my morning work hours which I really keep inviolate. So after breakfast I settled down in my study as usual in my
old shabby blue velvet dressing gown which I like to work in, and
was pegging away, a little low in mind—when my secretary called
up, all a-splutter that there was 'marvelous news,' that she had just
heard it from the Associated Press that I had been given the Nobel
Prize. I said what I am sure innumerable people have said since,
'Ridiculous, it can't be so!' . . . Then I had to dress at once for a
mass interview at the office. I found a great crowd of reporters and
photographers waiting and for an hour sat and answered questions.
To my disgust the first outcry was, 'How much money is it?' I said
I hadn't thought of the money. They all calculated excitedly 'how
much' and wanted to know if I didn't want a yacht or a fur coat or
jewels and when I said 'No,' that I was satisfied as I was and with
the life I had, they asked what I *was* going to do with it, to which
I replied that of course the government tax would be very heavy and
that I believe in income tax and had no objections to that. . . . With
the utmost care and reserve on my part, still absurd things have
been spread about purporting to have been what I said. Well, one
can't bother. . . . Then the official notice came from Sweden and at
12.05 there was the broadcast to Sweden in the form of a radio
interview with me. The prize, I am happy to say, is given for the
whole body of work of any writer and never just for one book. . . .
So the day went on. . . . Then we drove home to find an excited family . . . all the babies up, and it was lovely to find them all waiting. . . ."

Her sister was awaiting the birth of her fourth child. Pearl with
her ever-vivid humor went on, "My only anxieties are now two:
(a) Will you have your baby before I go? (b) Will my front tooth
inlay fall out just the day I have to receive the prize from the hand
of the only king I am likely to encounter? If so, I shall have to
whistle my gratitude through the hole that this accident always
leaves. I count on its falling out about twice a year—on July 4th
and at Christmas. Of course you can do nothing about (b) but
please see to (a) as far as you can."

That baby was born the afternoon before Pearl sailed for Sweden,
and talking to her sister over the long distance telephone, she said

half humorously, and yet with a touch of that sadness she is ever to have, "I wish I were having the baby instead of the Nobel prize!"

It is not in her words that one can tell of the real success of that trip to Sweden and of the awarding of the Nobel prize. She wrote to her sister one week after the day, telling of the journey, forever conscious of beauties of scenery and of the kindness and warmth of people. Of the occasion of December the tenth, she says:
"I went in on the arm of Dr. Pēr Halstrom, the secretary of the Swedish Academy, who represented the literature section of that body. Trumpets blared, curtains were drawn, music burst out, and we entered, the two recipients (Mr. Fermi's prize was for scientific work) and the members of the Swedish Academy and former Nobel prize winners, two by two from the back of the stage, facing what seemed to me the most enormous and glittering company I had ever seen—every seat full and much light and splendor We had to proceed to the front of the stage, bow and take our seats. . .Then my turn—and it was the longest few minutes of my life. First was a long speech by Pēr Halstrom. I had been given a translation of it and I knew it was a discussion of every one of my books, except *This Proud Heart* which had been translated too late to be considered. This means the prize is awarded for all my work. . . . Special emphasis was laid on the biographies. . . Then he turned to me and I had to rise. When he was finished, I walked across the platform, was momentarily dismayed by a blast of trumpets, but decided I must go on—which was, by the way, right—went down the steps to the King, made my curtsy, he shook hands and made a few pleasant remarks and handed me a large book in a box—my citation—a box containing the gold medal, and a big envelope I had to say, 'I thank you, Your Majesty,' and with these three things, curtsy again, go to the stairs and up, and then with every eye fastened on me and with my train to manage somehow, go across endless acres of deep Oriental rugs, piled one on top of the other—and not miss my seat!"
(This is all *backward* as court custom decreed) "I had made up my mind to keep the direction in my mind and not look back and *not* miss my seat. Well, I managed to do all those things and such a burst of applause as came forth! Everyone seemed to know it had been difficult, and it was appreciated, and every paper the next day

202

The scene of the Nobel Prize ceremony in Stockholm in 1938
Pearl is seated at left of center *(Photo by Karl Sandels, Stockholm)*

At Stockholm, December 10, 1938, the King of Sweden presents the
Nobel Prize for Literature — a gold medal, a certificate for the prize
money, and a leather-bound, hand-decorated "citation"

made headlines out of it. It was most amusing once it was over! Then we stood for the national song and two by two we walked out again, having to stop again for applause and bows. . . . Outside the door the book and medal were taken to be put on exhibition at the Town Hall for the evening. Then we went to the Crown Prince's dinner. I had been carefully coached as to the exact spot where I was to stand until the Crown Prince came to take me in to dinner—also in etiquette—never to begin conversation with him, never to say 'you,' but always, 'Your Royal Highness,' etc., which sometimes I forgot. Indeed, he begged me halfway through to feel it unnecessary. . . . The dinner was magnificent. The hall itself one of the finest in the world. . . . Well, the evening passed happily and pleasantly."

The next morning she had reporters and photographing; her speech (now in printed form as *The Chinese Novel*) to deliver at the Swedish Academy; a tea given her by Swedish women; then that evening the dinner at the King's palace. She continues, "I went in on the arm of Prince Wilhelm and found him very interesting. . . . We all had difficulty in keeping up with the King. who eats very fast, and whenever he is finished all the plates are changed, regardless. It was a magnificent feast—main dish reindeer roast. . . . After dinner we went into the other rooms, stood because no one can sit until royalty sits and, as a court lady sighed in my ear, 'Our *only* objection to the King is that he loves to stand!' Suddenly the King came up to me and ordered me, 'Come and sit down and talk.' So while he drank coffee out of a gold cup and I out of a fine china one we talked. . . He said he got very tired of being a king sometimes, especially when the government was so democratic, but he made it a rule 'always to follow the people.' Once a year he gets a vacation when he goes to the Riviera and plays tennis. He still plays, though eighty—and is much beloved by his people. . . . The next day was filled with numberless teas and dinners—the most memorable one being one at which I met the old and much honored woman, Selma Lagerlöf—herself a Nobel prize winner, who had a great deal to do, I know, with my award. She told me she considered *Fighting Angel* the best of all my books, which interested me very much . . . The dinner that night was a special one given me by the Swedish-American Society. . . . Well, so our story ended . . . The Swedish people are wonderful—friendly, idealistic, warm, united, kind, handsome—one of the world's most wonderful, and certainly they were *perfect* to me. It was a glorious occasion and certainly I am glad to have had it while

203

I am yet young enough to enjoy it and profit by it. I'll never forget a moment of it "

Thus Pearl tells of the great event but it is in the words of her husband that her success with the Swedish people is told in a note added to her letter. He says, "She has told you a lot, but not all, by any means. She has not, of course conveyed to you what a great personal triumph she had She did far more than please them and they were ecstatic. In the first place she is the most popular present day writer in Sweden, of any nationality. Then, in her very first interviews she spoke so simply of wanting to get home for Christmas with her children, and of having taken the day train so that she would see Sweden in snow. Walking backward for the King was regarded as a tremendous feat, as indeed it was. And she made eight speeches, ranging from her hour-long lecture to a short radio broadcast, and every time she said different things in exactly the right way. She gave many interviews, was photographed again and again, met all sorts of people and always in just the right way. I almost wept the night we went to the King's dinner when at the very door of the palace there was a crowd of plain people from the streets, with little children lined up in front, and to the dismay of all the flunkeys, she turned back to speak to them, and they set up a cheer. There were two phrases used about her in the papers—one was 'the magnificent Pearl Buck,' and the other simply, 'The Pearl' which they said everyone was beginning to call her. . . . The last night at the Lucia Festival before several thousand people, she was called to the stage at midnight and spoke a little farewell to Sweden, and then a little later as she was escorted out there was first normal applause, then a storm of it, and then at the end the crowd broke into cheering and men and women alike reached to pat her on the back and shoulders as she made her way out. Even an American Negro was at the door to give a last enthusiastic good-bye."

In the midst of this trip she had thoughts for her children and for her small new niece and for friends. She found time to write letters and send post cards of places she enjoyed seeing. She arranged for flowers to be sent to those in hospitals, and no moment of the triumphal affair could compare with her joy on setting out for home again with the knowledge that she was to be there in time for Christmas with her own. For she had made time, too, for Christmas shopping As she sailed homeward she lay abed, for the sea was rough, wrapping Christmas presents and keeping her mind occupied with the composing of "seasick" rhymes. She added a line to the postscript of her husband, saying, "I'm not reading what he wrote, knowing how he goes on. I couldn't have done without him. . . ." Below she scribbled a rhyme,

"The only thing 'twixt me and Sweden,
Is that the ocean is in betweeden
I think that all the Nobel prizes,
Should wait until the ocean dryses.
I thank whatever gods there be,
Somewhere a shore stops every sea, etc , etc.

"And so good-bye and Merry Christmas to all of you!"

PART SEVEN

XXIX EVERYONE WHO read the newspapers of those days came to be familiar with the face of Pearl Buck. And yet no one who came to know her so, knew her as she was that Christmas in her Pennsylvania home with her children around her. None of the excitement nor the popularity could touch her longing to be at home by Christmas.

That Christmas was the happiest she had ever had There was a sift of snow lying on the fields and garden and woods. Inside the stone house all was warm and bursting with the merriment of the children, and gay with Christmas tree and holly wreaths and candles. There were gifts from across the sea. Her husband gave her rare editions and some of the delicate things she particularly likes, French perfumes and soaps—"small frivolities which I love to have," she wrote, "but always forget to use, not being accustomed to them. I am like Mother—I'll never be a lady! I adore the idea of fripperies, but when it comes down to it, I am so busy that I give my hair a twist and put on what's nearest."

After she came back from Sweden those who knew her said, "She hasn't changed at all!" It has always been that nothing has changed her. Those who know her once, know her always

Soon she was hard at work again. The unforgettable Christmas was over, a Christmas special because it came after her longest separation from her children. She was back on schedule. Few knew how full that schedule was, and is, for it is her schedule still.

One day every week is spent in New York meeting the accumulated appointments waiting for her. Beside her bed in the apartment there is always a pile of manuscripts, some her own, more of others. Even by avoiding as nearly as possible purely social engagements, she can scarcely get everything in. When she starts for the country again she always carries a pile of books—all to be read and some of them reviewed in the next issue of *Asia*. As advisory editor of the John Day Company, she must spend much time in consultation, and she is eager always to discover a new writer of ability.

Her own writing goes steadily on. The morning of every day is given to it. She is able to do as much as she does because she is by nature a good organizer and because when she is at work she works swiftly and hard. She is at her desk every morning at nine.

Articles and speeches and some of her stories she writes directly on her typewriter. Her long manuscripts are sometimes written in ink by hand in large portfolio notebooks. When she sits down to write her episode is already formed, ready to set down. Her pen moves with incredible swiftness, filling page after page with small, compact script, illegible until one discovers its uniformity. She seldom re-writes a passage and usually she writes twenty-five hundred words in a morning.

Again and again people say, "But how can she keep it up?" The answer is that she has something to say and that something is based on her purpose, her old purpose which grows and deepens as time passes and the world changes. So long as the people of the earth misunderstand each other because they do not know each other, she will have plenty to write of. And as long as justice is withheld from any minority, her pen will move and she will speak in its cause.

It had been her intention to go forward with a group of books about Americans. The first of this group was *This Proud Heart*. But when the war between Japan and China broke out it disturbed her so greatly that she could not keep from interrupting her plan, to write of these peoples. She began a story of a young Chinese who was sent by his father to Japan in order that he might be safe from the disorders of China, and who married a Japanese girl. Here was a challenge to ability, the story of life between a man and woman of different nationalities and kinship of these two to all the world. She

207

had written much of the book before she sailed for Sweden. She continued the work on the voyage home, and then, once there, completed it swiftly.

Early in 1939 *The Patriot* was published. A passage tells of the Chinese man, Wu I-wan, now in the Chinese Northwest with the guerrillas after the Long March, famous in the history of the China war. He is watching Peony, once the maid in his father's rich home, now one of these under the leadership of En-lan, and in love with him, as she sits patching an old uniform in the sun. She had come those thousands of miles. . . .

"And I-wan, seeing the deep passion between these two, felt his own longing creep over him like a mist. For weeks he lived as though this were the only life he had ever had, and then, suddenly, as if his name were called by her voice, he longed for Tama. Over and over at such times he wanted to tell En-lan and Peony about her. But he could not. He could not be sure that they would understand. En-lan was as implacable as ever. The old calmness with which he had once told I-wan that he ought no longer to own his father (one of the Shanghai big-business men traitors) was in him still. He was ruthless in his simplicity. 'How,' he would ask I-wan, 'can you love a Japanese?' And yet I-wan knew that he loved Tama and would always love her and she belonged to no country, but only to him. . . . Once he had thought that he might tell Peony alone He had had that day a letter from Tama, sent as all his letters from her were sent, under an official seal from his father. This day Tama's letter had been long and full of what their children said and did. Jiro was beginning school. She had bought him a brown cloth schoolbag for his books and a little uniform and cap, such as the other boys wore. 'But at home,' she wrote, 'I teach him, too. We put flowers before your picture every day, and every day I explain to them how brave you are and how beautiful a country China is and how we belong to China—do I not belong to you, and they to us?' . . . Yes, since he was gone, she had written so '. . . we belong to China.' "

In April she went again to Lynchburg to speak at the annual celebration of Phi Beta Kappa held this year at Randolph-Macon There again were old friends. There again remembrance of those who could not come—a note to a classmate who had recently lost her father, a letter to one kept away by illness. One professor said that he saw more clearly than ever that she was led in everything by her deep love of human beings. To him it accounted for her interest in race, her willingness to work for understanding in whatever way it could be brought about. Pearl herself wrote simply of the event in a letter: "We had a successful trip to the college They were all very warm and enthusiastic and grateful and I feel only that they make too much over me."

And now she went back to her original intention of writing about Americans. Her experience of the American people in mass had deeply impressed her. The book she now began was perhaps more symbolic than any other she had undertaken. Its theme was hero worship, the impact of the crowd on individuals whom it chooses to deify. In 1940 *Other Gods* was published. It is a story almost too poignant because of its inevitability. The people changed the man— simple and good and well-meaning, into a hero, and into the mere shape of a puppet fit to meet their pleasure. But the story is a story even more of the girl whose clear, sad eyes watched the sacrifice and the whole enormous system which consumes the individual that the public may be fed.

In June of that year, 1940, Pearl's home state reached out to bestow an honor on her. The University of West Virginia presented her with the honorary degree of Doctor of Letters The rolling hills and the spreading fields and the heavy orchards all reminded her again of the old home in Hillsboro and of Carie.

In her own Pennsylvania home, meantime, her experience with her children was bringing into her mind stories of simple fundamental things, stories for children She put them together gradually and they were published that same year in a small volume called, *Stories for Little Children*. At first reading they seemed almost too simple and yet children ask for them over and over because they are to them stories of *how things are*.

Then the war in China made her undertake what she most hated, active part in a public campaign. For the relief of suffering in China she took leadership in raising funds for help of the Chinese refugees in Free China. Through the Book of Hope and the China Emergency Relief Committee, in which large contributors were later recognized by Madame Chiang Kai-shek herself, and later through her connection with United China Relief, she gave her name and effort to this work. And yet even with her warm partisanship for China, and her hatred of Japanese militarism, it was incomprehensible to her that anyone should expect her to hate the Japanese people. She said, "But I don't hate the Japanese people!" She wrote short stories trying to show the humanity of the ordinary people of the Orient.

She collected into one volume many short stories published in recent years in periodicals, arranging them in natural, climactic order and they were published under the title, *Today and Forever,* a book with significance for the time in which it appeared.

No one could tell what she was yet to undertake in her anxiety to bring about understanding among people. For what she had already done, the Chinese Government in the year 1941 conferred upon her a high decoration, the Order of Jade, White Cravat with Red and Blue Borders.

All this while she was writing more and more for the readers of magazines, concerned ever more deeply with the masses of people in the world. She wrote in the *Christian Herald* in May 1940, under the title, *"Speaking As an American,"* and said of the American trait of generosity, "To shut one's door while others suffer, to care only for one's own, disclaiming responsibility for humanity, is to destroy all good impulse and to build up a deadly selfishness which will be a boomerang in its effect upon ourselves. Let our own children see the opportunity now theirs for Americanism in the best and traditional sense. There was never a better hour than this to be an American "

In the days ahead she was to feel more and more that this was the hour for true Americanism. Clearly she saw what was involved and clearly she set out to write and speak and act in the cause of democracy. She was, as she is ever to be, concerned with all that leads in the direction of justice and freedom. She wrote that winter to Faith, "I am glad I inherited at least some of Mother's spirit and independence and want to go ahead and do what I know must be done. I suppose if I've had a rule of life—which I never consciously have had —it has been to decide what should be done, and having decided get it done somehow."

Her life spread more broadly than ever, for as she had said she could never live one life only. Yet her real center was her home and her children She wrote that spring, "I can scarcely tolerate the city these days when daffodils are blooming and everything bursting into beauty at home. I really hate cities and all their works. One occasional theatre is all I want out of New York. A year there is interesting but after that all is repetition."

It was that June that her husband gave her one of her most beloved gifts—a ring with seven small diamonds. She wrote to Faith, "It is rather Chinese, and somehow it suits me and I love it. Now of course I must keep my hands nice! Unfortunately on Monday I trimmed all my rosebushes and arrived in New York with my hands all scratches. Wouldn't you know I would!"

Later that summer she told of an occasion anticipated each year. "I am looking forward a great deal to our family holiday. I always enjoy family more than anybody else and never feel so relaxed as when I need not work and can be in the midst of home. I must have an exceptionally nice family—as indeed I have—a sort of handpicked family. By sheer force of obstinacy I have collected these beautiful children."

XXX   S HE HAD thus far given herself largely to the cause of the American understanding of the people of the two countries, China and Japan. Now with her years of experience in America, beginning sharply with earlier occasions in Harlem, as when she had that day spoken extemporaneously before a display of pictures of lynchings, she felt that she could not be silent on the subject of minorities in her own country.

She began deliberately to learn of these. They came to her knowing that here was an unprejudiced ear and a mind keen for justice. She visited organizations of women bankers, of women dentists, of housewives. She attended gatherings of Negroes. In her mind she classed women and Negroes as America's two chief minorities. She began to write articles based on what she had herself seen and heard. She spoke at a great meeting of the Women's Party in Washington, D. C. on the theme that upon women depends the success of American democracy. It was a tremendous speech.

Of the relative positions of men and women in society she has always said that there must be equality. Whether men and women are alike she says, as the Chinese say, is academic nonsense. How can two different entities equal each other? The value of a woman would be lost if she were the same as a man, and the man's value if he were the same as a woman. The balanced society needs the work of both. She believes in the balance between the sexes which means understanding, co-operation and appreciation

She wrote a series of articles for *Harper's* and other magazines. Sometimes she wrote sharply of women and of their failure to use their own powers and their opportunities. Sometimes she pointed out the fact that power in America rests in the hands of organized men. Her correspondence became enormous Yet no one is quicker to deny her alignment with any cause. It is for the people themselves she is working, whether there be a cause or not to meet their need.

She wrote her old friend Emma of her thoughts: "I have been thinking so much about this whole subject of war and what I as an individual can say or do that would be of any use. I feel so strongly that women can prevent war by refusing by all means to allow men to resort to it, but there is much to think over and reason through when one takes a stand. I am going to speak tomorrow in Philadelphia on women and war. To speak out on such a delicate thing at such a moment as this, one has to be sure that one's own convictions are clear and clearly expressed because people are so ready for prejudice and emotion. I feel so strongly, not on the grounds of pacifism or even religion, but on the solid grounds of practical accomplishment of any desired end, that war is completely useless. I am not a pacifist. I believe that force has to be used at certain times and upon certain persons, but never the force of war machines and methods. ... If we can maintain a rational attitude there is some hope of war being a temporary phase of human progress and not the inevitable thing it has been thought to be. Well, this *isn't* my speech, but merely my thinking these days!"

It was a tremendous undertaking, this attempt to clarify, and to suggest a remedy for the incomplete relationship between men and women of America. It meant a new kind of education—an education of men and women for each other. Her thoughts took shape and she set them in clear English in a small book which, since it was by no means to be a compendium on the most immense of subjects, she called humbly, *Of Men and Women*. All readers do not agree with her points of view. She did not intend to write an agreeable book but she did intend to awaken people to their situation, particularly

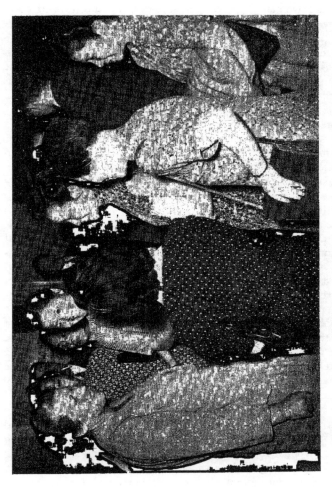

Pearl Buck talking with Chinese women in an interval of the hearings at Washington on the repeal of the Chinese Exclusion laws, May 20, 1943 *(Photo by Press Association, Inc)*

On the lot where the moving picture of *Dragon Seed* was being made in 1943, Pearl met for the first time the old water-buffalo who had been a leading character in the film of *The Good Earth* He is now an MGM pet (*Courtesy Metro-Goldwyn-Mayer Pictures, Inc*)

dangerous and acute in time of war. She did intend to stir up thought. She succeeded. Again her mails were stupendous. As though they had been waiting for a spark, men and women burst into flame, grateful, angry, contentious. She was satisfied that the book had accomplished its purpose.

While she had been thinking of this question she had been thinking, too, of that minority which existed for the reason of race. All of her old personal experience of being herself one of a minority in China rose up to renew her conviction. More than that, the necessity of action while there was yet time because a war for democracy throughout the world was impending, urged her to swift, strong, outspokenness.

She met more often with Negro groups, young educated Negroes in whom there was bitterness, older ones in whom the fire of race hatred had smoldered since slave days.

She had for a long time read what they wrote, listened to them, studied them. But now the war set her thoughts in clear relation to the times. With a sense of necessity she felt the hour had come when she must speak at whatever danger to herself and at whatever jeopardy to the esteem in which she was held as a writer.

She spoke on the editorial page of the New York *Times,* November 15, 1941. The occasion of her speaking was an answer to an editorial in the same paper, entitled, "The Other Side of Harlem." She denied that any amount of social work, as suggested, could be sufficient. She says further.... "the real point is that our democracy does not allow for the present division between a white ruler race and a subject colored race and we ought to make up our minds as to what we want and move to accomplish it. . . . But if nothing can (not even education) remove race prejudice from those in whom it is ingrained, they should not be allowed to violate our nation's democracy. At least our government should see to it that all Americans have equal economic opportunity and that colored people in this democracy shall not suffer insult because of their color. It can and should insist that colored citizens shall share responsibility with white citizens for the welfare of the nation and thus remove the half-tolerant, wholly patronizing contempt of the white for the colored and thereby build in the colored citizen belief in himself.... Is democracy right or wrong? If it is right, then let us dare to make it true."

That was written only three weeks before Pearl Harbor. By giant strides Japan took what she wished, in Thailand, in Malaya, in the Indies, in the Philippines. She looked toward India. The crisis became clear. The implication of the Japanese theme, "Asia for the Asiatics" was perfectly apparent. The race issue was enormous. The question of collaboration with Great Britain, the query of what the United Nations were fighting for, things as they had been in the East, or freedom for all, awaited an answer.

Her feeling and her necessity grew. In February, 1942, she sent a letter to all editors of colored periodicals in the United States and Canada. She clarified the position of the white man and gave the reasons for that position. She allied the Negro with all the colored races of the world. She said, "It may well be that in the future now very close, the peoples of Asia and Africa will look to you more than to any other Americans to see to it that the world does not divide as Japan would have it divide on the false line of color, but solely on the single issue of freedom for all. It is you who carry the flag."

In March she addressed a great audience at a Book and Author Luncheon at the Hotel Astor in New York. She spoke then of the danger of Japanese propaganda in Asia. The Japanese were, she said, making use of race feeling against the colored races as found both in the history of Asia itself and in the facts of America. She challenged the advocates of unifying the white races of the world, saying they are heading us toward an even greater war—the war between the races. She said distinctly that the trouble is that we do not know ourselves. On the one hand we believe in democracy to the point of sacrificing all we have for it; on the other we deny it in' practice. She closed, "Democracy, if it is to prevail at this solemn moment in history can do so only if it purges itself of that which denies democracy, if it dares to act as it believes."

She spoke again and again, through the *Christian Science Monitor* on April the twenty-fifth, over the Town Meeting of the Air, at a luncheon of the Federal Union organization, at the commencement of Howard University.

At Howard the exercises were deeply impressive. They were held out-of-doors on the open campus. An immense crowd, most of them colored people, for most of the students at Howard University are Negroes, waited beneath the beating sun to see her. Now as she came wearing the robe which was later to be decorated with the insignia of the honorary Doctor of Law Degree, there was silence. Then there were whispers, "There she is !"

214

She spoke simply, fully, of the opportunity of the Negro at this momentous time in history. She allied herself with them saying often, "We." A woman in the audience whispered, "She said 'we'!" She spoke almost an hour, and there was utter stillness. The great mass of colored people sighed and looked at each other when it was over. They applauded again and again. And yet she had asked nothing easy of them. She had not been sorry for them. She had asked for sacrifice and understanding and bravery and hard work. But she had understood and she had made herself one of them.

Dr. Mordecai Johnson in speaking before the awarding of the degree, outlined what she had done for their cause. It was in Washington, the capital of America, and a city where the relation of the white and colored races has least come to a solution, she had spoken what was in her heart and mind.

Afterward talking quietly with Dr. Johnson and his wife, she said, "I would like to come sometime just as an individual, to mix with the students and talk with them. A forward step is possible only if young people see it and are willing to undertake it Now while the war is on is an opportunity which must not escape from us."

She let no opportunity escape her. At a meeting of the India League for America the following September she said, "Of course I believe that freedom is a human right. If one stands by the Declaration of Independence it is un-American and undemocratic to say that anybody must 'achieve' freedom or 'deserve' freedom or any such nonsense. The only kind of a world fit for human beings is a world where everybody is born free. Yet people have often had to fight to assert that right, and so India, had there been no world war, would have had to assert her rights for herself. . . . We must now think of India for the simplest of reasons, one which even the realists (as contrasted with the idealists) honor, that of self-interest It is to our interest today, in this war still undecided, that we summon every possible ally to our one aim of victory—not only allies who are people, but allies of the mind, faith in our cause, and belief that our victory is victory for the right."

She spoke with tremendous power at a dinner given for Nobel Prize winners in New York, in December. She was moved to anxiety by the changing aspect of the war. She feared that military success might be taken for victory. She said, "You remember how heartily all of our allies, in Asia as well as in Europe, entered into the war for freedom. No war that has ever been waged was entered into with more devotion to freedom than was this war. Millions of people, dark and light, rallied to the cause of democracy. . . . One thing is true—the promise of freedom cannot be given one colonial people without being given to all, and therefore it may be argued prudently, that it is easier to make no promise of freedom. It is easier to cease talking about freedom at all. It is easier to say that we had better win the war before we discuss the postwar world. . . . So, in this fashion, the war has ceased to be a war for freedom and has become merely a war against the Axis. All Asia now knows and acknowledges, and so must we if we are honest, that the principle of human equality and human freedom may have nothing to do with our victory in this war. . . . Let us face this moment in this year, therefore, and not be deceived by military victories. . . . You who come from Europe must not be afraid to speak out . . . Let those who will, pass over to the side of those who oppress, our place remains on the side of those who are oppressed."

She could not be silent when all that has shaped the unity of her life and all that makes up the single purpose of her thinking and expression was at stake. In February she wrote for the New York *Times Magazine,* "It is not quite too late to unite all peoples by the one thing which all peoples value above everything—not freedom only for religion, not freedom only of speech, not freedom only from fear and want—but the great freedom to be free. Here is the true aim of this war and until it is so recognized, until it is so declared, we will fail in achieving democracy."

She has never been one to belong to organizations or work on committees. She is a member of the Advisory Board of the Common Council for American Unity. She is a member of the National Committee of the National Urban League. These all have to do with a meeting of races in America, particularly the white and Negro. But she is a member of the National Committee of the American Civil Liberties Union, and of the Advisory Board of the Japanese-American Committee for Democracy, as well, and these have to do with the rights and responsibilities of the citizen, whatever his color. On all of these she works, and through them she speaks, as well as through herself alone.

For in that year she was impelled also to write again a novel of China. She must write again of the common people of China, a people now trodden by the invader. She must tell how the peasant people are meeting the Japanese.

216

The first half of the novel being complete in itself appeared serially in *Asia*. In January 1942 the entire book was published. It was the sixth of her books to be a choice of the Book-of-the-Month Club. For many weeks it stood at the top of the best seller list.

Thousands welcomed this book especially because it was written in the style and mood of her trilogy and of *The Mother*. This was *her* writing, they said, having never fully accepted her change to the American scene or to the style which suited the scene. It was accepted by everyone as the novel of the occupied regions.

Here again were the large simplicities of earth and sky and human destiny. Here again the strength and shrewdness of the common man. Here was a China, old and yet newest of the new—China, invaded She called it simply, *Dragon Seed* She said briefly of the title, "To the Chinese the dragon is not an evil creature, but is a god and the friend of men who worship him. He 'holds in his power prosperity and peace' Ruling the waters and the winds, he sends the good rain, and hence is the symbol of fecundity. In the Hsia dynasty two dragons fought a great duel until both disappeared, leaving only a fertile loam from which were born the descendants of the Hsia. Thus the dragon came to be looked upon as the ancestors of a race of heroes."

The closing lines of the book are beautiful in their combination of the old and the young, hopelessness and hopefulness Ling Tan, the farmer over whom all the waves of suffering and bitterness have swept, went with his son, Lao Er, to hear the secret news brought by the cousin, an opium eater whose opium depended upon his smuggled trade in information from the outside. They sit on a narrow bench in the dark room to hear him. . . .

"The old man fumbled in his bosom and brought out a small piece of brown-stained paper, and then his horn spectacles. With much trouble he put his spectacles on his nose and they fell off because his hands trembled so and he put them on again and again they fell off, and all waited in great patience until a third time he tried and this time they stayed Then he lifted up the paper and read these words aloud ·

" 'The ordeal of the conquered peoples will be hard. We must give them the conviction that their sufferings and their resistances will not be in vain. The tunnel may be dark and long, but at the end there is light.'

"In this dark old room filthy with years and now with ruin, Ling Tan stood and heard these brave words ...

" 'Let us go,' he said to his son.

"So his son followed him and they went out from the city and Ling Tan said nothing.

"Soon they were beyond the desolate city, and the cobbled road grew narrow and wound its old way along the valley's bed. The hills were dark against the sky. This night there was no moon.

"Now Lao Er had all this time been unbelieving, and it was in his heart to say to his father, 'It is better for us not to count on sure help from anywhere. Are there men who give their help for nothing?' But he had waited for his father to speak.

"But when there was only silence he kept silent, too, and at last he thought to himself that he would let his father have his hope 'I am young.' Lao Er thought. 'I do not need a hope I can live.'

"And so with his heart cool and bitter within his breast, Lao Er let his father walk ahead of him and he saw him lift his head to look at the stars and put up his hand to feel the wind

" 'Is there not promise of rain?' Ling Tan asked suddenly out of the darkness There had been need of rain for many days.

" 'Only a promise,' Lao Er said."

XXXI SHE WAS in the months which followed sometimes weary. Keyed as she was to the necessity for understanding and action, she had been among the first to realize, when war broke out in China and four years later in Europe, that this time a world war would be global. She knew, from her experiences among the people of both sides of the world, that although there had been a little interchange on the higher levels of culture and between diplomats, the people of America knew nothing of the peoples of China and India, of the South Seas and of Russia, of the Near East as well as the Far East, and those peoples knew as little of the Americans. And yet if the principles of democracy were to prevail in the world, the peoples must understand each other, and they could not understand without knowledge about each other, expressed in the terms which they could understand.

218

When Japan attacked Pearl Harbor, she was convinced that somehow this knowledge of the East and West must be spread abroad. She founded the East and West Association, a non-profit, non-political organization, which has as its sole purpose the mutual exchange of knowledge between peoples of East and West about each other. It was a vast undertaking whose size and difficulty she fully understood. But as she often says, "Nothing is done that is not begun."

She said in a letter, "My real purpose in the East and West is to see if any way can be devised to spread accurate and human information about peoples to each other. I don't believe I would have done it if the war had not broken out, and it seemed necessary to do something, in order to endure this war, that would make people better allies for the war and better participants at the peace table I realized that after the last world war it was the ignorance of the people here in this country and in England and in France that ruined all of Wilson's fine ideas, the ideas that would have saved us from this war had people known enough to follow them and carry them out. But people were insular and stupid and wanted only to think of themselves—this because they didn't know enough to do anything else. If people could realize that their fortunes are bound up with each other, it might save us a second time. . . . It is something I want to try out—a technique for popular interchange of thought—if such a thing is possible. It has to my mind a direct relation to the practical working out of democracy and of course I believe in democracy."

She could not foresee the readiness of people for such an organization. She could not have guessed at the welcome given it by small groups in isolated spots, gatherings of teachers, students, librarians, women. She had pictured the size of the step she was taking in acquainting far-flung parts of the world with each other. She had estimated the means—written, spoken over the air waves of the world, dramatized. But she had not known how swiftly it would be accepted She was busier than ever.

She wrote one day when *Dragon Seed* was finished, "This has been one of the very few days when I simply could not, for some reason, settle down to work. With a lot of work waiting for me, I have been unable to settle my mind down to it I think this happens occasionally when I have had a long concentrated stretch of weeks as I have had and my mind, relaxed from the necessity to go on with a job, is just refractory. The brain is sometimes, I think, like a separate entity inside one's being. It has to be coaxed and coerced at times to come into harmony with what one wills for it ... It really is a matter of training. I fret sometimes over the years I had between twenty-five and thirty-five which, it seems to me now, were largely wasted. What was I doing in those years? Why didn't I get to work? I see now that I was in a queer dull submerged sort of state. ... It seems to me that I am now really myself. ... I feel I must somehow have more time. Does life grow so full as it shortens, I wonder? I seem never to have a moment I always hope for a long leisurely old age, yet with this war none of us will have that."

The autumn that the East and West Association began she was, if possible, more than ever in love with great simplicities and genuineness. She took even greater delight in her home and children. In speaking of a certain book which had just been popularly received but which seemed to her to lack real worth she wrote to Faith, "My favorite story in the world is that old fairy tale of the magic weavers who pretended to spin gold and silver tapestries to make the king's robes, maintaining that only the good could see them, and no one dared tell that he saw nothing and that the king was naked, until a little child cried out, 'Why he has nothing on !'. . It is fashionable for literary folk to exclaim over works of their own kind and insist that a great new literature has been born. To me they simply have nothing on .. Words are made, to my thinking, to convey, and when nothing is conveyed, what remains except empty words?"

Her relief and delight was ever the American country. Here she rested and was free even though she worked. Her garden grew more beautiful The border deepened and lengthened A small pool for goldfish was set where a tiny stream trickled down the slope She wrote of the pool, "We have had blue herons and white herons around our woods and the lake for two months—handsome stately birds that make pictures of themselves continually as they move among the willows or stand motionless among the reeds. I fear their long stay has been hard on the goldfish. Usually they only pass in migration and I cannot understand their long stay—unless it is that they grow constantly more plump while the goldfish grow more scarce !"

She wrote one winter day to Faith, "It is strange how one's life becomes entangled in the lives of all these peoples one is never to see. I often think, living here comfortably and safely, why do I ponder and puzzle over the lives of the Indians and Negroes and all these others? I have everything for happiness and am very happy, and yet in the night, or a dozen times a day, I find myself thinking furiously about the peoples of the world, as if they were my personal responsibility. It seems to me it would be easy to have a better world if only a few clear things were said and done. I don't think I over-simplify. It seems to me nothing was ever done in history except when out of complexities a clear question was simply asked and as simply answered—as when in our Revolutionary War we simply asked ourselves whether or not we could endure to be longer tied to England and said that we could not, and in spite of absurd difficulties, pursued our way to freedom "

She had in her usual way "taken on" the whole world of common people because she really meant democracy.

XXXII   IT IS MORNING on a bright day in June Rain has fallen in the night but now the sun is streaming down on rolling hills, broad meadows and swollen streams in the Pennsylvania countryside.

The woods are shining green this morning, and the long flower border against them is brilliant, rainwashed of dust The old stone house seems to have grown to meet the shape of the hill upon which it stands, changed from the small house it once was to fill the needs of all Pearl's family. But it is still essentially as it was—brown stone, deep-windowed, festooned with trumpet vine, shaded by its trees. The old farm bell still hangs on the narrow back porch and it is a signal to the children to come when it rings. Wrens are busy building under the eaves The stone-flagged terrace has grown and is enclosed at one side now reminding one of a Chinese court. The peony buds, Chinese too, will soon be bursting against the house wall. A vista shows irises in bloom, brush-daubs of blue and violet and gold beneath the weeping willows

The little stone house, once the summer kitchen, has grown, as well From one end there is the steady click of three typewriters, for a wing now added is an office, in which a staff is at work on the varied business of herself and her husband. At the other end is another addition, a high-ceilinged room in which she writes. Here on a balcony, are a sculptors' stand and tools, armatures and clay, and the modelled heads of her children. For she has followed the example of Susan in *This Proud Heart* and is making a hobby, at least, of sculpture Though she has never had any instruction, the likenesses she gets are remarkable, and the feeling in her models is evident From this room where she works an enormous window opens to the slope of the hill toward the stream and the small lake in the valley It is this scene which Pearl sees as she looks out sometimes, this, or the blaze of her roses in the stone-walled garden.

She is in her rose garden now, stooping to cut the blossoms Only a great garden hat and the soft green of linen is to be seen—then the hands cutting deftly the half-open buds—rich red, warm yellow, pinky-cream, pure white. The hands lay them in the basket which stands waiting.

Pearl rises She looks across to another bed, then goes swiftly to it. The low bushes are covered with rich yellow buds. She cuts a half dozen, looks deeply into them, smells them. They are the Pearl Buck rose, named for her four years ago. She wrote once to Faith, "One of the real pleasures of my life has been the rose named after me. It is absurd to enjoy that rose so much. I love roses with a feeling that is more than love for a flower, and this rose is so strong, so rich in its coloring. It improves its color, growing more golden as it gets older. It hangs onto life so strongly It is so hearty and energetic in its root system, that I have a feeling almost human for the plant."

Now her face is serene, pleased. Suddenly she remembers something one of the children said last night. She had dropped the newspaper she was reading. Her little girl picked it up, looked at it carefully and exclaimed in disgust, "These old papers, every day the same. They are full of nothing but ABCs all the time "

She cuts some tiny yellow rosebuds from an old Chinese bush for the little girls' room. Then this deep red bud, and this and this, for the boys'.

Her basket is full now. She lifts it and walks toward the house, stopping to examine the buds on a climber against the small house, and to clip a dead rhododendron blossom from a clump she passes.

Before she steps in the door to the living room, she turns to look out. The sunshine on the slope of the rolling landscape is making vivid greens, soft grays, brilliant yellows There is the distant moo of a cow and the whir of farm machinery. Full repose, deep satisfaction show in her face as she goes toward the pantry to fetch bowls

222

and vases. She thrusts the roses in without seeming plan or order. Yet when she is done they are there with the sure grace of an artist's touch This great bowl is for the table, that silver one for the piano, this small low bowl for the little stand there. These are for the dining room Before she is done every room has its roses, the playroom, the library—that sweet, quiet room lined with books—and every bedroom in the house. For she must have flowers. To her a room is dead without them They are beauty and beauty is a necessity, just as her home is a necessity, and her children.

It is here in her country home that she is most fully herself. To see her here is to see her as she truly is, for here she is in the midst of the surroundings she loves best, surrounded by those she loves best, giving expression to the many sides of her nature.

This year she belongs more than ever here. The good farm land lying idle around her, the need to produce for the war, her own instinct to develop everything around her could not be denied. She is farming in the Pennsylvania country. It is no unusual sight to see her trudging along the country road adjoining her land, a basket in her hands She eyes her steers with a canny eye She counts the cows She investigates the piglets And from that rich land she feeds her hearty children and her frequent guests, and cans and freezes fruits and vegetables against the winter She loves it. She says sometimes, "It rests me as nothing else could rest me. It makes the war more bearable to work here among the quiet fields and hills, to see the earth produce."

She is a sturdy figure dressed almost always in comfortable slacks and jacket. Her hair is brushed back from her face, light brown still except for a clear wing of white which accentuates the way she combs it. Outdoors she wears a large sun hat.

Indoors, as she settles in an easy chair to talk, one is not aware of what she wears. More than likely her clothes are a little wrinkled, or else touched with mud because of the rains last night, her bare feet thrust into play shoes, her lipstick put on absent-mindedly, her rouge, if at all, too much or too little One feels rather her intentness, for always she is intent, either upon some event of the children, or on news from some far-flung part of the world, or the bursting of buds on the fruit trees, or the first fall of snow, or a book she has "discovered" among the masses of manuscripts forever heaping upon her. One forgets what she wears, or how her hair is combed One sees only the clear gray-green eyes, the mobile lips, touched with dimples

223

like Carie's at their corners, the set of her jaw a little like Andrew's, the changing expression of intense interest, penetrating thought, humor If there is anything about what she wears that one is conscious of, it is of color. She loves color—deep warm color—plenty of it. For an instant one is conscious of her hands—artist hands, they are, not beautiful as hands are modelled, but slender, muscular, sensitive in the extreme and sometimes stroking the texture of the arm of the chair as she speaks

She might not be called beautiful if one measures each feature to test its perfect proportion. She has long been under the delusion that she has an enormous hook nose—"a beak" she is wont to say. Her nose is average of the aquiline type, her face is broad at the brow and across the eyes and narrowing in the well-set chin. But none of this matters. One forgets it, feeling instead only the personality, eager, alive.

It is not possible to talk with her long without being conscious that she is coming to the heart of the subject, whatever it is. Probing like a clean, sharp knife, her mind is cutting through all that is superfluous and reaching the central idea. Perhaps one was not certain himself what the center was before, but now he soon discovers it.

One cannot see her fully in any single way. Not in her rose garden, nor yet in conversation. One must see her pass through the room with a light free step going to the playroom to find the reason for a protest from the children; passing into the pantry to discuss dinner with Mrs Loris who turns out the magnificent apple pies, and pumpkin pies, and home made mince pies, or the roasted ducklings or perfect steaks which the table always displays She has no servants who stay in the house. Mrs. Loris is a neighbor, and a friend, who comes in for part of each day except Sunday to help in the kitchen. Another neighbor comes for mornings only to help in the rest of the house. By mid-afternoon there is only the family there. On Sundays Pearl does all the cooking, and the whole family helps. So it is on Christmas Day. "I think everyone should be at home, and not working in some one else's kitchen on Christmas Day," Pearl says.

One must see Pearl herself as she prepares a Chinese meal. She has Chinese guests and she has brought from New York's China-town all the makings of real Chinese food. Sweet pork is simmering slowly in a saucepan. There is the odor of chicken and red dates stewing. A puff of steam rises from the lid of the rice pot Vegeta-

224

bles are heaped ready for the quick-cooking just before they are to be eaten. Mrs. Lin Yutang and Pearl are sitting on high kitchen stools "picking" bean sprouts, which is the breaking off of roots which are not edible. There is a steady stream of Chinese chatter. One cannot tell except from the different voices who is speaking. There is warm amused laughter. After a long time Pearl's husband looks into the room and says with a twinkle, "What *are* you two jabbering about in here! You've been at it for hours!"

The food is done at last and set out on the table. Lin Yutang and his daughters with Chinese etiquette taste and appraise. "Exactly right! Perfect! The only real Chinese food I've had in America except what my wife cooks!" he says. He looks at Pearl, his eyes beaming behind his glasses "But then you *are* Chinese," he adds. "I insist you *are* Chinese. Your way of sitting, of walking, the angle of your head, the way you think, your philosophy, your expression." He would go on, but Pearl's hand rises in protest and she urges more food on him.

The children, too, are clicking their chopsticks in their bowls. They get down from their chairs and run to the kitchen for more rice. "The luckiest children in all the world," Mrs. Lin says and gives a little toss to her head.

One must see Pearl as she walks through the open country. She is pointing and sweeping the distance with her hand. Now she stops to examine a wild flower, now to pull a very large weed. "Before it goes to seed—I just can't let that one pass!" She is stooping to pick a wild strawberry. "They taste better than the others," she says and picks another.

Then she tells you how many young oak and pine and walnut trees she has put into the land that is not good for farming. She points out the garden where now one can make out the forms of the children stooping to pick beans for dinner, their chatter coming faintly in the breeze. She indicates the tennis court, and then looks in the opposite direction toward the small stone house across the stream which was to have been Edwin's but which now is hers. "I couldn't let it go into other hands," she says.

She is walking toward the flower border—immense, stretching for a quarter of a mile, it seems, and laid against a fringe of woods, trees and evergreens. Everything is here, everything luxuriant, spaced and timed to keep a continual bloom Two old men look up from their weeding to speak, saying the weeds are "turrible."

We are trudging down over the slope to the lake now. A small boat lies moored there. "The children swim like fish," she says, "so I need not worry when they play here. It is a wonderful country for children. There is nothing to hurt them They can grow up in the most wonderful surroundings the world can give—sunshine and rain and wind and mud and flowers and woods and streams. And now they are learning to work. I want them to know work and its satisfaction." We turn and start up the hill toward the house. She pauses and her eyes sweep the view. "I really think this is the most beautiful country there can be anywhere It is fertile, rolling enough and yet without the shut-in feeling of the mountains, open and yet without the unending space of plains. I don't want to go anywhere. The city smothers me. I don't want even to go to China, much as I love it "

And now there is a shout. Flying figures are coming down the hillside calling, "Mother! Mother! Wait! We want to come up the hill with you!" She stands and watches while they come, her face half-smiling, her lips on the point of speaking.

Then they are there, swirling around her, and clinging to her as they begin to move in a cluster toward the house.

The rest of the day is theirs. Every day at a certain time she stops work. (She has written *The Promise,* a sequel to *Dragon Seed,* and more books for children, and another book, *What America Means to Me,* has been published) Now the rest of the day is the children's for whatever they want to do. When they were very little she used to sit on the floor and let them climb over her, saying that it seemed to satisfy something in them, just that personal possession of her. It was a picture not to be forgotten, the mother with the four tiny things creeping over her and sometimes rolling off and shrieking with delight Today they lean against her while she reads a favorite book and sometimes they follow where she reads and tell her a word they know.

Each is different, each holding her love because he is hers and because he has some especial quality. One visitor recently said, "Visitors at the Walsh home over the week-end have the impression that the place is alive with kids. They pop in at the back window; they appear at the front door; they come chasing one another through the house. She likes children not only individually but in the mass.

" 'What I am going to do some day is to come home and find an orphanage has moved in,' says Mr. Walsh, presenting the thought as though he hoped it might happen."

It is late evening. There has been a picnic dinner in the court. The children are helping to carry in the dishes before they take a last dip in the pool, and so to baths and songs and bed.

Pearl settles back in her long chair when the last child has left. "Did I tell you of the conversation with my small daughter last night?" she asks, and smiles, remembering. "She had lost her scissors—she never puts anything away—and I took the opportunity to deliver a lecture on having a place for things. I said, 'Now I keep my scissors in my sewing basket, and when I have finished with them I put them back again and when I want them I know where they are.' She listened attentively and then asked, 'But, Mother, did you do that when you were a little girl?' I had to laugh and say I didn't, but that my mother taught me as I was trying to teach her."

Her face is serene and then it lights up with its usual intensity. She thinks aloud. "I do hope I have a long old age because there are so many things I want to do which I am having to put off until then I can see that after fifty life telescopes. I have at least twenty books I want to write, and it will be a race with old age And I want to enjoy every minute of the children, and the world, and beauty, and home, besides."

There is silence a moment. They are thinking of the past. Then someone speaks. It is her husband. "You are the most normal person in the world," he says. "All sorts of abnormal things have happened *to* you, but not *in* you. Your life could be called abnormal. But you yourself have not been changed by these things. You are the normal human being." She glances warmly toward him. Her lips open to answer, her old half-whimsical smile flickers, but a child's voice from an upstairs window calls suddenly, "I'm in my pajamas and ready for my song, Mother," and she is gone.

Her voice floats down, clear and sweet,—

"O beautiful for spacious skies,
For amber waves of grain ... America, America!"

BIBLIOGRAPHY

Books

(All published by The John Day Company, New York)

All Men Are Brothers, 1933
The Exile, 1936
Fighting Angel, 1936
This Proud Heart, 1938
The Patriot, 1939
The Chinese Novel, 1939
Dragon Seed, 1942
American Unity and Asia, 1942
The Chinese Children Next Door, 1942
The Water-Buffalo Children, 1943

Articles and Booklets

The Old Chinese Nurse, *Country Gentleman*, June 1932
A Debt to Dickens, *Saturday Review of Literature*, April 4, 1936
An Autobiographical Sketch of Pearl S Buck, The John Day Company, 1932
Literature and Life, Journal of the National Education Association, September 1938
Speaking As An American, *The Christian Herald*, May 1940
A Biographical Sketch of Pearl S Buck, The John Day Company, 1941 .
Preacher's Daughter, *Collier's*, February 7, 1942
Alumnae Bulletins, Randolph-Macon Woman's College, Lynchburg, Va.

Personal Letters

of family and friends, teachers, classmates

Printed in the USA
CPSIA information can be obtained
at www.ICGtesting.com
LVHW010225021023
759871LV00019B/309